The Corporate Environment

The Financial Consequences for Business

The Corporate Environment

The Financial Consequences for Business

John Collier

Prentice Hall
London New York Toronto Sydney Tokyo Singapore Madrid
Mexico City Munich

First published 1995 by
Prentice Hall International (UK) Limited
Campus 400, Maylands Avenue
Hemel Hempstead
Hertfordshire, HP2 7EZ
A division of
Simon & Schuster International Group

© Prentice Hall 1995

All rights reserved. No part of this publication may be reproduced,
stored in a retrieval system, or transmitted, in any form, or by any
means, electronic, mechanical, photocopying, recording or otherwise,
without prior permission, in writing, from the publisher.
For permission within the United States of America
contact Prentice Hall Inc., Englewood Cliffs, NJ 07632

Typeset in 10/12pt
by Keyword Typesetting Services Ltd, Wallington, Surrey

Printed and bound in Great Britain by T.J. Press Ltd, Padstow.

Library of Congress Cataloging-in-Publication Data

Available from the publisher

British Library Cataloguing in Publication Data

A catalogue record for this book is available from
the British Library

ISBN 0-13-355645-X

1 2 3 4 5   99 98 97 96 95

Contents

1	**Introduction**	**1**
2	**Environmental Laws**	**4**
	2.1 Introduction	4
	2.2 United Kingdom	5
	2.3 European Community	16
	2.4 Worldwide	19
3	**Key Environmental Issues**	**32**
	3.1 Introduction	32
	3.2 Compliance costs	33
	3.3 Waste	37
	3.4 Energy	42
	3.5 Contaminated land	44
	3.6 International	50
4	**Investment**	**61**
	4.1 Introduction	61
	4.2 Stock Market	62
	4.3 Banks and venture capital	67
	4.4 Insurance	71
	4.5 Environmental liability	75

5 Environmental Systems — 82

5.1 Introduction — 82
5.2 BS 7750 — 83
5.3 EC Eco-Management and Audit Regulation — 95
5.4 Life Cycle Analysis — 102
5.5 Accreditation — 104

6 Environmental Reporting — 108

6.1 Introduction — 108
6.2 Pressure groups — 110
6.3 Advertising — 112
6.4 Eco-labelling — 114
6.5 Employees — 117
6.6 Shareholders — 119
6.7 The future — 127

7 Environmental Auditing — 131

7.1 Introduction — 131
7.2 History — 132
7.3 Types of audit — 134
7.4 Financial auditing — 136
7.5 Environmental and financial auditing — 142
7.6 Due diligence — 157

8 Environmental Accounting — 164

8.1 Introduction — 164
8.2 Existing conventions — 165
8.3 Measurement — 176
8.4 Sustainable development — 180
8.5 Environmental bookkeeping — 181

9 Taxation — 184

9.1 Introduction — 184
9.2 In theory — 185
9.3 In practice — 186
9.4 In the future — 189

10 The Way Forward — **198**

Appendices — **200**

A UNCED 1992: Agenda 21 chapter headings — 200
B UK Ethical and Environmental Funds — 202
C EC Eco-Management and Audit Regulation:
  environmental management systems requirements — 203
D UK Statements of Financial Auditing Standards — 207
E UK Financial Reporting and Accounting Standards — 209
F ICC Business Charter for Sustainable Development: principles for
  environmental management — 211
G Environmental Action Checklists — 214

Index — **223**

1

Introduction

It is hard to imagine that any European businessman or woman would be unaware of the effect of 'the environment' on their business. Yet discussion with most middle managers (and some senior ones too) shows, all too quickly, that the main concern is the bottom line profit and environmental issues are only of interest to the extent that they might increase or reduce that profit. Most shareholders would be relieved to hear that but not all as, increasingly, people ask about the ethical values—including environmental caring—of the companies in which they invest. This is giving a whole new meaning to 'investor' relations and finance directors, accountants and auditors, as well as chief executives, can no longer turn their backs on 'green' issues as being for an eccentric idealistic fringe.

There is little written, as yet, that sets out the financial consequences of the environmental movement on business. There is a plethora of books, magazines, tapes, videos, etc., exhorting business to change and adopt best environmental practices but very little seen through the eyes of the finance director, accountant and auditor: the people responsible for measuring and reporting the bottom line and describing the financial standing of a business to all its stakeholders—shareholders, employees, the local community, customers, suppliers and the taxman.

There has also been very little written by accountants about what has become known as environmental auditing. Yet the approach, standards, methodologies and reporting procedures used in financial auditing can be readily adapted to deal with environmental issues.

It would be wrong to suggest that a trained financial auditor is able immediately to examine competently all manner of environmental data—on waste disposal and noise levels, for example—but financial auditors are used to working with other specialist professionals. There is every reason to suggest that both external and internal auditors could readily play a central role in systematically evaluating and checking compliance with company environmental policy drawing in technical expertise as needed.

The results of audit procedures need reporting and this should be done in a logical, clear, unemotional and unambiguous manner. Whether such reporting is internal—for managements' eyes only—or external for anyone who takes the trouble to seek it out, is the subject of heated debate. The accounting profession has an important contribution to make as the debate develops not least because the real world is as interested in costs as in benefits alone.

This book aims to describe, in terms that can be readily understood by a general reader, how finance directors, accountants and auditors view the enormously high level of interest in environmental matters. It includes an overall review of some of the legal and other environmental issues currently affecting British business, internationally as well as locally, and their effects on investment and corporate liabilities, and then looks at the function of environmental management systems and audits in helping address these issues. It tries to cut through the scepticism that is felt by many managers who believe that environmental auditing is but another fad that will pass by, before going on to look at how an environmental audit might be conducted in the real world. In doing so it looks at the role of a new standard (BS 7750) published by the British Standards Institution on Environmental Management Systems as well as the implications of an EC Regulation introducing, from April 1995, a voluntary Eco-Management and Audit Scheme to the industrial sector. It then goes on to look at the roles of financial auditors, technical specialists and lawyers in dealing with these developments. All have a lot to contribute.

An audit alone may not be enough or an end in itself. The process may raise expectations which will need to be met by some form of disclosure. Finance directors, accountants and auditors should know all about the problems of financial measurement, disclosure and reporting. So a further chapter (6) on environmental reporting includes comments on how accountants can apply this knowledge and help meet the demands of outside interest groups as well as managers, employees and shareholders.

There is also a chapter (8) which addresses directly accounting problems such as

- the identification and definition of environmental costs;
- the need to accelerate write-downs of assets whose value is permanently impaired by environmental factors;
- the disclosure and definition of environmental contingent liabilities;
- the need to account for environmental risks in carrying out due-diligence enquiries prior to a corporate merger, acquisition or disposal

and goes on to review UK Accounting Standards with the intention of identifying their environmental dimensions.

Chapter 9 covers the role of environmental taxes and their use in not only raising revenue but also in moulding corporate environmental behaviour. Whilst most of the world's businesses operate in relatively free markets it is suggested that, short of enforcing environmental laws, fiscal incentives or disincentives as well as other forms of economic instrument may have an important role to play.

Finally the threads are drawn together and a look is taken at the way forward for business in general, and the accounting profession in particular, both in the UK and around the world.

2
Environmental Laws

2.1 Introduction

Knowledge and awareness of the importance of environmental matters to business in Britain is increasing, but there is still a long way to go. Much seems to depend on the attitudes of senior management and, in particular, the man or woman at the top. Whether that person is environmentally aware for entirely practical and commercial reasons or because of some form of idealistic set of values held personally varies. But it tends to be those at the idealistic end of the spectrum who drive improvements in environmental awareness and management forward the hardest. Most business people only do what they have to so as to either stay in business or comply with the law.

There is certainly a growing body of environmental law that is affecting British industry, much of which arises at European Community level. Looking at these laws and those in the pipeline seems to be a logical starting point for this book, but they should also be set in a wider international context. It is worth remembering that environmental pollution does not recognise national boundaries and that ideas for its control should be freely borrowed and tried around the world. It is also vital for a business to know something about the content of environmental legislation in countries where it is operating.

There is no room in this book for a comprehensive review of the world's environmental legislation so this chapter will be confined to a description of the developing environmental legislative framework in the UK and at European Community level, followed by a closer look at two countries in the European mainland that are generally thought to have high levels of public environmental concern and legislation to match: The Netherlands and Germany. The sheer size of the USA and its relatively draconian environmental laws means that a closer look at the situation there is also needed. In a similar way Japan cannot be ignored and, in the light of the enormous strides it has taken to clean up the environmental impact of its continuing economic development, it may have lessons for the UK and Europe. In any case many UK companies now want to do business in Japan and need to understand what is happening there.

2.2 United Kingdom

In September 1988, Margaret Thatcher, then Prime Minister, made her now famous speech to the Royal Society in which she stated that the Conservative Party was not merely a friend of the earth but also its guardian and trustee for generations to come. That speech seemed to be a turning point for serious politicians in the UK and in the next few years environmental issues were firmly on the agendas of each of Britain's main political parties. That they needed to be was reflected in the 14.9% of the total number of votes that were won by the Green Party in the June 1989 European Parliamentary election. The first-past-the-post system of election in Britain gave them no MEPs but there were 30 Green MEPs elected across Europe.

But green political issues seemed to fade away in the UK over the next few years. In the General Election of 9 April 1992, the Green Party received 1.3% of the votes cast, which rose slightly to 3.2% in the June 1994 European Parliamentary election. To some extent this reflects the adoption of some of the Green Party's ideas and policies by the mainstream political parties. It also perhaps demonstrates that environmental disasters, such as the 1986 Chernobyl explosion and the 1989 Exxon Valdez oil spillage in Alaska, are needed to keep environmental issues on the popular political agenda.

The position is similar in many European countries. In the March 1992 regional elections in France, 18% of the electorate voted for France's two ecology parties, the Verts and the Generation Ecologie, but by June 1994 Greens across Europe could only win 23 seats in the new European parliament in comparison with the 30 they won in 1989.

This Common Inheritance

In the UK, however, it is to the party in power that one must look to see the likely direction of future policy development and associated legislation. That is why a monumental White Paper, published in September 1990, in pale blue covers and running to nearly 300 pages was of such importance. It is called 'This Common Inheritance' and subtitled 'Britain's Environmental Strategy'. Its introduction describes its remit as follows:

> This White Paper looks at all levels of environmental concerns and describes what the Government has done and proposes to do. It starts from general principles and objectives and it discusses the Government's approach to the environmental problems affecting Britain, Europe and the World.

It was therefore a look at problems, actions taken so far, and actions planned, and then went on to look at future issues and plans that the Government was considering which might give rise to legislation in years to come. It does not necessarily make firm commitments and has been described, rather unfairly, as a 'wish list'. But it is a starting point for any business that wants to review the environmental framework in which it is operating in the UK. Annual progress reports are being issued, the first of which was published in September 1991, the second in October 1992, and the third in May 1994. Reference to the overall direction of UK Government policy in the pages that follow will, where necessary, draw on the White Paper and subsequent progress reports for guidance, but the overall objectives are worth repeating here:

- protecting the physical environment through the planning system and other controls and incentives;
- using resources prudently, including increasing energy efficiency and recycling and reducing waste;
- controlling pollution through effective inspectorates and clear standards; and
- encouraging greater public involvement and making information available.

They show clearly that the UK Government has environmental principles that they are prepared to state publicly and which therefore set the context for a wide range of policy measures affecting UK business.

The Environmental Protection Act 1990

Hard on the heels of the White Paper came the first wide-ranging piece of environmental legislation for many years—The Environmental Protection Act 1990. The Act passed into law on 1 November 1990 and some of its provisions are still in the process of being put into practice by means of formal Orders by the Secretary of State for the Environment. Some encountered significant resistance, such as the provision requiring the preparation of a register of contaminated land, and have been deferred indefinitely, but the majority are now UK law. They are briefly described below together with other recent relevant legislation, although the contents of the 1994 Environment Bill which received its first reading in December 1994 have been omitted. It may be significantly amended as it passes through Parliament.

Industrial processes

Part I of the Act introduces the concept of integrated pollution control (IPC). It empowers the Secretary of State for the Environment to prescribe any industrial activity or process as requiring authorisation under the Act if it is capable of causing pollution of the environment. For these purposes, the term environment includes air, water and land—hence the name '*integrated pollution control*'.

The four main features of IPC are:

1. that an operator of a prescribed process requires a prior authorisation to carry it out;
2. that for the first time a single authority (Her Majesty's Inspectorate of Pollution—HMIP) controls releases to all three environmental media through a single authorisation for each process;
3. that authorisations are based on the use by the operator of 'best available techniques (including technology) not entailing excessive cost' (BATNEEC); and
4. that authorisations will be subject to review at the instigation of either the operator or HMIP as technology and techniques improve or as our understanding of the environmental risk develops—and must be reviewed at least every four years.

Further consideration of the accountant's role in dealing with and measuring the 'not entailing excessive cost' element of BATNEEC are set out in Chapter 3.

The prescribed processes to which IPC applies are basically those producing significant quantities of scheduled substances (such as sulphur dioxide and oxides of nitrogen, mercury and cadmium, benzene, carbon monoxide and hydrogen cyanide).

The processes requiring authorisation have now been identified and published as the Environmental Protection (Prescribed Processes and Substances) Regulations 1990. All process industries should check whether or not any of their processes fall to be looked at in the near future. If they do, steps should be taken urgently to establish the exact authorisation requirements of HMIP. The procedures can be drawn out and consume a lot of senior executive time. They might also result in technical changes requiring more investment or even scrapping and, in extreme cases, the closure of process plants. The control of pollutants from sources other than those prescribed is the responsibility of, for example, the National Rivers Authority for water and local authorities for air pollution control.

It should also be noted that environmental information collected by HMIP as part of the IPC process will, unless there are powerful reasons to the contrary, be made available to members of the public through the maintenance of registers of information. Copies of these registers are sent to local authorities so that the public can see them. As they include:

- copies of each IPC application;
- the authorisation issued and any amendments to it; and
- monitoring information on compliance

businesses may find themselves being forced to make sensitive and hitherto confidential information available to any competitor who chooses to look.

There is also, inevitably, a cost which is met by charging each applicant for authorisation—a practice that is consistent with the principle stated in the White Paper that 'the polluter pays'. The fee structure involves a flat rate fee for each application to cover authorisation of a new or substantially altered process and an annual charge to cover compliance monitoring costs. Existing prescribed processes attract fees when they are brought within the IPC regime and processes already approved under an earlier regime pay a reduced fee.

The scale of charges for each individual component of the process is set out below:

Application fee	£3750
Application fee if previously registered under the Alkali, etc., Act 1906	£2500
Annual subsistence fee	£1540
Substantial variation fee	£1250

As each overall process may be broken down into 'component' processes, costs can mount rapidly. When taken with management time to negotiate, administer and monitor the requirements of IPC with HMIP, the total costs can be considerable.

Water

Another recent and significant piece of environmental legislation directly affecting many UK businesses was the Water Act 1989 which created the National Rivers Authority (NRA). This, after HMIP, is probably the second most important environmental watchdog in the UK. It is independent of government, industry generally and the water and sewage industry in particular. Its major responsibilities are to control pollution and to improve the quality of the river systems in England and Wales which it does by:

- enforcing standards of environmental control; and
- raising awareness of environmental issues in industry, commerce, agriculture and the general public.

The Water Act 1989, however, did not last long. It was repealed on 1 December 1991 and replaced with five new acts that consolidated legislation relating to UK water. Two of these—the Water Industry Act 1991 and the Water Resources Act 1991—deal with water pollution. The former covers the control of trade effluent to the public sewerage system and is mainly administered by the water companies, while the latter deals with discharges to so-called 'controlled waters' (rivers, watercourses and the sea) and is mainly administered by the NRA. Emissions to the sewerage system or to controlled waters from prescribed processes under the Environmental Protection Act are controlled by HMIP although the NRA must be consulted for discharges to controlled waters.

There is also a confusing array of lists of prescribed substances which are subject to specific controls if discharged to water. The lists are:

- a red list produced by the UK Government in response to the wishes of several conferences of states bordering the North Sea to reduce discharges of red list substances to the sea by 50% from 1985 figures by 1995; and
- grey and black lists defined in an EC Pollution Directive: black list substances are controlled in UK law by the Trade Effluent Regulations which require that discharges are authorised and emission standards are set whereas grey list substances do not require authorisation.

In effect many of the prescribed substances, such as mercury and cadmium (and their compounds), chlorinated solvents and pesticides, are common to both the red and black lists.

The main impact of these laws and lists on businesses is the imposition of the need to obtain consents to discharge from either the NRA (controlled waters) or the local water company (sewerage system) or HMIP if the process is governed by the IPC regime of the Environmental Protection Act. And these consents have to be paid for. The water companies use a formula which takes into account the costs per cubic metre of reception, conveyance and treatment of sewage. The cost of disposal can vary widely throughout the country depending on whether the sewage receives a biological treatment or is disposed of via marine outfall. The NRA uses a formula based on the composition of the effluent, the quantity discharged and the type of receiving water.

Under the Water Resources Act 1991 it is a criminal offence 'to cause or knowingly permit any poisonous, noxious or polluting matter or any solid waste matter to enter controlled waters' without a consent or authorisation. For minor offences Magistrates can impose a fine of £2000–£20 000. For more serious offences, the Crown Court has the power to impose unlimited fines and imprison an offender for up to two years.

The sting in the tail is the power given to the NRA under Section 161 of the Water Resources Act 1991 to recover its clean-up costs from anyone who it can prove knowingly permitted the pollution. Careless or underfunded maintenance of pipes or storage vessels containing polluting liquids may give rise to higher penalties. Shell was fined £1 million for a discharge of oil into the river Mersey. If the company had to pay for the full clean-up the costs could have been many times greater. At present, however, the NRA has no budget for remediation and is unable to lay out the large sums required even if there was a good chance of recovering costs through the courts. But things may change.

Air pollution

The air pollution control regime is also fundamentally affected by the Environmental Protection Act. Before the Act, air pollution from major industrial processes was controlled by HMIP and was based on a number of statutes, the oldest of which was the Alkali, etc., Works Regulation Act 1906. Under the Environmental Protection Act the principal form of air pollution controls becomes IPC operated by HMIP and Local Authority Air Pollution Control (APC). HMIP regulates all discharges including those into the atmosphere from those processes which have the greatest potential for pollution, whilst local authorities only authorise discharges into the atmosphere from those processes with less potential for pollution. Transitional provisions apply so as to allow for the upgrading of processes to meet the full emission standards that are contained in formal process guidance notes.

There are, of course, a number of other pieces of legislation, such as the Clean Air Act 1993 (consolidating the Clean Air Acts of 1956 and 1968) and Regulations dealing with the control of dark smoke, dust and grit from furnaces, as well as Part III of the Environmental Protection Act which deals with statutory nuisances. In fact the Act strengthens the powers of local authorities in dealing with nuisances by allowing them, in some cases, to anticipate problems as well as merely reacting to them. Nuisances are those things that can cause personal discomfort or prejudice health such as noise, smells, smoke from bonfires, fumes, etc. Dust from a building site is an example.

Finally two international treaties relating to air warrant a mention. The first of these is the Montreal Protocol which had some 90 signatories and dealt with the control of ozone-depleting substances such as CFCs, halons, carbon tetrachloride and 1,1,1-trichloroethane. Under the 1992 Copenhagen Agreement of the Montreal Protocol, phase-out dates from 1 January 1994 to 1 January 1996 were agreed for these substances.

The second international treaty is the United Nations Economic Commission for Europe (UNECE) Protocol dealing with emissions of volatile organic compounds (VOCs). This Protocol requires the UK to reduce its emissions of VOCs by at least 30% by 1999 (compared with 1988). A consultation paper has been published on the UK Government's strategy for meeting this objective although the provisions of Part I of the Environmental Protection Act relating to reducing solvent emissions will achieve most of what is required.

Waste on land

Part II of the Environmental Protection Act deals with the reform of waste disposal and management in England, Wales and Scotland. It gives much greater powers to enforcement bodies such as County and District Councils and significantly strengthens the overall regime covering all stages in the waste chain and to the after-care of old disposal sites. It also encourages those involved in waste disposal to recycle waste.

The major new provision of the Act that has a direct impact on business and company directors is the introduction of a so-called 'Duty of Care'. This Duty is applicable to every person, other than private householders, who has control of waste at any stage from production to disposal. It requires each person—including company directors—to take all reasonable steps to prevent the illegal disposal or management of controlled waste by themselves or any other person.

Since the Act was passed, regulations have been issued by the Secretary of State requiring all who are subject to the Duty of Care to make records of waste they receive and consign, keep the records and make them available to the waste regulation authorities. Failure to observe the Duty of Care or apply the regulations is a criminal offence and as the Act extends the Duty of Care provisions to situations where the affairs of a company are 'managed by its members', in some situations shareholders may find themselves on the line too.

Part II of the Environmental Protection Act also makes some important changes to the overall local authority structure for waste regulation, disposal and collection. Waste Regulation Authorities (County Councils) now have full responsibility for the licensing and enforcement of waste disposal. They are required by the Act, and many have done so, to draw up waste disposal plans providing a strategic framework for waste likely to arise in their areas and they are encouraged to form regional groups to promote a greater consistency of regulatory standards. Waste Disposal Authorities (District Councils) are also affected by the Act and have been prohibited from operating disposal activities themselves. As a result they have transferred those activities to 'arm's length' local authority waste disposal companies (LAWDCs) or to private contractors. Waste Collection Authorities arrange for the collection of household waste and commercial/industrial waste too if requested by the Waste Regulation Authority.

Amended waste management licensing regulations were also announced in Part II of the Act but the need to ensure that the requirements of the 1991 EC Framework Directive on waste were also met meant the delay of the full introduction of new regulations until 1 May 1994. The Waste Management Licensing Regulations 1994 are now in place, however, and have been described as the most complex piece of waste legislation passed in the UK.

An important provision of these new regulations that affects businesses owning landfill sites is the requirement that a Waste Regulation Authority must refuse to accept the surrender of a licence to dispose of waste at a particular site until it is satisfied that the land is safe and there is no threat of pollution or harm. A licence can therefore remain in force long after the site has stopped being used for waste disposal making the company holding the licence, and not the Waste Regulation Authority, responsible for monitoring the site and carrying out any preventative or remedial work.

The regulations also greatly extend public access to information on licensed waste disposal activities through a system of public registers. Not only will various standard forms be available but so will be the Waste Regulation Authority site inspection reports which may create a precedent for other regulatory regimes.

The final provision of Part II of the Environmental Protection Act that will directly affect some businesses is the introduction of a system of 'recycling credits'. Under this scheme Waste Collection Authorities are encouraged to retain waste for recycling by receiving payment from the Waste Disposal Authority which makes savings in its costs of landfill in return for the waste retained. Provision is also made for payments to be made for savings in landfill or waste collection costs to other persons, such as voluntary organisations or groups of businesses, who organise recycling schemes in their areas.

Contaminated land

One of the most controversial proposals in the Environmental Protection Act was found in Section 143 which gave the Government power to require local authorities to compile and maintain public registers of all land in their areas that may be contaminated. The intention was that the registers should be open to public inspection free of charge and that their preparation should begin not later than 1 April 1992.

It seemed to take a long time before the main players with interests in contaminated land woke up to the full implications of this register. When it became clear that it was not just land that was presently contaminated that had to be included but all land that had at any time in its history, and regardless of whether or not it had been cleaned up, been put to a contaminative use there was an outcry. Property companies, developers, surveyors and holders of land as security lobbied hard and the Department of the Environment withdrew.

But it was a withdrawal and regrouping not a defeat for the proposal. In August 1992 the Department published new proposals which restricted the definitions of contamination but still left a lot of concerns—perhaps inevitably because the entry of a parcel of land on a register is going to raise questions about it and, indeed, about immediately adjacent land. To some extent that land will be blighted and, possibly, its value impaired. Nothing then happened for many months until a consultation paper called Paying for our Past was published in March 1994. The results of this consultation are included in the Environment Bill published in November 1994. The issue is of such importance for business, however, that a section is devoted to assessing it fully in Chapter 3.

A further concern is the suggestion in the White Paper that the Government will give local authorities grants for the reclamation of contaminated land in their areas. It may be that at some future time authorities will be able to recover these reclamation costs from private owners. Whether their powers will extend to cost recovery immediately or when the land is sold remains to be seen.

Litter, radioactive substances and much more

The Environmental Protection Act is an enormously wide-ranging piece of legislation. No UK businessman or woman can afford to ignore it but its sheer length and complexity deter many who should know better from taking a close interest in it. This is particularly true of the latter sections of the Act which may appear relatively innocuous but which may contain some real threats to some businesses. The titles of the sections do not give much away:

- Part III   – Statutory nuisances and clean air
- Part IV   – Litter, etc.
- Part V   – Amendment of the Radioactive Substances Act 1960
- Part VI   – Genetically modified organisms
- Part VII – Nature conservation in Great Britain and countryside matters in Wales
- Part VIII – Miscellaneous

In more detail, however, they cover such actions as the dumping of waste at sea, the control of dogs and the burning of stubble in harvested fields (the Act calls it crop residues) and financial assistance for certain environmental projects. The Act is a formidable piece of law that no business operating in the UK can afford to ignore.

Common Law

A review of UK environmental legislation would not be complete without a look at the importance of common law as well as statute-based law. The Common Law has developed over many centuries by a system of judicial precedent, and gives rise to environmental pollution actions in three main areas: nuisance, negligence and the rule under *Rylands* v *Fletcher*.

There are two forms of nuisance: public and private. Public nuisance creates a criminal offence and must be seen to affect 'a wide class of people'. Private nuisance, on the other hand, is a private offence and need only affect the person who owns or occupies a particular property. Nuisance is basically 'unlawful interference with a person's use or enjoyment of land' and might result from noise, vibrations, dust, smoke, poisonous or obnoxious emissions and accumulations which attract pests.

Negligence, on the other hand, only has real application in one-off pollution incidents when it must be established that a duty of care is owed to the plaintiff by the defendant who had breached that duty although the damage resulting from the breach was reasonably foreseeable. Accidental damage is not altogether excluded as negligence might be proven if the circumstances which gave rise to the damage were reasonably foreseeable. It may even be that environmental regulators such as HMIP and the NRA might be held liable in negligence if they fail to give adequate warnings about pollution incidents which subsequently result in damage.

The third main area where common law actions may be brought is in connection with the rule under *Rylands* v *Fletcher* whereby any person who brings onto their land and keeps there a substance which is likely to do damage if it escapes is liable for any damage resulting from that escape. Although at first sight the implications of this rule are wide ranging, in reality it seldom applies. The main problem is that the rule only holds if there is a non-natural use of the land on which the substance is being kept. Industrial use of land would normally be found by the courts to be natural use provided that the site is located with due care and consideration which might be said to have happened if, for example, planning permission has been obtained.

There seemed to be a likely further development associated with the rule under *Rylands* v *Fletcher* when, following a judgement in the Court of Appeal, it had seemed that liability could be imposed for acts which, it subsequently transpired, had caused damage to third parties even though when the acts were done nobody could have foreseen that damage would result. The case that gave rise to this judgement was *Cambridge Water Company* (CWC) v *Eastern Counties Leather* (ECL). The circumstances of the case were that ECL, through practices associated with the emptying of drains of perchloroethylene (which ended in 1974) unintentionally caused the contamination of the underlying chalk aquifer and, subsequently, a borehole used by CWC. A new borehole had to be developed at a cost of £1 million and CWC sued ECL under common law basing the case on nuisance, negligence and *Rylands* v *Fletcher*. In overturning the earlier High Court ruling, the Court of Appeal found ECL liable in nuisance for interfering with the right to abstract clean water from the aquifer and awarded damages of £1 million.

A ruling of the House of Lords in December 1993 revised the Court of Appeal decision ruling that in order for an individual to be liable it must be reasonably foreseeable at the time the acts are done that damage to third parties will result. In delivering the leading speech Lord Goff stated that:

> Given that so much well-informed and carefully structured legislation is now being put in place . . . there is less need for the courts to develop a common law principle to achieve the same end, and indeed it may well be undesirable that they should do so.

Much to everyone's relief, therefore, it seems that, for the time being at least, the courts are content to leave it to the Government to determine the nature and scope of environmental liability.

Environment Agency

Looking to the future and the way in which environmental law will be enforced, the Government's plans to set up two environment agencies deserve a mention. The plan is to have an Environment Agency in England and Wales bringing together HMIP, the NRA and the Waste Regulation Authorities. The Scottish version of the Agency will cover much the same areas but will include control of industrial air pollution as well. The Labour Party is opposed to the inclusion of the Waste Regulation Authorities within the Agencies, preferring to see local control with the Agencies having an oversight role only.

The intention to create these Agencies was announced as long ago as July 1991 but the Environment Bill in which firm proposals are made only received its first reading in December 1994. The target date set for the Agencies is April 1996.

2.3 European Community

Ever since the UK became a member of the European Community in 1973, UK business has had to look over its shoulder at developments in Brussels. Nowhere is this more true than in the field of environmental law and practice where the European Commission seemed to set the environmental agenda in a way that was well ahead of public opinion in many of the Member States.

British industry was shielded from the full impact of the many Commission proposals because most of them were blocked by the Council of Ministers under Article 130 of the Treaty of Rome which required that the vote be unanimous. In recent years, however, Commission protocol has changed and most environmental legislation is now ratified under Article 100 (relating to the harmonisation of national laws) where a qualified majority vote is sufficient. This change in protocol has forced the UK's hand and is behind the significant changes in environmental policy introduced by the Environmental Protection Act 1990 and the Water Acts.

There have been European Action Programmes in place since 1973 but it is the combination of the Fourth (1987–1992) and Fifth (1993–2000) Environment Action Programmes and the Single European Act 1987 that has put environmental matters at the centre of recent Community law making. In particular, the amendments to the Treaty of Rome introduced by the Single European Act set out the Community's fundamental environmental policy objectives as being:

- to preserve, protect and improve the quality of the environment;
- to contribute to the protection of human health; and
- to ensure a prudent and rational use of natural resources.

Underlying these objectives are the following fundamental environmental principles:

- preventative actions should be taken;
- environmental damage should, as a priority, be rectified at source;
- the polluter should pay; and
- environmental protection should be a component of other Community policies.

Clearly objectives and principles such as these have the potential to affect profoundly many business activities in the European Community. Businessmen and women must therefore look closely at existing Community Regulations and Directives and then keep an eye on those that are in the pipeline. The difference between a 'Regulation' and a 'Directive' should also be borne in mind. The two words are often used as though they mean the same thing—but they do not:

1. Regulations, once passed, are directly applicable law in Member States and require no further implementation within the national law.
2. Directives are binding on all Member States but leave the means of introducing the changes required to the States' discretion, although a time period for enactment is stated. Further local legislation is usually required and may be considerably delayed if there is a full parliamentary agenda.

Directives are the traditional way by which Community environmental legislation has been implemented and allows each Member State to use its existing systems of environmental control. The Environmental Impact Assessment Directive, for example, was passed at Community level in July 1988 and became law in the UK through The Town and Country Planning (Assessment of Environmental Effects) Regulations 1988. Environmental Impact Assessments are now a required part of all UK planning applications, covering developments such as radioactive and nuclear installations, motorways, oil refineries and waste disposal projects.

In mid-1994 there were approximately 300 Regulations and Directives in force with a further 140 proposals in the policy pipeline. Two important measures that are in force, but not yet fully implemented, are the

Regulation establishing a European Environment Agency in Denmark and the Directive guaranteeing freedom of access to information on the environment.

The Regulation establishing the European Environment Agency was made in May 1990 but could not take effect because there was no agreement about where it should be located! It has finally been decided that the Agency should be based in Copenhagen. Its main objective will be to gather information about the 'present and foreseeable' state of the environment in the Community and to provide 'objective, reliable and comparable' data which can be used as a basis for preparing and monitoring environmental protection measures. It is also planned to produce a public report about the state of the Community's environment every three years. In the future, the Agency may take on a role involving 'the monitoring of the implementation of Community environmental legislation' as well as the promotion of environmentally friendly technologies and awarding labels for environmentally friendly products, technologies, goods, services and programmes.

The Directive guaranteeing freedom of access to information on the environment had to be implemented in Member States by 31 December 1992. This has been done in the UK through the Environmental Information Regulations 1992 and the various measures proposed in the Environmental Protection Act 1990 and the Water Acts. The Directive requires that information held by any public authority (which not only includes local authorities but also HMIP and the NRA) for any company or individual should be freely accessible. There are exemptions for data affecting national security or which is industrially or commercially confidential.

Of the 140 proposals in the European environmental policy pipeline some are more important to UK business than others. Three are worth a special comment.

- Civil liability for damage caused by waste. Under this proposal there would be a system of strict liability on producers of waste for damage caused by that waste until it is transferred to an authorised disposal facility. Damage to the environment would be a form of civil liability and a holder of waste could become liable in cases where the producer could not be found.
- Packaging. The draft packaging Directive includes targets for increased collection, sorting and recycling of packaging. Germany, France and the Netherlands have already imposed some targets and as a result are better placed to implement this Directive than other Member States as well as having put in place what amount to non-tariff barriers to trade.

- Carbon taxes. There has been much discussion of a Commission proposal that a carbon tax is introduced, equivalent to $3 a barrel on the price of oil, rising to $10 by the year 2000. (A fuller discussion of the implications of this proposal and, indeed, the role of taxes in bringing about environmental improvements is given in Chapter 9.)

A brief comment on the EC's Fifth Environment Action Programme is also called for as this sets the European scene through to the end of the century. The Programme was published in final form in May 1993. It contains a series of long-term environmental objectives and proposals for specific measures to achieve them. The overall goal is to set the EC on the path of 'sustainable development'. An accompanying Resolution agreed by Environment Ministers acknowledges that existing environmental protection measures 'do not appear to be sufficient to meet the increased pressures on the environment likely to arise in consequence of current and anticipated trends in economic and social activity', and accepts that 'the achievement of sustainable development calls for significant changes in current patterns of development, production, consumption, and behaviour'.

2.4 Worldwide

It is beyond the scope of this book to review environmental laws affecting business all around the world. Most UK businesses are now aware of, if not actively involved with, one or more European countries and many have strong links with the USA, which invested heavily in the UK in the immediate post-war years and which is now, in turn, the subject of many takeovers by British companies. So a few words, by way of example, about the legal background in one or two mainland European countries and in the USA is needed. Looking to the future, there is one country which has already transformed its environment as a result of terrifyingly high levels of pollution 25 years ago. Japan may not be the way forward but it is worth a look.

The Netherlands

Whilst only just across the North Sea geographically, The Netherlands is much further away from the UK environmentally. Given the way its environmental laws and policies have evolved over the last 10 years most environmentalists would say it was in front and that it has shown a way forward which other countries will follow.

Environmental policy making and the reactions to the environment of business are often jerked forward by an environmental disaster or scandal.

So it was in The Netherlands when, in 1980, it was discovered that housing in Lekkekerle, a village south of Rotterdam, had been built on a landfill site. Such was public concern, and in the light of an estimated 35 000 industrial sites needing cleaning up, the Dutch government set tough standards for acceptable levels of soil contamination. Dutch local authorities now issue annual lists of contaminated sites in the areas for which they are responsible and then clean them up. They then try to recover the clean up costs from the polluters—usually through the courts. As is so often the case elsewhere, however, making the polluter pay, whilst fine in theory, depends on being able to find the polluter. Records of ownership of a particular site are often inadequate and in any case underground water or some other physical movements may be the cause of the pollution and not the activities of the present site owner. Such are the problems in The Netherlands that cases wait a long time pending a Court hearing.

A key feature of the Dutch business/environment interface, however, is the extent of mutual co-operation between government and industry. An example is the government initiative in setting up the Oele Committee, comprising senior statesmen and industrialists, to deal with soil pollution. Companies voluntarily join a system of corporate collaboration looking at soil pollution which then leads to government aid in the conduct of a sequence of surveys that may either lead to the public reporting of what the surveys revealed or to clean-ups—it depends on the environmental risk shown by the surveys. Each Dutch province has a foundation overseeing the system and reporting regularly to Parliament. Those companies which do not take part may find that expensive investigations and clean-ups are forced upon them.

Another example of environmental co-operation is the setting up of a commission on the environment by VNO, the biggest union of employers in The Netherlands with some 10 000 company members and the second biggest employers' union. The commission has 10 full-time employees and appoints boards drawn from some of the country's biggest companies to deal with specific environmental topics. One of these has been to draw up a framework for corporate environmental management systems which industry hopes may, in time, allow government to relax its environmental guard.

Yet another example of a government/industry agreement has been the negotiation of a covenant on the recycling of packaging materials. Legally the covenant is enforceable in law but it is more like a gentleman's agreement than a piece of legislation. One hundred and fifty Dutch industries, accounting in aggregate for over half of the country's sales, have promised that by the year 2000 there will be no more packaging waste dumped in Holland. A maximum of 40% is to be incinerated and at least 60% recycled. The amount of packaging to be used is also significantly reduced and more use is to be made of recyclable materials.

But this spirit of understanding and compromise between Dutch industry and government may be coming to an end. The Netherlands has a very complex set of environmental laws and regulations which have been introduced on an *ad hoc* basis over the last 20 years or so. Plans are now afoot to pull many of these together and to see that they are properly enforced.

A curious aspect of Dutch governmental enforcement of its many and varied environmental laws has been the lack of it! Although, for example, a system of requiring emission permits exists it has seldom been rigorously enforced and in some cases local authorities have gone so far as to point out in a letter to a company that whilst it does not comply with its permit the situation will be tolerated. This too may be changing as public opinion lets it be known that such cosy relationships between enforcers and the enforced are not acceptable and are going to court to see that permits are properly adhered to.

So The Netherlands is a paradox from the point of view of its environmental laws. On the one hand they are complex and tough but on the other hand the regulators have been quite prepared to turn a blind eye. In any case Government has looked for co-operation with industry in bringing about environmental change and not confrontation. Any UK company considering moving up there could do a lot worse than to consult an environmental lawyer before it makes any commitments, particularly relating to land or property, whatsoever.

Germany

Another European mainland country with a reputation for tough environmental laws is Germany—and with good reason. Its laws are amongst the most stringent of any country in the European Community and, some would argue, amount to a non-tariff barrier to free trade in the Community. Certainly any British business looking to set up there would be well advised to put environmental matters high up its list of priorities for consideration.

Obviously there are real differences between what was the German Democratic Republic (East Germany) and the Federal Republic of Germany (West Germany) although following formal unification in October 1990 the environmental legal structure of the former West Germany now applies throughout the country, including the newly formed East German States of Brandenburg, Mecklenburg-Vorpommern, Saxony, Saxony-Anhalt, Thuringia and Berlin. These States, together with those of West Germany, are known as *Laender* and form the second tier of government in Germany with the main responsibility on a day-to-day basis for administering laws set by the German Federation or *Bund*.

The brief review that follows covers water, waste (including packaging) and contaminated land before saying a few words about the German legal framework for the enforcement of liabilities.

The Acts which govern water resources work to the general rule that all measures which may affect water should avoid any negative impact on water quality and ensure the economic use of water. Water use, including anything that might bring about harmful changes to the physical, chemical or biological properties of water, is subject to specific authorisation as is the discharge of waste water into surface water. Strict polluter liability also applies whereby anybody who adds or discharges substances into water in such a manner as to alter its physical, chemical or biological properties is required to compensate for any damage arising to another person—this includes accidental damage unless caused by *force majeure* and so is extremely onerous.

The German environmental law probably giving rise to most concern in British business circles at present is the ordinance on the avoidance of packaging waste (*Verpackungsverordnung*). This ordinance has established a comprehensive system of waste management aimed at avoiding waste from packaging materials. It applies to packaging manufacturers, makers of materials from which packaging is made and the suppliers of goods in packaging. In principle both manufacturers and distributors are obliged to take back used packaging and to provide for its reuse or recycling. Packaging for drinks, washing and cleaning detergents and dispersion paints are subject to mandatory deposit schemes. The only way a business in Germany can now avoid the obligation to take back, reuse and recycle, or use a deposit scheme is if they are part of an approved collection arrangement which guarantees a regular household collection of used packaging within a distributor's catchment area.

The aim of the *Verpackungsverordnung* is said to be the wish to set up a dual waste disposal system consisting of the existing public system and a new, privately owned, second one operated by and at the expense of the industries that create packaging waste. The effect, however, is not only to reduce waste but also to increase costs and to put a barrier in the way of foreign-made goods being sold in Germany which may not be able to organise or take part in an approved collection scheme.

As in many other countries waste disposal itself is a local authority responsibility that is regulated by the *Laender*. Some wastes, such as builders' rubble, cannot go into the public waste disposal system and have to be disposed of in licensed installations which may be operated by the waste-maker or someone else. Whatever happens, however, there is a general requirement that disposal must be done in a way that does not affect the health and well-being of human life, endanger fauna and flora, damage water, soil and plants, or endanger public safety and order.

There is also a Federal ordinance which defines 350 types of waste that need special supervision. This is supplemented by a Technical Waste Instruction that sets out mandatory disposal requirements and routes. Paint thinners and solvents have to be disposed of in hazardous waste incinerators, galvanisation sludges containing cyanide have to be disposed of by chemical and physical treatment and waste containing arsenic has to be put in underground waste disposal facilities. Residual substances from industrial processes which are to be recycled are controlled by another Federal ordinance with provisions that are broadly similar to those for the determination of waste. Effectively both hazardous waste and residual substances are subject to cradle-to-grave supervision.

Germany, however, has not always looked after its hazardous wastes in such a rigorous manner. In the former West Germany alone it is estimated that there are some 70 000 sites suspected of old contaminations (*Altlasten*) where soil and groundwater or both have been affected by industry or waste disposal activities long since stopped. The problem in the former East Germany is certainly much greater although no really reliable estimates are available. As a starting point, however, it is likely that most, if not all, of the 750 licensed waste installations and many of the 5000 uncontrolled and 7500 illegal waste dumps in East Germany will need cleaning up.

In spite of this widespread problem as yet there is no single piece of legislation requiring the assessment, investigation and clean up of old contaminated sites. The laws governing such sites are numerous and exist at both Federal and State levels. Often the relevant law depends on the time the contamination occurred, the circumstances, the type and the origin of the contamination. It is the general Police Acts, however, which need the most careful watching. Under these Acts the authorities are entitled to order, at their discretion, appropriate investigatory and clean-up measures wherever there is thought to be danger to public safety and order. The scope of the clean-up measures will obviously depend on the type and scope of the old contamination, previous and present use of the site together with its geology and hydrology. Several *Laender* have issued helpful regulations and guidelines.

The key issue for business is what next? What powers do the authorities have to seek compensation from the polluter or the present owner of the site? As is so often the case in other countries here too there is no clear answer. The German Police Acts, however, do make a distinction between the actual polluter and the person 'responsible for the disturbing condition'. The latter could also be described as the current user whether it is the owner, tenant or lessee.

Several court decisions suggest that the polluter is normally held primarily responsible but that later contractual agreements between the polluter and any subsequent user should be taken into account. So a purchaser of contaminated land could find himself responsible for old contamination even though it was caused by a previous user. If only the confusion ended there—but it does not. The authorities seem to have the discretion to select the polluter with the best financial standing or to hold several people liable for the contamination.

Obviously buying property in Germany that may be contaminated is beset with potential problems making careful investigation of legal succession and obtaining proper indemnification more than normally important. This is also true of purchases in former East Germany although the Federal Government has issued guidelines granting certain exemptions to purchasers in their agreements with the *Treuhandanstalt*—the body responsible for disposing of former state-owned East German enterprises.

Finally, in this brief review of German environmental laws, mention must be made of the Environmental Liability Act 1989 which provides for strict liability on the owners of some 100 types of installation for any environmental damage they cause. The list in the Act includes furnaces, gas turbines, cooling towers, chemical manufacturing and pharmaceutical plants, paint shops, stores for hazardous substances, etc.

In general the Act assumes that the cause of environmental damage is a particular nearby installation 'if taking into account the circumstances of each particular case, an installation is found to have been capable of causing the ensuing damage'. On the other hand, the Act waives this assumption if an installation has been operated according to legally imposed permits and conditions. Perhaps this is a carrot that will prove more effective than the big stick. Unusually the Act also requires some owners to carry mandatory insurance if the installation is thought to be particularly hazardous and gives an injured party rights to information about an installation's operators from the environmental authorities particularly when claiming for damages.

USA

The 1980s saw many British businesses look to the USA for takeover opportunities so as to make the most of its 240 million high-earning consumers as a potential market. Whether or not this continues at the same rate throughout the 1990s we cannot ignore the world's largest, richest and most sophisticated economy in this review of environmental laws and their effects on business around the world.

Sad to say the story of recent environmental laws in the USA is not one that most other countries would want to follow. Environmental law has become one of the major sources of fee income for lawyers and shows every sign of continuing to be so. Some would argue that if the fees paid to lawyers in helping companies and individuals avoid or reduce environmental claims made against them had been spent on clean-ups the USA would be a visibly cleaner country today. The root of the problem however is not at the lawyers' door but at that of Congress because myriad federal laws and statutes have resulted from the efforts of many different and often competing Congressional committees over the past 20 years. Today at least 80 sub-committees dabble in environmental legislation.

Another key factor adding to the immense complexity of US environmental laws is the Federal/State duality. There are a number of major Federal statutes which set uniform national programmes in place and encourage states to adopt parallel programmes as well as take on the main role of administering and enforcing them. In many States, most noticeably California, stricter standards than those set Federally are adopted together with supplementary laws not found at Federal level. As a result there can be significant differences from State to State. The application of Federal environmental laws can also give rise to differences from State to State as there can be extensive public consultation before local regulations are drawn up which govern the awarding of the relevant permits to industry. The regulations themselves can also be subject, if challenged, to further administrative and judicial review.

Civil penalties for violations can be high. Approximately $25 000 per day of violation is relatively normal with, in some cases, fines of three times this amount. Criminal penalties not only involve large fines but also imprisonment which may extend to company officers or managers who were only negligent or who knew of the offence but were not the perpetrators.

The power of the ordinary citizen in the USA also should not be forgotten. Public participation is actively encouraged in developing most regulations and awarding permits with relevant information (excluding trade secrets, etc) being publicly available. Companies are, in many cases, also required to report non-compliance themselves which has led to many private-citizen led enforcement suits to force companies to comply. Attorneys specialise in this sort of action and work on a contingent fee basis—with particular success where overworked or underfunded agencies have overlooked a company's environmental failings.

The overall legal framework for environmental control in the USA is set by four main Federal laws covering air, water, waste disposal and the clean-up of contaminated land. The overall national pollution control framework is administered through the Environmental Protection Agency—widely known as the EPA—three letters which cause fear and loathing in the minds of many corporate executives.

The first of these laws are the Clean Air Acts, whereby the Federal Government sets national standards and guidance for certain types of emissions which the States have to implement. They do so by means of State implementation plans which also require EPA approval before they can be enforced by the Federal Government and private citizens, as well as by the State itself.

There are four main parts of the Clean Air legislation:

- The National Ambient Air Quality Standards programme which is designed to protect public health and control levels of sulphur dioxide, ozone, nitrogen oxides, carbon monoxide, particulates and lead.
- The introduction of National Emission Standards for Hazardous Air Pollutants which imposes strict emission limits on sources producing some 189 hazardous air pollutants. In due course these sources, which are mainly manufacturing plants, may be subject risk-based standards which are technologically unachievable. Some plants may have to close.
- An acid deposition control programme, which is to take full effect by the year 2000, imposes stringent sulphur-dioxide emission limits on most existing fossil fuel-fired steam electric generators. The most novel aspect of this programme is the use of annual emission allowances by which regulated units will be awarded for every ton of sulphur dioxide they are allowed to emit. The number of units issued is to be capped at approximately 9 million tons so that new sources will have to buy allowances from existing sources. It is hoped that this will provide a market-based incentive for existing units to overcontrol their sulphur dioxide emissions so as to provide surplus allowances which they can then sell.
- A so-called 'mobile sources program', brought in as a part of the 1990 amendments to the Acts, introduced more stringent exhaust standards for cars and trucks, cleaner fuel standards, vehicle inspection regulations and much more.

The second main Federal law is the Clean Water Act which has as its ambitious objective nothing less than 'to restore and maintain the chemical, physical and biological integrity of the Nation's waters'. It does so by authorising the EPA or delegated States to issue water discharge permits to industrial and municipal dischargers, to others involved in the filling of wetland and also provides measures for the prevention and clean up of oil and chemical spills.

The main regulation is the National Pollutant Discharge Elimination System permit programme which makes it illegal to discharge any pollutant into surface waters without a permit. Most of the standards are set by the EPA for particular types of industry and work on the principle that all industrial sources of a certain type, wherever they are, must meet the same limits on the quality of pollutants discharged using the best pollution control technology available to the industry. Many people think that this system has worked particularly effectively because the permits are based on nationally available standards of technology and not the particular impact of a pollutant on its immediate environment.

Enforcement of the permits is based on self-reporting by permit holders. The effectiveness of such a requirement is greatly enhanced by private actions, which increased very significantly in the late 1980s using publicly available discharge monitoring reports. These actions seem to have spurred government agencies into action and there has been a big increase in civil and criminal actions brought by them in the last year or two.

The third main Federal law dealing with hazardous waste is known as the Resource Conservation and Recovery Act 1976 (RCRA). It provides for cradle-to-grave control of hazardous waste and covers generators and transporters as well as the owners and operators of treatment, storage and disposal (TSD) facilities. Detailed documentation is required which ensures that anyone who has handled a load of hazardous waste at any point in its life-cycle can be traced and made liable should any problem arise.

The EPA regulations which implement the RCRA are highly complex and cover specifically listed types of waste or waste which is ignitable, corrosive, reactive or toxic. The most stringent of these rules relate to TSD facilities which have to obtain detailed operating permits that prescribe minimum technology, emergency contingency plans, financial assurance, groundwater monitoring and plans for closure and post-closure care. Still further regulations are found in the Hazardous and Solid Waste Amendment of 1984. Two of the most important of these are:

1. A ban on the disposal of untreated hazardous waste in landfills.
2. A requirement, administered by the EPA, that the owners and operators of TSD facilities investigate and put right virtually all soil and groundwater contamination on their sites—not just that related to the handling of hazardous waste.

The effect of this second regulation is similar to that of the fourth major piece of Federal environmental legislation: the Comprehensive Environmental Response, Compensation and Liability Act 1980. It is generally known by its acronym—CERCLA—or as 'Superfund' because of its main provision which is the enforced clean-up of past contamination financed initially by an EPA administered 'Superfund' trust but ultimately, if they can be found, by the responsible parties. Because it was one of the first such pieces of legislation anywhere in the world requiring compulsory clean up of past contamination and because of the immense legal problems associated with making it work it has acquired considerable notoriety. Most British businesses who have first-hand experience of operating in the USA know something about it—some, to their cost, wish they had known more.

CERCLA gives the EPA the power to take action over the release or threat of release of any hazardous substance from any 'facility' into the environment. The definitions used are very broad, making these powers quite formidable. The EPA's actions may involve emergency removal as well as something more permanent which has been decided on after extensive investigation. This process can take several years and may result in a waste site being included on the National Priorities List (NPL) that the EPA may then clean up itself. More than 1200 sites are on the NPL at present and this number could expand to 2000 although the EPA has more than 30 000 sites catalogued and under scrutiny for possible listing. It does operate, however, a system of evaluating and ranking hazards and risks, reflecting, for example, direct threats to human health as a priority.

EPA clean-ups are financed by the Superfund, which is a Federal trust funded largely by special industry taxes. But CERCLA and a later amendment (the Superfund Amendments and Reauthorization Act of 1986—or SARA) authorise the EPA to recover its costs and additional compensation for damage to natural resources from four types of responsible party:

- the current owner or operator of the site;
- the owner or operator at the time of disposal;
- the waste generators who arranged for treatment or disposal; and
- transporters who selected the site.

The last three types on this list may find themselves liable retroactively. The cause of the liability may predate CERCLA by many years and might have been quite lawful at the time. This search for parties with deep enough pockets to warrant an EPA claim against them has given rise to another acronym—PRP—or Potentially Responsible Parties.

Furthermore, liability is generally strict—it exists regardless of knowledge, fault, degree of care or intent. It is also joint and several so that any responsible party may be held responsible for the entire cost. This is a considerable threat as the average CERCLA clean-up cost is now some $30 000 and many cost over $100 million. A study by the Rand Institute suggests that 88 cents out of every dollar spent by insurers on clean-ups in 1989 went to cover legal fees and the like, rather than dealing with the contamination itself, although most of this is not directly spent on clean-ups. And almost no-one is in the clear—the US courts have interpreted these liability provisions very broadly so that they may cover individual shareholders, past or present parent companies, lessees, and even lenders who, as a result of their actions, can be said to have stepped into the shoes of the owner or operator.

The EPA also has powers to issue unilateral administrative orders to force a company to clean-up itself. Failure to do so can result in swingeing penalties of as much as three times the EPA's clean-up costs. CERCLA also authorises companies to recover their clean-up costs from other responsible parties. Such actions are not now limited to sites on the NPL. There can be few places in the world where the warning of '*caveat emptor*' can have more importance than when buying real estate in the USA.

Before leaving this brief review of environmental law in the USA a further word is needed about the EPA or Environmental Protection Agency itself. It may become a model for other similar agencies elsewhere in the world—beginning with the proposed European Environmental Protection Agency or its British equivalents? The EPA was established by President Nixon in 1970 to bring together under one roof the disparate federal pollution control programmes of a number of federal agencies. It is independent and acquired Cabinet status under President Bush. Its headquarters are in Washington DC and it has 10 regional offices which implement either directly or indirectly national regulations and policies developed in Washington. In the early 1990s, it had a staff of over 26 000 and an annual budget of some $5 billion, of which $2 billion is its operating budget and $3 billion is grant money. It regulates discharges from more than 200 000 industrial and commercial sites as well as 30 000 sites under scrutiny for clean-up and 1400 sites which it believes threaten harm to the public health where it is now conducting or monitoring clean-ups.

Japan

No survey of environmental law around the world would be complete without a look at at least one of the Asian economies. The most obvious one, which had some of the worst industrial pollution problems to be found anywhere only 25 years or so ago, is Japan. The fact that many of these problems now appear to be resolved suggests that there may be lessons for the rest of the world to draw from the Japanese example.

The root cause of Japan's pollution problem was the post-war focus on rebuilding its industry which had been largely destroyed during the closing stages of World War II. Government and industry worked closely together to bring this about but scant attention was paid to the environment. Manufacturing plants were built in densely populated areas without land use or pollution controls and attempts to enforce laws on water and air pollution passed in the late 1950s and early 1960s failed because preventing harm to public health and the environment had to be harmonised with sound industrial development. The post-war focus on rapid economic growth meant that the latter prevailed.

This state of affairs continued until several high-profile cases of poisoning changed public attitudes. The most prominent of these were the mercury poisonings which caused brain damage and deformity at Minimata. The poisoning was caused by drinking polluted water and eating polluted fish from Minimata Bang. The importance of the case was not just the horrible results of the poisonings but an interpretation by the court of the Japanese Constitution which, the courts decreed, conferred upon the country's citizens, the right to enjoy a healthy environment. Much tougher environmental legislation followed, beginning with a Basic Law for Environmental Pollution Control in 1967. This law sets the framework for nationally enacted environmental laws being enforced by local laws and administrative procedures throughout Japan's 47 prefectures and then lower level municipal governments.

At a national level there are three principal environmental agencies each reporting to the Prime Minister's office. The first of these is the National Environmental Agency which studies environmental pollution problems and the second is the Environmental Pollution Control Committee which controls them. Both can propose legislation. The third agency is the Pollution Adjusting Committee whose role is to resolve environmental disputes. Western governments could do worse than look at this tripartite approach which allows specialisation and concentration of effort without creating an all-powerful environmental body—such as the EPA in the USA—whose powers can have a devastating effect.

It may be that cultural factors are just as important in making Japanese environmental legislation work. In practical day-to-day terms the law is of less significance than so called 'administrative guidance' which is an informal, more-authoritative process by which government seeks and gets industry's voluntary co-operation. It involves discussions and consultation and may take the form of unwritten directions, requests, warnings, suggestions or encouragement—most of which will be tried before a formal enforcement action starts. Perhaps the reason for the success of administrative guidance is the back-up discretionary enforcement powers of local government. If the guidance given is ignored, future government co-operation may be withheld.

Private agreements between individuals or citizen groups and companies are also often used to establish environmental controls. Some 30 000 exist now and more, perhaps 2000 a year, are appearing all the time. Government does not rely on such agreements but may take them into account and could, for example, delay issuing a licence or permit until a company and the local citizens have sorted things out between themselves. They can cover virtually anything but agreements on emission limits and inspection rights are two of the more common examples. In some cases they can involve establishing a trust fund to compensate individuals for environmentally related personal injury.

Consistent with this general theme of negotiation and conciliation is the low level of criminal actions, although provisions do exist in an Act going back to 1970 which codifies environmental mediation and dispute resolution procedures. The Act provides for an environmental counsellor for each prefecture who helps in obtaining information and expert assistance and makes his own independent assessment of the facts.

Further legislation at a national level covers air emissions, water effluent and waste disposal and is enforced, sometimes more stringently than as set nationally, by the prefectures and municipalities. Environmental Impact Assessments are used widely. There is no law however, nationally or locally, which can force private parties, companies or individuals, to clean-up contaminated land. Where clean-ups happen it is normally as a result of administrative guidance.

The Air Law dates back to 1968 and provides for an emissions control programme to control plant emissions so that ambient air quality standards are observed. It seems that the administering prefectures take their responsibility seriously. There are regular inspections of Japan's 180 000 registered facilities but these seldom result in fines or criminal penalties and only occasionally in administrative guidance.

The Water Law of 1970 establishes water quality criteria for designated public water areas, such as rivers, lakes, ports, and harbours, and sets effluent standards for industries and businesses discharging certain pollutants into water. Again inspections of the 280 000 registered facilities result in very few fines although administrative guidance is rather more widely used.

Finally, the Waste Law of 1970 (amended in 1976 and 1983) deals with industrial and domestic solid and hazardous waste that is disposed of in inland and coastal landfills, in offshore reclamation sites and in the ocean. Coastal reclamation is widespread and is a particular feature of Japanese waste disposal. It involves the construction of box-like structures on the sea bed which are filled with waste and soil to create land which can then be built on. There are now regulations in place governing reclamation and use, but prior to 1976 land reclaimed in this way was not considered to be a waste disposal facility. Perhaps there are latent clean-ups required around the Japanese coast which may cause problems for landowners in years to come. There is no Japanese Superfund at present but there may be a need for one in the future.

3

Key Environmental Issues

3.1 Introduction

An underlying theme of this book is that nearly all so-called environmental issues are business issues too, and most business issues have their financial side which the finance director, accountant and auditor has to understand and explain. The aim of this chapter is to identify a few of those environmental issues which are likely to be of more importance to financial people. It has to be highly selective; leaving out is just as hard as putting in.

A start is made by looking at the costs of complying with legislation and best practice both in general terms and specifically in certain industrial sectors. Waste management and disposal followed by energy and energy conservation come next. These are areas where costs can be offset by savings and which are some of the more obvious cases for early action. The following section looks at contaminated land, its valuation and responsibility for its clean-up, which are topics of increasing importance for any business owning or occupying land. The chapter then concludes with a more far-reaching review of international issues, such as free trade and the latest GATT round, which are of particular relevance to multinationals.

There is insufficient space to do more than outline each issue but they are described from a business point of view and, in particular, from an accountant's perspective. It is hoped that this will make the descriptions relevant and focused.

3.2 Compliance costs

It is easy to say much about the business challenge represented by the cost of complying with the environmental laws, regulations and pressures currently confronting British companies. Indeed all the way through this book are examples of changing patterns of investment, revenues and expenses which, when brought together in one place, show the large financial cost of what is involved.

This section looks first at the overall findings of a UK Department of the Environment (DoE) statistical survey of the costs of environmental protection, then looks to the future and, in particular, to the EC where the legislative agenda is fairly visible. There follows consideration of the cost aspects of the UK's Integrated Pollution Control regime, the capital investment programme of the chemical industry and the effect of environmental compliance costs on export markets before concluding with an example of how additional costs can be more than offset by savings.

The UK DoE survey estimated that in 1991 environmental protection cost some £14.0 billion or about 2.5% of the country's Gross Domestic Product. Nearly half of this total, £6.7 billion, was the cost of cleaning up river pollution and purifying water. Much of this figure is eventually paid for by water consumers whose bills, the survey estimates, may double in real terms over the next 10 years as the UK water companies comply with EC regulations. The next most significant category of cost was the £3.0 billion spent in 1991 reducing pollution from all kinds of waste, followed by £2.4 billion spent by industry mainly on curbing air pollution, with the balance of £1.9 billion going on cleaning up contaminated land and reducing noise. The survey suggests that the Government paid about one-third of the total bill with industry and households paying the rest.

These figures are but an indication of the total of all kinds of environmental costs. They only represent direct, 'pure' environmental spending and almost certainly underestimate more general additional 'green' costs of changing working methods, promotion and consumption in response to increased concerns about the environment. They also need to be seen in the context of benefits reflected in reduced levels of recorded pollution where the results are, at best, mixed. The report shows that carbon monoxide emissions rose by 30% between 1980 and 1991. Lead emissions from vehicles, however, have fallen by 70% since the mid-1980s with the arrival of unleaded petrol.

Turning to the wider European picture, a report produced by the Environmental Policy Consultancy (EPC) in July 1992, called 'Anticipating the Future EC Environmental Policy Agenda', estimated that prospective European Community legislation may cost British business more than £15 billion annually when fully implemented over the next few years. It reviewed 86 environmental proposals and concluded that they could have very substantial cost implications.

One of the most significant is the latest EC proposal for reducing sulphur in diesel fuel and gas oil used for heating, which might cost the European oil industry £2.4 billion in desulphurisation equipment at refineries. EPC estimate that for gas oil alone the proposals could cost British refineries £262 million. Another major area of concern is the fast rising cost of disposing of waste brought about by much higher incineration standards and a shortage of acceptable disposal sites. EPC estimate that the price of dumping domestic waste might increase 20-fold over the next decade and the cost of special waste disposal might rise 100-fold.

Jobs are at risk too. EPC believes that EC proposals for harmonising energy efficiency requirements, admittedly still in the early stages of consideration by the Community, might lead to a significant loss of jobs among British boiler manufacturers.

Is it all worth it? In some quarters serious questions are beginning to be asked. In a leading article in *The Economist* on 8 August 1992, entitled 'Environmentalism runs riot', a warning note is sounded drawing particularly on experience in the USA where more hard financial data seems to be available. The article stresses that 'nothing—not even cleanliness—comes free' which could well mean that the recent popular enthusiasm for environmental controls and clean-ups will not survive unless these enthusiasts 'learn the language of priorities, and of costs and benefits'. One response perhaps is to ask the question about how much environmental laws cost in preventing a single early death. The office of Management and Budget in the USA has had a look at the cost-effectiveness of a number of the Environmental Protection Agency's rules and calculated that the answers range from US$200 000 a life saved (for a drinking water standard) to US$5.7 trillion a life saved, roughly equivalent to the US Gross National Product (for a rule on wood preservatives)!

Coming down to earth and back across the Atlantic to the UK, questions such as these are at the heart of Integrated Pollution Control (IPC) as administered by HMIP. The Environmental Protection Act 1990 requires operators of prescribed processes to demonstrate that they are employing BATNEEC—the 'best available technique not entailing excessive cost'—to prevent and minimise releases of prescribed substances and to 'render harmless' all their releases. But easy answers are not forthcoming and for the first few years of the IPC regime, HMIP have tended to interpret BATNEEC on a case-by-case basis.

A new system for more consistent environmental and economic assessments of IPC applications, however, has been proposed by HMIP in 1993, but there is still a long way to go. In principle, the new system is based on the idea that the overall environmental impact of a process can be quantified as a 'BPEO Index'. BPEO—or 'best practicable environmental option'—must be considered if a process discharges to more than one of air, land and water. The process option which gives the lowest value of this BPEO Index will then be the 'best environmental option' (BEO).

Although simple in concept, drawing the BPEO Index is fraught with difficulties, not least in applying the 'not entailing excessive cost' part of BATNEEC. The current attitude of HMIP is that if a firm wants to use an option other than the BEO it must present annualised costs for all the different options. This requires estimates of capital costs, annual operating and maintenance costs, cost credits from waste or energy saving, and details of the expected operating life of the process. A graph of the BPEO Index for various options plotted against the annualised costs will show 'break points' where large cost increases will yield little reduction in the pollution potential.

Clearly this approach will require a lot of confidential financial information being passed to HMIP—unless, of course, it is expressed in relative rather than absolute terms showing incremental costs between the various options. A report published by Environmental Data Services (ENDS) in December 1993 entitled 'Integrated Pollution Control: the first three years', however, showed that of the 328 process applications that were authorised by 1 April 1993 'only a tiny fraction of firms supplied cost data to support claims that a process option had been rejected on the grounds of excessive cost'. But the signs are that in future this may no longer be acceptable.

It is arguable, however, that the costs of complying with IPC and other requirements may not be as high as at first thought. An annual investment survey carried out by the Chemicals Industry Association (CIA) showed that earlier predictions of a growing burden of environmental capital investment have been exaggerated. The latest CIA survey results reveal that the chemical industry's capital spending in 1993 totalled £1.9 billion of which 14% was on environmental investments. Two years ago, CIA members predicted that environmental investments would account for 21% of their total capital spending in 1993. That would have been a steep increase on figures of 10% in 1991 and 14% in 1992. On the other hand, the results show that chemical companies have consistently planned for a sharp increase in environmental expenditure three years ahead. It should also be noted that by no means all of the industry's spending on environmental protection is being forced by legislation. Only about 60% of 1993's investments were driven in this way.

The CIA's report states that increased environmental expenditure brings 'both costs and opportunities'. This should not be overlooked by other industrial sectors, not just the chemical industry. In a perverse way tough local legislation, and its effective enforcement, force companies to develop new technologies which can then be used to take advantage of rapidly growing overseas demand for environmental technologies and services.

A study for the DTI published in early 1994 (*The UK environmental industry: succeeding in a changing global market*: HMSO) reported that the global environmental market was worth US$ 210 billion in 1992—comparable to the aerospace sector—and is predicted to grow to US$ 320 billion in 2000 and US$ 570 billion by 2010. In 1992, the UK had a trade surplus on environmental equipment of $ 350 million which rises to over $ 1 billion if environmental services are added in. The UK's trading position in water and wastewater treatment is now particularly strong.

Tough domestic regulations, however, have forced other countries to develop sophisticated environmental technologies too. A Labour Party paper published in 1994 identified Germany (with desulphurisation technology), Japan ('deNO$_x$' equipment), the USA (catalytic converters), The Netherlands (contaminated land remediation) and Sweden (incinerator emissions abatement). Clearly one country's compliance costs are another's export opportunity.

Compliance costs, both immediate and prospective, however, can be relatively neutral in their effect if other environmentally related costs savings can be found. Nissan UK, the owner of a major car manufacturing plant in Sunderland, won one of the Royal Society of Arts' annual environmental management awards in June 1993 for doing just this. The annual cost savings of £260 000 per annum are derived as follows:

	£
Plant environment—costs of noise, health and safety	200 000
Plant impact—including costs of solvent emissions and effluent treatment	620 000
Conservation—savings of energy and other resources	(120 000)
Waste management savings	(980 000)
Neighbourhood protection costs	20 000
Net annual cost savings	£(260 000)

The high plant impact costs of £620 000 per annum are largely due to Nissan's move to water-based paints (which complies with forthcoming restrictions on emissions of volatile organic compounds) including the cost of an effluent treatment plant and the use of fluidised bed pyrolysis for cleaning contaminated plant items making caustic cleaning chemicals redundant. Waste management savings of £980 000 per annum were largely derived from recycling fuel tank cut-offs for reuse in new fuel tanks.

So environmental compliance costs need not always be seen in a negative light but they are increasingly real for a wide range of business activities.

3.3 Waste

Most kinds of economic activity generate waste of one kind or another. By definition 'waste' is something that is surplus to requirements and as such it has become the legitimate focus for the attentions of environmentalists as well as for those who want to save costs. In fact, any UK business asking questions about its environmental performance finds that waste is one of the first issues raised and, equally quickly, that there are all manner of challenges that its management presents.

Perhaps, in practical terms, the first issue to look at is the legal framework now operating in the UK putting a Duty of Care on everyone who produces, transports, carries, keeps, handles, treats, disposes, or deals with controlled waste to ensure that it is properly disposed of. The scope of these provisions, introduced with effect from 1 April 1992 by Section 34 of the Environmental Protection Act 1990, is potentially so wide that every company director or manager is affected. Then, when the legal background is better understood we can go on to look at recent developments affecting particular types of waste and the scope for its treatment and recycling that provide some real opportunities as well as threats for British business.

The most striking threat posed by the Duty of Care provisions is their imposition on most company officers and even shareholders in some circumstance. Officers (directors, managers, company secretaries, etc) may be personally criminally liable where they have consented to or 'committed' an offence or where an offence is attributable to their neglect. They must take active steps, therefore, to satisfy themselves that their company has taken the necessary steps to comply with the legislation.

It may not end there because the Duty extends to shareholders as well as officers where the affairs of a company are 'managed by its members'. This area of law is untested in the Courts but it raises questions about the responsibilities of venture capitalists, holders of securities, and receivers or administrators who exercise some control over the management of a company and may find that they have unexpected liabilities which are personal and tough as the following table shows:

Offence	Magistrates' Court	Crown Court
Dumping any waste or treating it without a licence	£20 000 fine and/or 6 months in prison	Unlimited fine and/or 2 years in prison
If the most poisonous form of waste was involved	£20 000 fine and/or 6 months in prison	Unlimited fine and/or 5 years in prison
Breach of Duty of Care or its regulations	£2000 fine	Unlimited fine

More needs to be said here about the nature of the offences and, indeed, about the meaning of the expression 'controlled waste' which is defined as being all waste, including domestic household waste (other than when it is in the hands of the occupier of the household), but excluding agricultural, radioactive, explosive and mineral waste. The Duty of Care means that anyone who has the Duty must ensure:

- that the controlled waste does not escape from their control or that of any other person to whom it is passed;
- that any other person disposing of controlled waste does not treat, dispose or treat it without a waste management licence—or break the conditions of a licence, or keep it or store it in a way that causes pollution or harm to health; and
- that if the controlled waste is transferred there is also transferred a written description of the waste that is sufficient to enable each person receiving it to avoid committing any offence and to prevent its escape.

For many businesses it is the last of these three conditions that is potentially onerous. A copy of the written description or transfer note, which must be completed and signed by both parties, has to be kept by both sides for two years from the date of consignment. Fortunately repeated transfers of the same kind of waste between the same parties can be covered by one transfer note for up to a year. Weekly collections from shops are a good example of this. And the Waste Regulation Authority has a right to ask for and inspect these transfer notes.

Businesses producing waste from a manufacturing process may well have found these provisions a burden but have coped by changing their existing routines. They should already have systems and procedures in place to control their waste, although the need to know how and where their waste is disposed of has caused some difficulties. It is offices and shops producing mainly non-hazardous paper and cardboard waste that inadvertently may be caught out, particularly if the Waste Collection Authority has authorised a private contractor to do the collection work or such a contractor is employed directly. It is then the duty of anyone consigning the waste to the contractor to make sure that the contractor has a current, valid certificate of registration under the Control of Pollution (Amendment) Act.

In practical terms, the biggest danger from the Duty of Care provisions is if a company's waste was found, by the Waste Regulation Authority, to be in the wrong place—in the street, at an unlicensed location, at an unsuitable site or being mishandled at a site. The first three on this list would, *prima facie*, be a breach of the Duty of Care. The fourth would depend heavily on the description on the transfer documents. If the waste producer has done all he should then his liability will be much reduced. Proving that he has is a another matter but can be achieved more easily if a properly designed and documented waste-management system is in place.

Now, having reviewed some of the more onerous legal provisions, is the time to turn to some of the wider waste management issues affecting UK business. Such issues affect both liquid and solid wastes and cover not only general waste management but also the scope for recycling, including cost savings and potential recoveries.

A good starting point is one of the excellent short booklets in the Environment Means Business series published by the CBI's Environmental Management Unit, entitled *Managing Waste:Guidelines for Business*. It sets out in a straightforward way the steps that companies need to take to improve waste management standards and performance. Apart from the legal requirements, which have already been discussed, it looks at the responsibilities of the waste producer and, in particular, at:

- knowing what wastes are generated,
- management's responsibilities,
- waste minimisation,
- management of waste on site,
- choice of disposal option,
- use of contractors,
- information to the public.

Most of these headings require little further comment, their meaning is obvious, but one or two do.

The first of these lies behind 'management's responsibilities' which recommends that a company should publish its waste disposal policy, which itself should be the responsibility of a director or senior manager. The second is to re-emphasise the need for keeping proper records on site showing the waste management process in action, which is necessary if good handling and proper disposal is to be proved to an outsider. The third is the suggestion that information on waste disposal practices should be made available to the public which the CBI suggest is helpful in gaining public confidence. Details of what is needed will vary between industries but should include something about the quantities and nature of the waste, the disposal routes used and the reasoning behind using the routes chosen. Whether or not such information would ever allay public concerns about the generation and disposal at sea or in landfill of radioactive waste is another matter but in most cases it could make a real difference, especially if an incident occurs.

Another way of dealing with criticisms of industrial waste management practices is to have a good story to tell about the amount of non-renewable resources used. Not only will this help allay some external criticism from the public and customers alike but it can also save real money. When, for example, the Dow Chemical Company decided to launch a waste minimisation programme in the UK in the late 1980s, one of its first targets was the 'Staraue' weedkiller production plant in Kings Lynn, East Anglia. It now estimates that the 'greening' of the process, largely through recycling, has saved it more than £500 000 a year. Previously, two organic process solvents used during the production of the weedkiller—methanol and DMF—were collected as they became contaminated, transported to a commercial high temperature waste incinerator and destroyed. One of the solvents alone accounted for 2000 tonnes of waste burned each year. Now both solvents are recycled. One of them is cleaned using an in-house loop with relatively unsophisticated technology. As a result the company now buys less 'virgin solvent' and reduces its disposal costs whilst at the same time helping enhance its environmental image.

The Dow Chemical programme in the UK was introduced from the USA in late 1988 and is known as WRAP (Waste Reduction Always Pays). WRAP is to continue indefinitely with constant monitoring of processes and continual improvements attacking the most wasteful as soon as possible. In fact it is a part of the company's ongoing total quality management programme. Recycling as well as direct waste minimisation is at the heart of WRAP and is generally held out to be one of the major planks in the building of a platform of truly sustainable industrial activity and development.

It is nothing new. It has always been accepted as common sense that the most should be made of materials before they are discarded but with the UK government's commitment that, by the year 2000, 50% of all recyclable material will be recycled and an almost 300% increase in landfill prices since 1985 recycling is centre-stage. But Dow still has a long way to go, particularly for paper, glass and plastics, although metals are better—currently some 82% of ferrous metal, 74% of copper and 66% of lead are recovered. Only 33% of paper and board consumption, 20% of glass consumption and 6% of plastics are recovered.

A key factor in making recycling work is the existence of markets—a market for the reclaimed materials and a market too for the products made out of secondary materials. These markets can be influenced directly by purchasing policies and indirectly by waste disposal costs. Taking paper and board as an example the CBI's figures show that although recycling is already very active there is the potential to go very much further. In 1989, 2.8 million tonnes of paper and board were recovered which provided 53% of the UK paper and board industry's raw material needs overall. On the other hand some 10 million tonnes of paper and board are consumed each year so that there is much more that could be done. 59% of newsprint is recovered but another 200 000 tonnes is available and only 8% of the 1.2 million tonnes of high-grade printing and writing paper is recycled each year.

One of the main problems is the way in which market prices vary, especially for newsprint, making forward investment planning difficult. Another is the low (but growing) demand for recycled paper products and a third is the low level of collections presently achieved from offices and other commercial premises.

There are also wider commercial knock-on effects if recycling takes off. A 1991 study by a London-based consultancy, Clean Systems, has shown that the growth of plastics recycling will make a serious impact on sales of new plastics in Western Europe. This will exacerbate the overcapacity which already threatens the profitability of the petrochemical industry. If the 7 million tonnes of plastic currently handled every year by Europe's municipal waste authorities is augmented by a further 8 million tonnes from 'long term' waste such as cars and televisions, making a total of 15 million tonnes in all, and if the proportion recycled rises from 6% in 1991 to 16% in 1996, the consumption of virgin polymer (freshly manufactured plastic) could be reduced by 2 million tonnes a year.

A final word is also needed about packaging which is one of the main contributors to the waste-stream. In 1993, 68% of all UK packaging went to landfill, 30% was recycled and 2% was used in waste-to-energy schemes. It was figures such as these that prompted the Secretary of State for the Environment to ask all businesses in the 'packaging chain' to prepare proposals for recovering 50–75% of packaging waste by the year 2000. The response came from a specially formed Producer Responsibility Industry Group (PRG), which was reported in February 1994.

Some of the key recommendations in the PRG report, in response to the Secretary of State's pre-determined key tasks, were:

1. To set up an organisation, provisionally called VALPAK, to put the proposals into action.
2. To raise, through VALPAK, funds (initially some £100 million per annum) via a levy on packaging to meet the costs of new collection capacity, material-specific price-support, the development of waste-to-energy and some reprocessing operations that are not economic.
3. To achieve a 'recovery' rate of 58%, encompassing material recycling, composting and waste-to-energy by the year 2000. Within this

material, recycling will rise from 30% to 50% and waste-to-energy from 2% to 8%.
4. To continue actively to encourage packaging specifiers to use more recycled material.
5. To seek statutory backing for its proposals.

Packaging going to landfill will reduce from 4.9 million tonnes in 1993 to 3.4 million tonnes in 2000, according to the PRG, if its recommendations are adopted.

The proposals are not without critics. There is no commitment to avoid unnecessary secondary packaging but instead reliance is placed on market forces working against increased packaging. Similarly some argue that there are insufficient measures proposed by the PRG to promote markets for recycled packaging. Even if the PRG's proposals work packaging consumption is still expected to increase by 10% over the next 7 years from 7.29 to 8.05 million tonnes.

3.4 Energy

Having looked at waste one of the next areas examined by most businessmen and women who develop some form of environmental awareness is energy. In particular, they want to look at the scope for efficiency so as to reduce their own costs as well as contribute to the wider issues of global warming, acid rain and other forms of atmospheric pollution. It is one area where the benefits can be both to the company and the wider world at the same time.

Energy is a big world environmental issue; indeed one of the biggest of all. Over the past 30 years the world's energy demand has grown at an annual average rate of 3.3%. The fastest rise, particularly since 1970, has been in the developing countries where, in the last decade alone, energy demand increased by 49% in comparison with 14% in developed countries. This pattern is likely to persist because it is the developing countries which have accounted for 87% of the world's population growth since 1960 and where the present levels of energy consumption per head at some 1.2 toe (tonnes of oil equivalent) per annum are very low in comparison with developed countries. In North America the equivalent figure is 7.8 toe and in Western Europe it is over 3.1 toe.

There have been many studies of the factors behind this trend and suggestions about what to do in response. Before looking at the more detailed actions that UK companies should be taking it is worth considering some of these factors and responses to put more local actions in context.

- According to the World Energy Council it is broadly agreed by the world's industrial nations that improved energy efficiency could lead to savings of the order of 30% overall on current consumption.
- It is often cheaper to invest in energy conservation than in additional energy supply. Conservation measures and technology are often simple and well tested; planning permission is rarely needed and the risks, both financial and technological, are low.
- Over the next 30 years it is unlikely that alternative forms of energy to those we have at present will be developed on a significant scale and there can be adverse environmental side effects for renewable energy sources just as there are for non-renewable ones. Tidal power for example can have catastrophic effects on estuarine habitats including bird populations and migrations of international importance as well as visual, siltation, fish and shipping impacts.
- Strenuous efforts to develop renewable energy sources will nevertheless have to continue apace with developed countries pursuing multi-energy strategies and actively encouraging the development of the necessary technology, finance, management, facilitating institutions and political climate.
- Proper pricing is also important. The World Bank has estimated that energy is often sold in developing countries at prices which cover only 40% of traditional economic costs. But wider non-traditional economic costs, such as the environmental impact of new energy developments, also need to be taken into account even though at present there seems to be no adequate or acceptable method for doing so.
- Pollution from non-renewable energy sources may be of critical importance. Approximately 70% of Britain's SO_2 emissions and a large proportion of NO_x emissions come from power stations. Legislative controls to combat acid rain will require large-scale investment thereby increasing energy prices. The total cost forecast for Britain to comply with the EC Large Combustion Plant Directive is £6 billion.
- The need to reduce CO_2 emissions arising from energy production and consumption to combat the Greenhouse effect (global warming) is a major international priority. As described in Chapter 9 the EC is currently considering the introduction of an energy or carbon tax aimed at reducing energy consumption.

If these are the big global issues, which should be borne in mind by all businesses considering their long-term strategies, practical action requires that we focus on the company and look at the initiatives being proposed and implemented at present by the UK Government.

An early attempt to get UK companies to do something was the October 1991 launch of the Making a Corporate Commitment Campaign when the UK's top 2000 businesses were asked to sign a declaration committing them to set energy saving targets and report publicly on their performance against them. Since then the campaign has been extended to other businesses and public bodies.

By February 1994 the campaign had 1600 signatories but not all are very good at disclosing their energy efficiency targets. In response to a request from the Secretary of State for the Environment in September 1993 only 30 companies submitted details of their targets. Most who did respond aim to improve their energy efficiency by 10–15%, though not necessarily in all their operations, over varying periods but most commonly around five years.

3.5 Contaminated land

One of the biggest potential challenges arising from the present changes in law and attitudes to environmental matters is the need for and cost of clean-ups. Nowhere is this more important than the cleaning up of contaminated land.

The earlier description of the US Superfund laws in Chapter 2 and the extensive powers of the US Environmental Protection Agency make the point particularly graphically because there are some signs that enforced clean-ups, with the costs being recovered from owners, previous owners and lenders as well as the polluters, may be a feature of business life in the UK as well as the USA in a few years time. There is already real interest awakening in this possibility not least because the proposal to create a register of land which had been put to certain contaminative uses, announced in the Environmental Protection Act 1990 and described in Chapter 2, has focused landowners' and tenants' minds on the question.

In fact, the proposed registers are not now going ahead, for the time being at any rate. The idea caused such a storm of protest that, after a second attempt to produce a workable approach, which was the subject of wide consultation in late 1992, the whole idea was shelved. Instead the problem is still being looked at and has been the subject of a formal Review which was carried out by the Department of the Environment and the Welsh Office. A report, entitled 'Paying for our Past', was published in March 1994 and is described more fully in what follows. The results of the consultation were published in November 1994 and will be put into effect through the Environment Bill, which received its first reading in December 1994.

In the absence of registers, however detailed, comparable knowledge of the scale of the problem of contaminated land in the UK can only be guessed. This is not true of some other mainland European countries: in The Netherlands an inventory of contaminated land identified 110 000 sites, and even Denmark has identified 20 000 sites. This sort of data suggests that the number in the UK will be very large in the light of the country's land-use history.

An authoritative statement on the scale of the problem in the UK came from the Ecotec consultancy in October 1991. Ecotec said that it is generally accepted that the UK has some 75 000 to 100 000 contaminated sites—or in excess of 100 000 hectares—which will need investigation and treatment at some stage. These estimates are broadly comparable with the 100 000 sites mentioned in the Friends of the Earth 1993 booklet *Buyer Beware: A guide to finding out about contaminated land* and the 200 000 hectares suggested in the CBI's paper *'Firm Foundations: CBI proposals for environmental liability and contaminated land'*. Ecotec's experience suggests that the cost of site investigation and remediation currently range between £100 000 and £300 000 per hectare. This implies a national bill of up to £30 billion (or £60 billion on the CBI's figures), but Ecotec believe this figure could rise significantly given the growing involvement of the National Rivers Authority (NRA) in clean-up projects. The NRA is developing clean-up standards of its own for individual contaminants so as to be in a position to protect groundwater quality. Applying these standards is forcing developers and landowners to undertake much more extensive site-investigation work, to carry out tests on soils to determine the mobility of pollutants and to undertake thorough post-treatment validations to ensure compliance with the agreed clean-up standards.

All this must sound very depressing to developers or landowners. Remediation and monitoring costs are on the increase but one man's cost is another's opportunity. The demand for land remediation services in the UK seems set to grow very rapidly. Ecotec estimate that £157 million was spent in 1989 and £240 million in 1990 and that spending will carry on rising by 15% each year. If on the other hand the UK's stock of contaminated land was to be cleaned by the end of the century much more would need to be spent. The spending in 1989 of £157 million represents only 19% of the £828 million of spending *per annum* that Ecotec reckon would be needed to accomplish this task by the year 2000.

The problems of course do not end with the costs of clean-up. Blight caused by public recognition of contamination could have as big a cost impact when looking at values of adjacent properties or of existing developments on potentially contaminated sites. Many property buyers can be expected to demand investigations to assure themselves that the property they want is neither contaminated nor requires clean-up. Perhaps government grants will be made available especially if there is scope for demonstrations of new clean-up technologies?

In the absence of such grants however the largest clean-ups of derelict land at the public's expense in recent years have been carried out by the Urban Development Corporations. One prime example of this is to be found at Bowman's Harbour to the East of Wolverhampton where the Black Country Development Corporation has the responsibility. The situation at Bowman's Harbour formed the basis for a feature in the *Financial Times* on 23 June 1991 because it is a problem of industrial dereliction and carelessness that is typical of much of the Black Country. Its 57 acres cost about £4.5 million to clean up and the biggest problem is dealing with landfill gas which contains methane but not quite enough to allow it to be harnessed and used as a fuel as happens elsewhere. This gas therefore had to be vented so it can gradually escape and the site sealed off so that there is no lateral seepage into adjacent areas of either the gas or any other contaminates.

Bowman's Harbour is not just a landfill site, however; the waste is just the topmost layer. Other problems are the result of mining from the 1700s to 1944. There are some 60 shafts, some of which are filled with pulverised fuel ash and topped with concrete and some of which are not. In the nineteenth century there were no requirements to record mine workings so there is always the danger of collapse into an unidentified shaft. All of this means that most of the site cannot be used for commercial or residential property development which gives it a value for recreational purposes or sheep grazing but not much else. Sad to say there are many Bowman's Harbours throughout the UK.

So what might be done? In answering this question the findings of the 1994 government review 'Paying for our past' provide the only recent authoritative statement in the UK. The review takes into account the Council of Europe 'Convention on Civil Liability for Damage resulting from activities dangerous to the environment' (which opened for signature in June 1993 and is known as the Lugano Convention) and the May 1993 EC Green Paper on 'Remedying Environmental Damage'. Section IV of the review identifies seven key issues in the form of questions, some of which are also referred to in Chapter 4 of this book. They are discussed below.

(1) What should the objectives of a contaminated land policy be?

The review concludes with a number of fairly modest objectives including the requirement that polluters pay and that owners need only act on existing contamination 'which poses unacceptable, actual or suspected risks to health or the environment'. Clean-ups of each and every contaminated site to a pristine state are not required.

The aim would also be to encourage an 'efficient market' in land which is potentially or actually contaminated or has been cleaned up, and to minimise financial and regulatory burdens. The review specifically mentions the question of whether, when, and on what terms to bring the liability into a business's annual report and accounts but does not begin to provide an answer.

(2) How should the statutory framework meet the objectives?

The overall conclusion is that there is a need for a regulatory framework to prevent or minimise new pollution and to require action in respect of existing pollution. Most importantly, the review concludes that regulators must be able to take action themselves and to recover costs. There is no comment however about claiming the costs of remediation work *in advance* from those liable. This is a crucial point. The National Rivers Authority for example has no money to institute remedial operations which its report '*Contaminated land and the water environment*' (NRA, 1993) estimates to be £0.5 million per site in the Severn Trent region.

The review also calls for greater co-ordination amongst the regulators and looks to the proposed Environment Agency to help do this.

Perhaps the most telling conclusion of the review is that in appropriate circumstances statutory liability for contamination should attach to current landowners, lenders, receivers and others who can be deemed to have taken over responsibility for contaminated land as well as the polluters themselves. What these appropriate circumstances might be is not made clear but it is suggested that the extent of liability should not be determined by 'availability of resources'. The review goes on to say that it would be inequitable and would damage markets if regulators were able to pursue the financial sector to an extent disproportionate to their responsibility or ahead of others who had more direct responsibility.

(3) What relationship should the statutory framework have with the Common Law?

As explained in Chapter 2 the Common Law enables individuals and organisations to seek compensation for actual or threatened damage or injury to their private interests even though no statute has been breached. This is because statutes set standards which are usually considered sufficient to protect human health and the environment, bearing in mind other factors such as the costs involved, rather than to protect all the interests of every individual who may be affected. As statues do not cover all polluting activities and as standards set may not be very high, private interests may be injured although there has been compliance with all relevant statutory provisions.

The review recognises these principles and therefore recommends a cautious approach to any statutory changes to Common Law.

(4) Should there be any extension of strict liability?

This question is posed because some people argue that strict liability is more appropriate for cases of environmental damage than fault-based liability. In the case of strict liability it is only necessary to prove casual connection between the act and the resultant damage whereas in fault-based liability the injured party needs to prove legal culpability on the part of the wrongdoer. The review concludes that the current needs of the two forms of liability strike a reasonable balance although the consequences of the Court of Appeal judgement in the *Cambridge Water Company* v *Eastern Counties Leather* case in December 1993 (which is described in Chapter 2) need some time for consideration. The Common Law defences as a result of this case appear to be the 'no-one could reasonably have foreseen' and the 'what a court would have thought at the time' approaches. The danger, recognised by the review, is that if these defences are given statutory backing they might weaken the ability of regulators to secure remediation and would pass costs on to the taxpayer.

(5) Who should pay for putting right environmental damage?

This is a question of fundamental commercial importance with the review commenting that the polluter pays principle 'must be *central* to any regulatory regime'. The Advisory Committee on Business and the Environment, the CBI and bankers argue, however, that the polluter pays principle *alone* should apply and that where no-one can be found against whom a case can be proved or where such a person lacks the necessary resources the burden should become a 'social cost'.

The review concludes, however, that the regulator should not only be able to enforce obligations on the polluter but also on anyone to whom the polluter has transferred 'the burden of meeting the obligations however that transfer took place'. It then goes on to say that the regulator should not be inhibited from taking urgent action because of the need to investigate the history, legal relations and recoverability of costs. It does not say how this aim will be achieved although it does stress that where contaminated land has been dealt with at public expense and its value enhanced, the landowner 'should not make an uncovenanted gain' and that financial hardship might be taken into account.

It is all very well, however, deciding *who* should pay but funding that burden also needs considering. The concept of advance payment through insurance, bonds or levies to provide a fund are briefly considered. The review's conclusion is that its outcome, presumably by defining parameters and drawing away some or all of the uncertainties, will be to make it more likely that the insurance market will be ready to insure businesses against contamination and, in doing so, will encourage risk assessment and preventative measures. The hope is also expressed that individual sectors will build their own voluntary funding arrangements to spread liabilities.

(6) How should markets be provided with information?

The review asks this question in the light of the decision to abandon the introduction of registers of land subject to potentially contaminative uses proposed in the Environmental Protection Act 1990. The registers would have been open to the public but responses to the consultation exercise suggested that the information could have been misleading or blighting in too many instances.

The review does not suggest a clear alternative but instead stresses that it is in the interest of all concerned to see that the conveyancing process is as economic, efficient and effective as possible in assembling information about contamination for relevant transactions. Particular reference is made to a proposal from the Royal Institute of Chartered Surveyors that all or some selected planning applications should be accompanied by a Land Quality Statement which would remain on the planning register to be available as a source of information to regulators and would-be-purchasers.

The difficulties of getting information on contamination into the hands of domestic and small company purchasers are mentioned but no indication of the way forward is given. Major commercial transactions on the other hand are already subject to extensive disclosures which identify contamination and consider the remedial action required.

(7) What other roles should public sector bodies have?

The review stresses the role of policy planning guidance in reminding local authority planners of the place of contamination issues in development plans, the job of English Partnerships and the Welsh Development Agency in making funds available for land remediation and the responsibilities of the planned Environment Agency in establishing a framework of guidance within which remediation of contaminated land would be addressed and high-risk closed landfill sites monitored.

Unfortunately there are more questions than answers. Perhaps this is to be expected given the complexity of the issues involved and the mistakes made in doing the wrong thing—the role of the Superfund in the USA comes to mind. Some general principles are beginning to emerge, however, which should help businesses assess their likely response and its financial consequences on their balance sheets and future plans. What eventually becomes law when the 1994 Environment Bill is enacted will also need to be considered with care.

3.6 International

What the UK Government is planning for business and the environment has already been discussed but only passing reference has been made so far to international developments. Yet the environment is one of those issues that transcends national boundaries—air pollution and acid rain affect everyone and are no respecters of frontiers. World business is also increasingly dominated by multinational corporations or indeed transnational concerns which almost operate as nation states in their own right. Organisations such as these, as well as national governments, have a vested interest in the environment—whether to exploit it or to sustain it—and are playing an increasingly important part in influencing pronouncements at world level.

The trouble is that world pronouncements, visions and shared-ideals agreed at major inter-governmental conferences, such as that at the Earth Summit in Brazil in June 1992, can be very far removed from day-to-day business decisions taken with a view to profit—and short-term profit too. But the fact that the Earth Summit took place at all is perhaps a sign that things are changing. It provides a starting point before brief attention is paid to issues such as the role of development banks, free trade and international aid agencies.

The Earth Summit

The Earth Summit, or the United Nations Conference on Environment and Development (UNCED) to give it its full title, took place in Rio de Janeiro in June 1992. It was the high-profile culmination of a long process of discussion and consultation with over 100 Heads of State or Government attending the final sessions. Nearly all of the UN's 180 or so members were represented together with 5000 officials and 7800 accredited journalists. Nothing quite like it had ever happened before. The earlier conferences with broadly similar agendas—wanting world-level government-backed environmental actions—had, in retrospect, been very significant but none involved Heads of State or Government in quite the same way. The UN's idea was that, as environmental matters are of such importance, discussions and follow-ups could not be left simply to Ministers of Environment or their equivalents. They had to be dealt with at the very top.

The two previous events that were of similar intent if not public profile were the 1987 Conference of the World Committee on Environment and Development under the Chairmanship of Gro Harlem Brundtland, the Prime Minister of Norway, and in June 1972 the UN's Stockholm

Conference on the Human Environment. The key concept that was given a major push forward by the Brundtland Conference was that of sustainable development, whilst the Stockholm Conference was the first major world event when the ultimate limits to economic growth were discussed.

In each case, business was represented but the impact on the day-to-day operations of most businesses anywhere in the world was very limited. This seems to be the outcome of the Earth Summit too. Out of the cast of thousands there were only some 50 business-based executives in attendance, many of them accredited through the International Chamber of Commerce (ICC) and similar business organisations. The ICC was particularly active as was the Business Council for Sustainable Development led by Stephen Schmidheiny, a leading Swiss industrialist, but their impact overall was small in comparison with that of governments and environmentalists although the ICC believe that, broadly speaking, the output of UNCED in the form of agreed text 'can be regarded positively by the business community'.

There was a real risk that the whole UNCED process would produce a result that the business community would prefer to ignore or would actually oppose. Environmental discussions might have been dominated by extreme environmentalist opinions that questioned or rejected the need for economic growth in all countries. In the event the ICC believe 'there is an implicit and often explicit, recognition that the business community can and must play an indispensable role in moving the world towards a sustainable development path'.

In order to play the role in the way that the ICC describe, UK business needs to know what was actually decided at Rio de Janeiro in June 1992 and have a clear picture of the way forward. Surprisingly, in spite of all that was written and the millions of words spoken before and during UNCED, there has not been much publicity given in the business press and media to the outcome. As the outcome does pose some real challenges for business a few words about each of the five main agreed texts is called for.

(1) The Rio Declaration on Environment and Development

This Declaration sets out 27 principles in language that is clear and to the point if not exactly inspirational. It is certainly not the 'Earth Charter' for which some people had hoped. It also refers constantly to what States should do or not do and not once is the word 'business' used. Every reader will take something different from a reading of the declaration but a few of the principles that undoubtedly do affect business directly are summarised below.

- Principle 8 states that to achieve sustainable development and a higher quality of life for all people States should reduce and eliminate unsustainable patterns of production and consumption and should promote appropriate demographic policies.
- Principle 10 includes a statement that at the national level each individual shall have appropriate access to information concerning the environment that is held by public authorities, including information on hazardous materials and activities in their communities and the opportunity to participate in decision-making processes.
- Principle 12 talks about international economic matters and trade and, *inter alia*, says that States should co-operate to promote a supportive and open international economic system that would lead to economic growth and sustainable development in all countries to better address the problems of environmental degradation.
- Principle 15 describes the precautionary approach which is that where there are threats of serious or irreversible damage lack of full scientific certainty shall not be used as a reason for postponing cost-effective measures to prevent environmental degradation.
- Principle 16 says that national authorities should endeavour to promote the internationalisation of environmental costs and the use of economic instruments taking into account the approach that the polluter should, in principle, bear the cost of pollution with due regard to the public interest and without distorting international trade and investment.
- Principle 17 endorses the use of environmental impact assessments and says that they should be undertaken for proposed activities that are likely to have a significant adverse impact on the environment and are subject to a decision of a competent national authority.

(2) UN Framework Convention on Climatic Change

This is the second major agreed text coming out of UNCED which caused much controversy along the way and was only approved after the USA had successfully insisted on the exclusion of specific targets for the stabilisation of greenhouse gas emissions.

The Convention imposes an obligation on signatories to draw up plans to limit emissions of CO_2 and other greenhouse gases which are believed to lead to global warming and climatic change. The Convention may lead (without specific targets it is not possible to be certain) to much tougher controls on energy use, carbon emissions and 'dirty' industries and its impact might extend beyond industry to affect transport systems and life at home too.

(3) UN Convention on Protection of Biodiversity

This is a much more focused Convention that is of great interest to the pharmaceutical and bio-technology industries as well as to researchers because it contains legal measures to protect plant and animal life and lays down certain rights to their commercial exploitation. The USA was the only State that refused to sign the Convention although a number of others had serious reservations about parts of it.

(4) Declaration of Principles on Forests

When the UNCED process started it had been hoped that one of the major outputs would be agreement on ways of managing the future of the world's forest resources. In the event, and well before delegates started to arrive in Rio de Janeiro, it was accepted that a full Convention was going to be impossible and therefore a Declaration of Principles would have to do instead.

The key objectors were developing countries with substantial natural forest resources of their own. They argued that the OECD's interest in preserving forests is hypocritical in view of the freedom that the industrialised world had to exploit its own forests in the past. They also see the control of their forests as an important, high-value bargaining counter in future negotiations over world environmental policies.

A word is needed here about so-called sustainable forest management given the high-level of consumer interest in the UK in seeing that wooden products, especially those made from tropical hardwoods, come from such producers. This issue was caught up in a debate about the meaning of the words 'environmentally sound forests' on which there was no final agreement. Perhaps Principle 7(a) comes closest to helping with its statement that 'efforts should be made to promote a supportive international economic climate conducive to sustained and environmentally sound development of forests in all countries which include *inter alia* the promotion of sustainable patterns of production and consumption, the eradication of poverty and promotion of food security'.

(5) Agenda 21

Apart from Conventions and Declarations the main outcome of the Earth Summit is 'Agenda 21'—a shorthand way of describing the 40 chapters and 500 pages which set out the detailed recommendations for implementing the Rio Declaration. The lawyers call the contents of Agenda 21 'soft law' in that the contents are advisory to governments and should be taken as strong guidance which is to be followed in the absence of anything stronger to the contrary. The Conventions are, in contrast, 'hard law' which establish a framework of basic rules leaving their detailed practical application for future negotiations, which will take years rather than months to complete.

There is no room in this book to do justice to what Agenda 21 contains so Appendix A lists the chapter headings to given an idea of the scope and contents of the Agenda. Perhaps it is worth quoting a spokesman from the consulting firm Arthur D Little who is reported in the magazine *Environment Risk* (July/August 1992) as saying that companies will now see the hastening of 'a number of changes already set in motion: the growing involvement of management (in sustainability issues), recent strides towards environmental excellence, development of management tools, attention to the needs of corporate stakeholders and a new focus on environmental issues across key business sectors'.

It is also worth putting a few figures on the potential scale of what Agenda 21 might imply. The UNCED Secretariat estimated that its full implementation could cost US$625 billion annually in developing countries alone, of which US$125 billion could be financed by industrialised countries. Some developing countries and environmental pressure groups want a new international Green fund to disburse such new financing but in reality this is unlikely to happen for a long time.

What is happening is that developed countries (other than the USA) reaffirmed the aim of expanding official development assistance to 0.7% of gross national product (GNP) by the year 2000 and the existing Global Environmental Facility (a joint operation by the World Bank, UN Development Programme and the UN Environmental Programme lending to projects which bring global benefits) is being refocused to include developing and developed/industrialised countries' governmental representatives in its management.

Finally, Agenda 21 proposed establishing a UN Commission on Sustainable Development which would oversee the implementation of the Agenda's recommendations and direct multi-lateral financial assistance for social-economic development.

The World Bank

If the Earth Summit was the single most important international environmental event of the early 1990s the World Bank has probably been the single most important international institution affecting the environment throughout the 50 years since the end of World War II. In the year ending 30 June 1993, it lent US$ 2.0 billion to free-standing environmental projects alone. Its direct effect on the UK might not have been great but its influence on the country's trading partners in the developing world has been profound. No review on the environmental challenges to British business is complete without some understanding of what it has done in the past and plans to do in the future.

Frankly, so far as environmentalists are concerned, the World Bank's past record has been a disaster. It has lent money to projects that have encouraged deforestation, moved settlers to lands that could not sustainably support them and, in doing these things, has financed dams, roads and power plants. Its attitude in the past has been seen as being that, should a conflict arise, economic development comes before environment. But this is now in the past, more or less at any rate. Increasingly the Bank insists on some form of environmental impact assessment being carried out before a decision is made to lend funds, and much greater emphasis overall is placed on projects that will not damage the environment. Financing of commercial logging in primary rainforests for example will not be financed under any circumstances.

Nevertheless the Bank still gets caught out. Its involvement in the funding of a huge dam project on the Narmada River in North West India is a case in point. In 1985 the Bank approved a US$450 million loan as part of the US$3 billion project which is designed to supply irrigation and drinking water to about 30 million people through a 75 000 km network of canals and to generate large amounts of electricity. Very laudable objectives; and, as the Bank was conscious of criticisms about its early lending to environmentally damaging projects, it insisted on a detailed environmental master plan taking particular account of the need to relocate 240 000 very poor tribal villagers. It also insisted that the three Indian States leading the scheme compensated the displaced villagers in ways which safeguarded their economic and social well-being.

The problem has been that the States failed to meet their obligations. In response to complaints from many environmental activists, the World Bank commissioned an independent report from Bradford Moss, a US development aid administrator and Thomas Berger, a former Canadian Supreme Court judge. In mid-1992 they wrote:

> The projects as they stand are flawed; resettlement and rehabilitation of all those displaced by the projects is not possible under prevailing circumstances, and the environmental impacts of the projects have not been properly considered or adequately addressed.

They were also concerned about compensation for those villagers whose rights to land had never been recorded and about the continuing absence of any environmental master plan. A worldwide press and media campaign followed to get the Bank to bring about the changes needed. This did not show the Bank in a good light and has fostered continued doubts about the

Bank's environmental credentials. It has now stopped spending any further money on the scheme and has withdrawn its support—the Indian States, however, are still pressing on with the construction work.

Perhaps it is fairer, and also more relevant to business, to look at the way that the World Bank sees its ongoing role. There is no better place for finding this than in its 1992 World Development Report—'Development and the Environment'—which was published a few weeks before the Earth Summit began. It is a practical document that should go some way to reassuring both environmental lobbyists and business that the World Bank now has its environmental feet firmly on the ground. It stresses over and over again the need to consider costs and benefits when evaluating different policies—which should please the business world—and also places much emphasis on the kinds of environmental damage that harm human health or wealth in the poor countries: dirty water and dirty air or soil erosion, for example. This emphasis should satisfy some environmentalists although they may not be too happy that issues such as conserving biological diversity and preventing climate change are not given more attention.

Fundamentally, however, the World Bank remains committed to economic growth as the cure for poverty. Also, it believes that environmental quality is an important aspect of human welfare. One billion people in developing countries have no access to clean water and 1.7 billion lack access to sanitation. Improvements to these can significantly reduce disease and deaths. Environmental damage can also undermine economic progress. Some estimates suggest that the productivity of a tenth of all irrigated land has been adversely affected by increased concentrations of salts which are a direct result of bad irrigation practices. And environmental degradation affects the poor the most. The rich, for example, can afford to buy clean drinking water, the poor cannot. Hence, economic growth is important to the environment just as the environment is important to economic growth.

The World Bank Report also places much emphasis on the importance of pricing policies to make sure that resources are put where they are most needed and plans to put its funding in places where it will assist in the effective working of these policies. A striking example that the Report describes is that of clean drinking water where conventional policy in the past assumed that clean water should be provided cheaply to the poor. The effective price charged for water is only about 35% of the average cost of supplying it with the result that supplies have often failed to keep up with the needs of fast-growing populations.

Even if they have kept up the supply is often unreliable. The World Bank Report says that the level of water leakage in Latin America is four times higher than is normal in industrial countries and the number of pipe breaks is twenty times higher. As a result the very poor have to rely on privately provided drinking water which, when bought from street vendors, can cost between 4 and 100 times as much as piped water. In Lima, a poor family uses only one sixth as much water as a private household but its water bill is three times bigger.

The Bank's argument therefore is that developing countries sell their resources too cheaply for the good of their economies and of the environment. In the case of water, sensible pricing policies would provide more revenue to install and maintain supplies. They would encourage farmers to use irrigation water less wastefully and so make more available for the cities. In the case of electricity, developing countries' prices are about half of those of OECD industrial countries resulting in irregular supplies and enormous losses. In Bangladesh 31% of electricity is lost during transmission and distribution compared with 8% in the USA.

So the World Bank is still in favour of economic development—but in a much less gung-ho manner than before. It believes that solving problems of the lack of clean drinking water or air pollution require more development but in such a way as to take into account its environmental effects.

If anyone doubts whether policies that improve economic efficiency will also improve the environment they need look no further than the pollution found in the former Soviet Union and Eastern Europe where subsidised energy prices and industrial protection are largely responsible for the terrible environmental mess found there. The challenge for business is to make the most of the opportunities arising from further economic growth in the developing world whilst recognising, in the way the World Bank now seems to, the environmental consequences of their actions. Failure to do so can be very damaging for profits and, as the World Bank found, for reputations.

Trade

For many years the world of business has readily accepted the notion that free trade is a good thing and, therefore, that every effort should be made to foster and encourage it. Environmentalists tend to see things differently and question whether economic growth encouraged by free trade will do anything good for the environment. The irony is that they are now finding themselves aligned with real protectionists who are happy to wear environmental clothes if they will provide a cover for inefficiency or political ideology.

In recent years these issues have moved up the international agenda and are now very near the top. On the other hand the Uruguay Round of trade talks, concluded in 1994 under the auspices of the General Agreement on Tariffs and Trade (GATT), had enough problems in dealing with such issues as the EC Common Agricultural Policy and so gave less time than the lobbyists and pressure groups would have liked to environmental matters.

GATT did produce a report, however, specifically on trade and the environment in February 1992 which set out some basic thinking that bears repeating here. Probably the most fundamental GATT belief is that there is a close link between wealth and improved environmental protection. Trade barriers which frustrate developing countries' ability to improve living standards will also frustrate efforts to raise standards of environmental protection. GATT also says that tariff walls are no more justified in protecting competitiveness where companies have incurred the cost of meeting strict environmental standards than they are in protecting companies paying more corporation tax or spending more on research and development. In fact, they point out, such companies may become market leaders in due course as a result of having to invest heavily in environmental compliance.

The GATT report also warned against unilateral action by a government to export its own domestic environmental policies. A graphic example was a controversial GATT ruling in 1992 against a US decision to ban imports of Mexican yellowfin tuna because fishing methods led to the killing of dolphin that swim above tuna shoals. But, almost in contradiction of the principles behind this ruling, GATT defended a country's sovereign right to set its own environmental priorities although a logical consequence of this might be to encourage a country to keep its environmental standards poor so as to encourage the migration to it of polluting industries. There is no easy answer but the report does have one or two helpful recommendations.

One of these is that the advanced industrial countries, whose emissions of carbon dioxide account for most of the global warming, should compensate forested countries for their 'carbon absorption services'. If no payment is made for these 'services' then a country like Brazil 'has little or no incentive to take such services into account in deciding on the optimal management of its forest resource'. This may seem a little far-fetched at present but such economic incentives may prove to be the way forward.

They are now being advocated by the UN Conference on Trade and Development (UNCTAD) which, in another 1992 report, suggested that countries should be allocated an annual quota of tradeable carbon emission entitlements with developing countries getting more than they need and industrialised countries getting fewer. Surplus permits would be tradeable on an international exchange so providing poorer countries with some additional development finance. It would nevertheless still pay such countries to invest some of this finance in clean technologies so as to keep to a minimum the number of permits they really need to cover these existing industrial activities. It might even help bring on board big potential polluters, such as China and India, both of which have large fossil fuel resources who would be better able to afford to buy the technology they need to exploit these reserves in a non-polluting way if such an arrangement was operating.

Apart from innovative ideas such as these, most of the GATT negotiations were about such things as disagreements between the USA and the European Community on support for farming and farm trade. GATT officials, however, have shown a willingness to consider the views of environmentalists and interested politicians. They met with 300 of them in Geneva in June 1994. Such meetings have brought about a level of focus on key topics that is unusual. Perhaps they set the agenda for GATT and trade in general and as such warrant repeating here. They are certainly the sorts of issues that business needs to be aware of over the remaining years of the decade.

The first of these issues is the need for internationally agreed standards, particularly on food and farm products, to provide a floor from which environmental standards should rise rather than a ceiling which governments can aim for. The campaigners are concerned, for example, about plans to harmonise the EC's 'E-numbers' of permitted food additives. Ahead of harmonisation, the UK has 300 approved additives and Germany or Greece only 150 but after harmonisation all EC countries will have a list of 411 approved additives. This hardly seems a step forward for many EC countries!

The second issue is the need for the Multilateral Trade Organisation (MTO). The MTO would be a powerful new body to oversee international trade and to give high and formal priority to environmental concerns, in particular sustainable development. Without it many of the initiatives the environmental and development campaigners want to see pursued would never get off the ground.

The third issue is the need for 'pace-setting' governments to be free to set environmental standards that are higher than the international norm. Although it is controversial, the campaigners believe that such pace setters should have a right to act unilaterally in blocking imports from countries with lower standards or dirty industrial processes.

Another issue is the need for industry to 'internalise' the environmental cost of a product—ranging from electricity generators incorporating the true cost of treating unclean waste to timber prices which include reimbursement to exporting countries for their loss of biodiversity. How this should be done is dear to an accountant's heart but there is as yet no sound method that has general support.

A further issue, the fifth, is the need for industrial countries to recognise that they bear the main responsibility for the cost of environmental improvement in poor countries because not only can they afford it but also because they are and have been the main cause of pollution. Once recognised, then various schemes need to be considered, such as recycling cash raised through tariffs back to developing countries to improve their environment.

Finally, the sixth issue is the need as the campaigners see it for international trade bodies to be more open and answerable. They do not just include GATT here, but also organisations such as the Rome-based Codex Alimentarius which sets international food standards.

The list is long and far-reaching but there is nothing on it that is impossible or too threatening to UK businesses. The fundamental philosophical issue remains unanswered however. Is economic growth not only the cause of many of the world's environmental problems but also the means of generating the wealth to provide the resources needed to protect the environment? For most governments free-trade and economic growth go hand-in-hand.

4

Investment

4.1 Introduction

Environmental issues have not been of much concern to the financial and investing community in the UK over the last few years. Probably more than in many parts of business, 'greenery' was seen as a temporary fad of more relevance to the world of consumer goods and marketing than to the City. For many this is still the case, but, as environmental issues continue to receive widespread publicity and as the law tightens its grip, the wide ramifications of contaminated land, process licensing under IPC and much more are beginning to raise serious questions in some financial minds.

In a sense raising awareness of these issues is what this book is all about. Its aim is to look at them from the point of view of the finance director, accountant and auditor who individually or collectively are usually closely involved in investment decisions and dealing with City institutions. What, then, are the attitudes of the Stock Market and investment community to environmental issues? How are the banks and venture capitalists, the main sources of funding to most of the UK's smaller businesses, reacting? And what about insurers who may find themselves covering environmental risks they were unaware of when policies were written a few years ago?

What follows is an attempt to give answers to these questions and then to look at the whole question of 'environmental liability' which affects all the answers. The current legal framework of environmental law is being challenged. The financial community is responding and making its views known at both UK and EC levels. In the absence of final decisions about the way forward a review of the issues involved provides an important concluding section to this chapter.

4.2 Stock Market

Introduction

Investors in the Stock Market, whether they be institutions or private individuals, approach environmental issues in two ways. The first, and much the most important at present, is actively to seek out companies making the most of commercial opportunities created by the surge in environmental interest and laws or to avoid those which are most likely to be damaged by such interest or laws. Either way 'the environment' is a factor to be taken into account in the same way as war, unemployment or exchange rate fluctuations. The second is to screen companies for their environmental performance and to invest in those that meet certain criteria—usually of an ethical nature. Companies producing CFCs, for example, might be avoided. This group is part of the wider ethical investment movement which is playing an increasingly important part in investment decisions in the UK markets.

Commercial opportunities

The first approach—the commercial one—is presently the most important one for Stock-Market investors. Clearly, a good environmental performance in ethical terms might also result in enhanced demand for certain shares and therefore affect the price—a commercial impact if ever there was one—but making such a judgement is highly dependent on the use of published information and, therefore, is dealt with in Chapter 6 where environmental reporting is discussed more fully. Inevitably there is an overlap in that during the last few years some UK institutions have been applying environmental criteria to all their funds under management. The Norwich Union, with more than £18 billion under management, builds environmental criteria into all its investment decisions. Research done by a public relations firm, Dewe Rogerson, found that in late 1991, 40% of fund managers said that they believed that they ought to consider a company's greenness before buying its shares. But, overall, the City and the Stock Market react to environmental information because of its impact on the commercial prospects of a company, which are in turn reflected in its share price. Tessa Tennant of pension specialists NPI believes that fund managers react to three types of information.

The first of these are straightforward news stories. After the Exxon Valdez foundered on Good Friday 1989, Exxon's share price fell and the volume of trading increased dramatically. It took about two months for the price to settle again.

The second type is general information that has an effect on a particular industrial activity. Fossil fuel power generators, for example, are affected by information on acid rain and the threat of taxes on greenhouse gases. Waste management companies can find positive benefit in stories about companies' pollution fines and exposure to potential liabilities from land contamination. Insurance company share prices may be marked down by fears of exposure to claims ranging from storm damage and subsidence to land contamination.

The third type is historic information about a specific company such as Royal Insurance's provisions to cover its potential exposure to Superfund clean-up claims in the USA which have contributed to the shares' big discount to assets. Similarly Turner & Newall's share price still suffers from market sentiment over claims relating to the company's interests in the asbestos industry, even though some of the claims are for incidents that occurred over 20 years ago.

On the other side of the same coin, however, a number of institutions believe that there are some real investment opportunities in companies which might benefit from new environmental expenditure on such things as recycling (metal, glass, paper, plastic), energy efficiency and conservation, alternative energy (solar, wind, geothermal), site remediation, instrumentation, monitoring equipment, and much more. Commercial Union, for example, launched a £17 million CU Environmental Trust on 25 March 1992 which aims for long-term capital growth from companies which stand to benefit from new environmental protection expenditure.

Another example is provided by Ecofin, a London-based environmental financial services specialist, which launched an environmental fund of US$ 75 million in June 1992 to coincide with the start of the Earth Summit in Brazil. It invests in companies in the environmental services and technology sectors concentrating on small and medium-sized companies in the US and Europe and with up to 25% of its resources in unquoted companies. And James Capel, the stock broker, has now produced an annual edition of its Green Book which aims to identify companies making the most of environmental business opportunities. The interest is clearly there and there are signs that it is growing.

Ethical screening

Interest is also growing in the second approach to stock-market investment in the environment: the screening of companies for their environmental performance. But the evidence to date also suggests that there is a long way to go. In the UK it is estimated that by 1994 more than £140 million was managed in specifically green funds, with a total of £800 million being managed ethically (including greenly)—over 1% of the total UK funds managed through unit trusts, pension funds and investment trusts.

In the USA, however, the figures are many times this size. It has been suggested that ethically screened investments now total as much as $625 billion although the exact figure must be treated with caution. Many institutions have some sort of ethical screening even if it is not at the centre of their investment strategy. The inclusion of their funds in this total may exaggerate the picture.

In the UK the idea of ethical screening of investments has been around for about 10 years. The first screened unit trust was launched by Friends Provident, the life assurance group, in 1984 as the Friends' Stewardship Unit Trust. It still is the biggest socially orientated fund in the UK.

Perhaps one of the reasons for the slow development of ethical (and green) screening in the UK is the existence of unhelpful or confusing trust laws. A high profile and precedent-setting case that happened at about the same time as the Friends Provident Unit Trust was launched was *Cowans* v *Scargill* (1984). The case involved the Coal Board's pension fund whose aim, according to its governing trust deed, was to provide pensions for retired mineworkers. The trustees appointed by the National Union of Mineworkers, led by Arthur Scargill, refused to agree to a new investment plan in 1982 unless it was amended to forbid investment in other energy industries and to lower levels of overseas investment in the future. The Coal Board trustees took the NUM trustees to court.

The upshot of the judgement was that trustees must not accept lower rates of return or a reduced spread of investments in order to further political, social or moral objectives not laid down in the trust deed. In effect this means that either new funds have to be established or existing trust deeds have to be modified (which can be administratively complex and expensive) to give trustees the specific powers that they need to carry out some form or other of ethical screening. This has meant that pension funds, in particular, whose beneficiaries have clear and focused interests in their funds, have had to continue investing widely looking for the best return, without necessarily minding too much where it comes from.

On the other hand, the best advice to trustees seems to be that they must at least consider investments that might be thought in some quarters to be socially or morally questionable. If, after careful consideration, the trustees believe that they will get as least as good a return on their ethically screened investments then they are protected. Which brings us to the question of returns on screened investments, unit trusts in general and green ones in particular.

Investment returns

There is no hard evidence one way or the other that ethical or green screening results in bad investments and poor returns. This should not be a particularly surprising conclusion: there is so much to managing a business and producing profits that environmental factors may make a contribution but not, in most cases, a decisive one. Having said that one important factor seems to be the average size of the screened companies, particularly those that have been environmentally screened. Ethical funds tend to be invested in smaller companies which, in general terms, were hit harder than larger companies during the recession of the early 1990s but which were very successful during the boom years of the late 1980s.

The ethical/environmental unit trusts, investment trusts and similar funds on offer in 1994 (according to the Ethical Investment Research Service) are set out in Appendix B.

The future

What about the future for green/ethical investment in the UK? Should green/ethical considerations be an integral part of management's thinking and reporting, or will they always be there but in the background rather than high up the agenda?

The answer to these questions seems to be that the ethical investment movement as a whole and green screening in particular are growing in importance all the time and cannot be ignored. There is a growing realisation that ethical considerations are influencing the demand for shares, and not just profitability, dividend yield and asset backing. Whilst the weight of funds that are ethically invested is relatively small this influence may not be profound, but the ethical movement in the USA—known there as socially-responsible investment or SRI—suggests that the amounts invested could increase substantially in a very short period of time. Most attention so far, however, has been paid to avoiding involvement with South Africa and much less to the environment.

Perhaps the way forward is going to be for an all-round increase in environmental pressure from investors who want to have a stake in companies that not only work in the environmental sector, such as waste management, but at the same time operate in an environmentally friendly way. Eagle Star's Environmental Opportunities Trust, with £8 million under management, aims to satisfy this dual approach. It says that whilst it does not make moral judgements, and will not list sectors or companies that it will not invest in, its objectives are 'to invest in companies which take a positive attitude to environmental issues and share in their success'. It has three criteria for selecting suitable investments:

1. management with a good track record and a sound positive plan;
2. at least average earnings per share growth and a prospective earnings out-performance; and
3. hard evidence of a positive attitude to environmental issues.

The first two are straightforward and commercial; the last requires some further comment.

The management of the Eagle Star Environmental Opportunities Trust say that, for example, they *will* invest in a company involved with making products that increase energy efficiency in buildings or industrial processes, or which has connections with recycling, pure foodstuffs or environmentally safe waste management. They *will not* invest in companies which continue to harm the environment significantly, even if they have a programme for improvement, which provide funds to environmentally destructive projects including Third-World lending, which derive significant profits from oil exploration or nuclear energy and which promote non-environmentally friendly products.

Obviously some pretty tough moral judgements have to be made and it is up to the fund managers to act as God and make them. But the fund managers themselves are not always above criticism. In March 1993, the Merlin Research Unit (part of the Jupiter Tyndall Group) published a Survey of Ethical and Environmental Funds in Continental Europe which concluded that some of these funds could lose the confidence of investors because of poor definitions and a low level of supporting research. In some cases funds depended on the advice of brokers, rather than environmental scientists, as to whether a company was 'green' or 'ethical'. Other funds allow up to 10% of a company's turnover to be in 'undesirable' areas, but this was not always made clear to investors.

So a good financial performance for a fund may no longer be enough in itself. Other criteria of an ethical or green nature may be employed. But the world of company reporting has yet to catch up, as will be seen in Chapter 6, and 'green' investors have to rely on independent research from organisations such as EIRIS (Ethical Investment Research Service) on which to base their decisions. In the absence of systematic, comprehensive and regular information on the chosen criteria that is independently audited there will always be a question in some investors' minds about the way in which fund managers can be held to account.

4.3 Banks and venture capital

Introduction

The banks, and venture capitalists too, are looking to make the most of the commercial opportunities afforded by the environment. But they also have to look, every day, at the downside risks involved in the loans they make. There are signs that commercial lending managers in our High Street banks are now making themselves aware of the sort of questions they should be asking their corporate customers before increasing (or decreasing) their overdraft facilities. Most are doing so for practical reasons: to avoid bad debts or to make the most of, for example, some new technology with environmental benefits. But some managers work for banks that are now taking a much stronger ethical or green policy line. On 6 May 1992, shortly in advance of the Earth Summit in Brazil, commercial banks in 23 countries with combined assets of US$ 1500 billion made a formal commitment at the United Nations to pursue common principles of environmental protection in all their operations. In particular they committed themselves to ensuring that they use the best practices in environmental management, including energy efficiency, recycling and waste minimisation. The group of 31 signatory banks did not include any from the USA or Japan but did have three British banks in its ranks: National Westminster, Midland (through its parent company Hong Kong and Shanghai Banking Corp) and the Royal Bank of Scotland.

The lack of involvement of banks from the USA and Japan as well as some major British banks may cause some to ask how far ethical considerations will permeate the entire banking industry. Will those that adopt the principles agreed to at the United Nations put themselves at a competitive disadvantage? In the UK the Co-operative Bank does not think so. It has positioned itself as aspiring to sound ethical principles in all that it does and has backed this up by a high-profile advertising campaign. It is too soon to tell whether this strategy will have benefited the Co-operative Bank at the expense of their competitors but what is certain is that business ethics and environmental concerns are now more in the minds of lenders than they were a few years ago.

Risk, security and return

The most fundamental concerns of the majority of lenders, however, are risk, security and return. The new environmental laws in the UK, as well as the enhanced awareness of the problems of, for example, contaminated land, can have a profound effect on each of them.

Bank lenders have two main fears. The first is that the company will be fined or sued heavily for some environmental transgression which may impair its ability to service its debt or to repay it. The second is that the lending bank itself may be liable for clean-up costs should it exercise its security over a company to which it has lent money. Arguably, the first fear can be covered by making appropriate enquiries: there are many business risks and now environmental concerns are higher up the risk-list than they were before. The bank's own position, however, is much less clear and there are developments in the USA, the EC, as well as in the UK, which do not help. A few words about each follows.

USA

As has already been discussed, awareness of environmental problems has a much higher profile in North American business circles than in the UK at present. This is largely because of tough legislation of which the Environmental Protection Agency's powers to enforce the clean-up of contaminated land and recover the costs under the Superfund provisions are the best known. Lenders, however, whilst needing to be aware of the effects of such costs on their customers' financial standing, had thought they were protected by legislation which excluded secured lenders from the environmental liability of an 'owner and operator' provided they did not participate in the day-to-day management of the business. But a recent case has changed all that and sent waves of consternation through North American banking circles that are now reaching the EC and the UK too.

The case in question was heard in the State of Georgia in 1990 and involved a debt factoring company known as Fleet Factors. The Environmental Protection Agency sued Fleet Factors for $376 000 to cover the cost of removing asbestos and for other clean-up operations at the site of a bankrupt cloth printer. Fleet's advances to the cloth printer were secured on its plant and equipment. When the cloth printer's plant closed Fleet management took charge and ran down the business so as to exercise its rights under its security. The court held that Fleet could be liable as an 'owner and operator' because it had the capacity to influence the cloth printer's treatment of hazardous wastes. It went on to stress that a lender did not have to exercise that capacity to be liable.

This judgement has created enormous concern in US banking and business circles and has certainly restricted the availability of banking funds to some higher-risk polluting industries such as scrap merchants, producers and handlers of hazardous chemicals, pulp and paper mills and even petrol filling stations. A 1991 survey, carried out by the American Bankers Association, of 1741 community banks (those with assets under $500 million) showed that 62.5% had rejected loan applications or potential borrowers because of concerns about environmental liabilities and 13.5% actually had had to pay pollution clean-up costs on property held as collateral for loans. Not surprisingly nearly all US property involved in a financing transaction now undergoes some form of site assessment. There are signs that this could become the norm in Europe too.

Europe

A recent European development that makes this seem more likely was the 1991 European Commission draft Directive on Civil Liability for Damage Caused by Waste which said that 'the producer of waste' would be liable 'irrespective of fault on his part'. It was not clear whether or not a lending bank counted as a 'producer'. Whilst the draft Directive has been withdrawn—in response to vociferous protests from banks in particular—the commission has prepared a Green Paper on Civil Liability for Environmental Damage which addresses the issue again. Whether or not this is, as Commission officials claim, to provoke discussion or whether it is a sign that they plan to define precise borders for environmental liability remains to be seen.

Whichever it is there is likely to be a considerable time-lag before effective laws are in force in the UK—directives can only be put into domestic law when local legislation has been passed. And this may not result in an even-playing field across Europe. Legal definitions of liability tend to be more tightly drawn on mainland Europe than in the UK (and USA), which may not help UK lenders.

UK

Further recent developments in the UK, such as the provisions in the Water Act 1989 allowing the National Rivers Authority to recover clean-up costs from anyone it can prove knowingly permitted the pollution, the White Paper references to grants for clean-ups and the proposals for a register of contaminated land, all served to heighten banks' sensitivities. And with good cause. Under existing UK law if a lender forecloses on its security and becomes an 'owner in possession' then they become technically liable for the property they hold. If that land is contaminated or was a factor in causing the river pollution which the NRA has cleaned up, then, if the original owner cannot pay up (as is likely if a lender has foreclosed), the lender will have to do so risking loss not only of the original loan but also of the clean-up costs. All may still not be clear even then as the lender may find it hard to sell 'blighted' property particularly if adjacent land has not been cleaned up and there is a risk of recontamination. Perhaps we will see lenders walking away from their security. Whilst forfeiting the primary loan, they will then avoid incurring the secondary clean-up costs.

Not surprisingly there is growing talk in UK, as well as US, banking circles of the need for a 'secured lender exemption' in such circumstances. A balance has to be struck allowing banks to do business on a reasonable basis without imposing a liability, which would be an active deterrent to the provision of finance. Banks are worried, quite rightly, that they will be turned into environmental policemen unless something is done and are now beginning to engage actively in a public debate on the issues. They were active contributors to a Financial Sector Working Group set up by the UK government's Advisory Committee on Business and the Environment (ACBE) which issued its report in February 1993. Their views, as set out in this report, are described fully in the final section of this chapter.

Venture capital

In some ways the issues affecting the attitudes of venture capitalists are similar to those already discussed concerning Stock-Market attitudes to ethical/green investment and environmental opportunities but, in the UK at any rate, specialised environmental venture funds are very thin on the ground.

In early 1992 Charterhouse in the UK and Alex Brown and First Analysis Corporation in the USA raised some $100 million from institutional investors in Europe and the USA for environmental venture capital funds. Companies in the UK, France, Germany, Italy and Spain are said to be attracting most of the money. Stuart Janney, managing director of Alex Brown, which is based in Baltimore USA, is reported in the *Financial Times*, 29 January 1992, as saying:

> We think that the next 7 to 10 years are going to afford an unprecedented opportunity to invest in companies that are small now but which will be very big at the end of this decade. And these companies are going to be European companies.

So, in one investor's mind at any rate, the future looks very bright although the environmental risks posed by conventional venture capital investments are increasing—as they are for Stock-Market investors and lending banks.

4.4 Insurance

Given the types of environmental risks described earlier in this book, and the attitudes of investors and lenders in particular, a natural reaction is for companies to take out appropriate insurance and for their investors and lenders to insist that they do so.

This was the reaction in the United States of America too when new legislation in the 1970s and early 1980s raised the profile and costs of pollution. This in turn led to insurance claims that were eventually so large and numerous that the environmental insurance market there all but collapsed in 1984. The US experience, therefore, may be worth looking at first before turning to the situation now in the UK and the wider European Community where developing legislation is creating conditions similar to those in the USA 10 years ago.

In the early 1970s, and the years before, most US insurers regarded product liability as their main concern. Where public and product liabilities were combined, as they often were, most US underwriters virtually ignored the potential exposures under the public liability element which were covered on a blanket and occurrence basis. Although limits were normally set for each occurrence there were no limits set to the number of occurrences for each period of insurance. In such cases, public liability cover had virtually no limit.

The unforeseen consequences of this were brought home to the US insurance market with the introduction of the Resource Conservation and Recovery Act in 1976 and the Comprehensive Environmental Response Compensation and Liability Act in 1980. Both Acts are discussed more fully in Chapter 2. The 1976 Act was aimed at preventing the indiscriminate dumping of toxic waste and establishing systems of managing hazardous waste from cradle to grave. The 1980 Act set up Superfund and the Environmental Protection Agency (EPA). Superfund gave the EPA the resources and power to clean up sites affected by hazardous waste endangering human health or the environment and to recover the costs from all the parties involved—producers, carriers and waste-site operators. Liability imposed under the rules governing Superfund is strict, retroactive and joint and several. As a result a site owner may find him or herself partly or wholly responsible for pollution caused at any time in the past history of the site regardless of who or what caused it.

There are now over 1200 Superfund sites and there could be over 2000 by the end of the century according to the EPA itself. Other authorities think the number could be over 30 000. With an average clean-up cost of US$ 25 million per site, a recent Congressional report noted that hazardous waste could be a '30-to-60 year, US$ 500 billion problem'. Not surprisingly with potential clean-up bills of this magnitude US industry tried to recover its costs under Comprehensive General Liability (CGL) insurance policies which most held.

The initial reaction of US insurers was to put such CGL policies onto a 'claims made' basis (only honouring claims made during the period when the cover is in force) and restricting pollution cover to 'sudden and accidental' events. But in spite of these measures there were many occasions when the US courts ruled in favour of the insured and made insurers pay for gradual pollution incidents.

The final reaction of US insurers was to delete all forms of pollution liability—gradual and sudden—from their CGL policies. The result was a search for a new form of pollution insurance which was realised in the form of the first Environmental Impairment Liability (EIL) policies in the late 1970s. By 1983, 40 insurers were offering various forms of EIL policy but disastrous claims led to the collapse of the market in 1984. Since then there have been only two or three insurers offering a reasonably broad range of pollution-related products.

The litigation goes on. In December 1992, a decision by an Illinois court freed Outboard Marine Corporation, an outboard motor manufacturer, to pursue its insurers for the costs of cleaning up polychlorinated biphenyls (PCBs) which it had dumped into Lake Michigan between the 1950s and 1970s. In 1978, Outboard was ordered to clean up the PCBs which had been present in pydraul, an hydraulic fluid the company had used in die-casting. The mainly US insurers had restricted their coverage under CGL policies to cases where pollution was 'sudden and accidental' and resisted claims from Outboard on the grounds that pollution had occurred over a long period of time. The ruling of the Illinois court however was that the term 'sudden' was ambiguous and that cover was available no matter how rapidly pollution had occurred if it could be shown that pollution had been 'unexpected and unintended'.

Nine other US courts have also ruled on the interpretation of the 'sudden and accidental' clause with five courts ruling that there is cover only where the pollution is 'sudden' in a temporal sense. In the absence of a genuinely definitive ruling, it looks as though the litigation could go on for a long time yet in the USA and, if the lessons are not learned soon, it could start in the UK.

There are a number of forces at work in the UK at present that might bring this about because the increasing volume of actual or pending environmental legislation is forcing companies to look at ways of reducing their risks. The first piece of such legislation is the Environmental Protection Act 1990 which not only raised the idea of registers of contaminated land, as described earlier in this chapter and in Chapter 2, but also requires that local authorities separate waste regulation from waste disposal. Many have done this by setting up independent Local Authority Waste Disposal Companies (LAWDCs), some of which are now privately owned, but all of which are looking at some form of insurance to protect them from problems with the waste disposal sites and facilities they are taking over.

There was also an EC draft Directive on the Civil Liability for Damage Caused by Waste published in 1991. The draft Directive, which has since been withdrawn, aimed at providing a means of compensating those suffering from environmental damage caused by waste disposal activities and was based on the principle that the polluter pays. This in itself should be enough to raise interest in environmental insurance but the draft Directive also contained a requirement for waste disposers to demonstrate some form of financial security which may be a bank guarantee but could also be insurance.

It seems likely that the demand for environmental insurance will grow in the UK but insurers are, not surprisingly, nervous about what to expect in the light of events in the USA. In fact in April 1991, the members of the Association of British Insurers decided to delete cover for gradual pollution from all General Public Liability policies and also from All Risks policies unless caused by fire and perils. In fact most have deleted all forms of pollution from their policies and then written back sudden and accidental damage to third parties and their properties so that the scope of coverage is restricted to 'a sudden, identifiable, unintended and unexpected incident which takes place in its entirety at a specific time and place during the period of insurance'. But even then General Public Liability policies do not cover the costs of cleaning up the insured's own site and only protect the insured from claims brought against him or her by third parties for damage to their property.

The response to these trends in the UK, as in the USA a decade or more before, has been to develop special types of insurance under the Environmental Impairment Liability (EIL) umbrella. EIL policies generally have several features which distinguish them significantly from most General Public Liability policies:

1. They are written on a 'claims made' basis, covering all claims brought by third parties in the policy period. In practice such policies also stipulate a retroactive or past date and exclude all claims arising from occurrences before that date.
2. Although criminal fines and penalties are not covered, legal costs and expenses incurred in defending a criminal prosecution for a breach of regulations are covered provided the prosecution relates to a risk which is covered by the policy.
3. Clean-up costs are expressly included but usually only to the extent that they are incurred in preventing or minimising a claim by a third party.

4. The policies are site-specific and site-audits are normally required before cover is given.
5. Cover is usually limited to a specific amount.

Even these sorts of policies do not resolve all insurance problems. Deliberate acts or omissions are expressly excluded so that cover is not available where, for example, the insured's management should have realised that the damage would be inevitable. Similarly excluded are claims where the damage is a consequence of senior management having failed to take reasonable steps to remedy a breach of law or regulations of which they should have been aware.

There is also no rush by the insurance market to provide such cover, which is presently available from very few sources and which is not only hedged about by the conditions described above but is also likely to require independently conducted environmental surveys by approved environmental consultants, carried out at the insured's expense, and rigorous controls of risk. And what cover there is can also be very expensive depending on the results of the survey and the history of the previous occupation of the site concerned.

Perhaps, in due course, the UK insurance market will follow precedents set on mainland Europe where groups of insurance companies form 'Pools' to share environmental risks. In France, for example, Assurpol is one of the longest established Pools, comprising some 50 insurers, and has issued over 200 contracts to date. Its capacity is over FF 130 million. Cover is subject to strict environmental audit and, if all sites operated by a company are covered, the policy might be written on a blanket or non-site-specific basis. In Holland, MAS is a Pool operated on a similar basis to Assurpol although the majority of policy holders are in the agricultural or small/medium industrial business sector. Premium income is relatively low as a result and therefore overall capacity is low. The Italian Pool is known as Inquimamento, has a capacity of up to L40 billion and uses Assurpol for reinsurance purposes. Other Pools are in the early stages of development in Germany, Denmark and Spain.

Clearly insurance is not presently the whole answer to dealing with environmental risks. The wider role of risk management, therefore, is very important to the well-managed UK company. This process, put simply, involves the identification and evaluation of the environmental risks a company faces. The consequences of holding contaminated land, for example, on the financial standing of a company can be very serious. A full audit may be needed before land is acquired, therefore, and good housekeeping in the widest of senses may significantly reduce exposure to other environmental risks at minimal cost. Planned maintenance and a company-wide strategy for environmental compliance can play a vital part. Perhaps as a result of this process a company will decide to bear any loss as and when it arises. Alternatively a captive insurance subsidiary may be more appropriate rather than going to the insurance market for cover.

4.5 Environmental liability

From what has already been discussed in this chapter it is clear that uncertainties about the legal framework for environmental liabilities is causing problems for the financial markets. All markets work best when the rules are known and are relatively unchanging and the financial markets are no exception. With this in mind, therefore, there is a need for a review of the present position and developing agenda. Fortunately, a high-powered Financial Sector Working Group for the Advisory Committee on Business and the Environment (ACBE) under the chairmanship of Derek Wanless, Chief Executive of National Westminster Bank, published a report in February 1993 giving just such a review. What follows draws heavily on that report.

The US, European and UK legislative backgrounds to current views on environmental liability have been described already. All seem to point to stricter liability regimes for industry, or at least for specified industrial sectors, and to extend these to include environmental impairment. There is growing pressure for further changes too: some people argue that a strict liability regime with minimum defences would increase the incentive for business to take all the measures it can to avoid damaging the environment. Such a strict regime might also release new resources from the polluter to deal with the problems that arise after pollution has occurred—such as clean-up costs, restitution of a site and/or compensation. But, as has already been seen, insurance is not presently available for such things and may be even less available under a stricter regime.

The ACBE Group had these sorts of thoughts in mind when it reviewed the options for government over the nature of a future environmental liability regime. The eight options that the Group considered are described below:

(1) The retention of fault-based common law with strict liability in some areas; and
(2) The introduction of an absolute liability regime

The distinction between strict and fault-based liability has already been discussed. In the USA, Superfund is a form of strict liability which can result in little correlation between the degree of involvement and the degree of responsibility for a polluted site. Furthermore, it is retrospective. In The

Netherlands, on the other hand, a fault-based system prevails but, when combined with a stringent concept of Duty of Care, enables regulators to clean up contamination and then seek recovery from polluters whose liability is determined by the extent to which a polluter should have known that his actions would cause harm.

There are two other bases of liability: 'no fault' and 'absolute'. In the former case it is not necessary for the harmed party to identify a wrongdoer and then to proceed against that wrongdoer. Instead the injured party can obtain compensation for his damage from a fund or pool as is the case with road accidents in the USA. In the latter case of absolute liability there are no defences whatsoever available (in contrast to strict liability where defences are available in certain circumstances).

The ACBE Group concluded with a strong preference for the existing fault-based liability regime although lenders and insurers accepted that they could, in principle, work in a strict liability regime subject to an acceptable structure of supporting rules. They were opposed to the introduction of any new concepts of liability and to an absolute liability regime. The Group also looked at defences and suggested that a 'State of the Art' defence would be vital to industry, lenders and insurers. This, they suggested, could be based on the sort of wording to be found in the Consumer Protection Act 1987 whereby:

> the state of scientific and technical knowledge of the relevant time was not such that a producer of products of the same description as a product in question might have been expected to have discovered the defect if it had existed in his products while they were under his control.

They would also like a *force majeure* defence so that industry could obtain adequate insurance and suggest that the exposure of lenders should be confined to the amount of their loan/funding which they stand to lose if the borrower's environmental liabilities result in the borrower's bankruptcy. A further suggestion is that there should be a statutory obligation on borrowers and vendors to disclose information about possible contamination of sites owned or occupied by them.

(3) Extending or restricting (as appropriate) the application of the concept of joint and several liability

Joint liability occurs where one person involved in, say, a pollution incident can be liable for the whole of the damage caused. Several liability can either involve personal liability being restricted to the actual identifiable damage caused by that person (which can sometimes be difficult to prove) or each person being liable in full for the entire damage to which each of them contributed in different ways but for which their individual contributions cannot be identified. In effect, therefore, the concept of joint and several liability means that a plaintiff has the option of either suing someone for the personal environmental damage that person has caused or suing that person for the whole of the damage.

The ACBE Group concluded that such a concept is likely to encourage the so-called 'deep pocket' approach which may be very unfair on someone who has contributed to the damage in a very minor way yet is required to bear the cost of the whole damage. Whilst being in favour of joint and several liability, therefore, the ACBE suggest a financial cap on the joint liability element in the case of clean-ups possibly complemented by the right to recover the shortfall from a compensation pool. Alternatively, there could be a system under which an individual's proportion of liability could be calculated according to the length of time during which his or her activity was conducted and/or the potentially hazardous nature of it.

(4) Widening the categories of individuals who can seek relief for environmental impairment

As the UK law stands at present a regulatory authority or a plaintiff has to prove that 'but for' a particular action the damage would not have occurred. Where there are several potential causes or several potential sources of the cause, only an 'immaterial' contribution to the damage will enable an individual to avoid being responsible for the entire damage.

Proving such a causal connection can be difficult and may depend on complex scientific evidence. This has led to suggestions that such a requirement be relaxed and, as in the case of the US Superfund's site clean-up plans, liability be attributed on the basis of simple connection, not cause.

Perhaps not surprisingly, the ACBE Group comes out against such a widening of the categories of individuals who can seek relief for environmental impairment. They do suggest, however, that where a site has been occupied over a period by different people and for different lengths of time liability could be based on the length of time an activity was carried out and the potentially hazardous nature of the activity concerned.

(5) Extending the categories of damage recoverable for environmental harm and the circumstances within which they can be recovered

Under English Common Law if a clean-up is a consequence of physical damage to property then it is a form of recoverable economic loss. If, on the other hand, a landowner cleans up polluted groundwater under his land, which had not actually been damaged, then this is an irrecoverable economic loss. This then raises the question of the aim of the present environmental laws: if the intention is to prevent and/or reduce pollution then should measures to prevent or contain damage also be recoverable?

Two important points are worth noting here. The first is that the ACBE stress the need for a balance between the cost of remedies to repair 'damage to the environment' and its benefits. Restoring the environment to its 'original state' would be unduly onerous on industry and ignore that we live in a commercial and industrial world. The second point is that punitive damages to reflect irreparable harm to the environment would be 'inconsistent with the English principle that damages are to compensate and not to punish'.

The ACBE, therefore, came out against extending liability in this way 'beyond the normal concepts of injury to persons or damage to property or the circumstances which currently exist for the recovery of economic loss'. They go on to say that such extension 'could, without adequate safeguards, encourage vexatious or misguided actions, damaging industry, insurers and lenders'.

(6) Altering the limitation periods for seeking remedies for environmental harm

One of the problems with some forms of environmental liability is that they can be 'long tailed' with a potential defendant being on the hook for many decades. The ACBE therefore recommends that consideration should be given to providing a long stop date for personal injury claims, such as the 30-year period under the Nuclear Installations Act 1965, and as outlined in the EC draft Directive on Civil Liability for Damage caused by Waste.

The ACBE also maintains that consideration needs to be given to simplifying the legal rules applied in identifying when a polluting event, that may be the cause of a subsequent legal action, occurs. This is a particular problem for continual or repetitive pollution where it may be difficult to distinguish one from the other and therefore establish whether limitation periods for action have expired.

(7) Introducing retrospective liability

The ACBE Group believes that it is necessary to take steps to clean up past pollution if that pollution is causing continuing harm or is in any way threatening. But it goes on to say that there are many circumstances where no threat exists and no action is needed beyond monitoring and, possibly, additional containment.

The Group also addresses the question of who should pay for historic pollution and points out that, under Section 61 of the Environmental Protection Act 1990, current landowners could be required to clean up polluted sites even if predecessors were responsible for the pollution. The current owner may have a right of action against predecessors particularly if, in the light of the judgement in *Cambridge Water Company* v *Eastern Counties Leather* described in Chapter 2, the predecessor should have 'reasonably foreseen' at the time the pollution occurred that damages to third parties would result. This judgement goes some way to meeting the ACBE's recommendation that retrospective liability should not be imposed for acts which were legal or met the established environmental standards of the day—which would impose significant costs on industry, discourage lenders from financing high-risk industries and damage the market for pollution insurance.

If, in due course, there is a policy to clean up where possible all past contamination then, according to the ACBE, consideration will also need to be given to covering the costs from a central fund generated from levies on the commercial sector generally. This is the subject of the group's eighth option described in the following paragraphs.

(8) Forming a financial pool to compensate for and remediate environmental harm

The starting point in evaluating the need for a financial compensation pool is the recognition that there are bound to be some circumstances in which the person liable for the pollution cannot be found or has no insurance or other financial means of meeting the claims. On the assumption that a pool or fund is to be set up, the next two questions are: in what circumstances should claims be made and how should compulsory contributions to the fund be raised?

The ACBE suggests that compensation funds could have their place where:

    i   there are no identifiable liable parties;
    ii there is no specific incident that caused the damage;
    iii there is no basis for liability;
    iv there is no causal link determinable;
    v   there is no party with a sufficient legal interest to bring proceedings;
    vi the polluting party is insolvent; and/or
    vii the claim is statute-barred.

Also, a fund could be raised by a general tax on society (likely to be politically unacceptable), or an EC-wide compensation scheme (for example, from resources provided by a carbon tax), or a general levy on business, or a more specific funding mechanism directed at polluting products or industries.

The ACBE go on to conclude that it would be a mistake, even if such a compensation fund existed, to abandon the general concept that the polluter should pay. They suggest that compensation schemes should be a safety net which should come into play when the mechanisms of civil and public liability fail.

That concludes a review of the ACBE's eight options which they prepared for UK legislators. They were published in February 1993 and were strongly welcomed by both the DTI and the DoE at that time. Taken together with the EC Green Paper published in March 1993 on civil environmental liability, the ACBE's report was an important contribution to the debate on the future shape of the EC and UK environmental liability regime.

The subject has since been taken further by the House of Lords Select Committee on the European Communities which reviewed the EC Green Paper in autumn 1993. In its report, published early in 1994, the Select Committee recommended that:

1. landowners should take on responsibility for past damage unless they 'did not know and could not reasonably be expected to have known that environmental damage had or was likely to have occurred';
2. where a present landowner should not bear responsibility, consideration should be given to setting up a compensation fund by the industrial sector concerned or to paying for remediation from tax revenues;
3. a phased programme of land remediation extending over several decades and based on accurate data on existing contamination should be introduced in the UK;
4. a statutory regime of strict liability for 'new' pollution damage should come into force from a date set some years in advance;
5. the principal defence available to a polluter should be that he could not have known in the light of scientific and technical knowledge at the relevant time that his activity could cause a damaging outcome;
6. a lender's liability 'should be restricted to circumstances when he exercises effective control of the activity';
7. plaintiffs should make claims only within three years of the date they become or should have become aware of the damage with a long-stop period of 30 years from the date on which the first instance of pollution gave rise to the damage occurred;
8. although at present compulsory insurance for environmental impairment would be unavailable, some financial security should be obtained for any firm wishing to carry on an activity which may cause environmental damage be it insurance, self-insurance or a compensation scheme;
9. the interest of society at large in protecting the environment should be served by placing a statutory duty on a public body, such as the

proposed Environment Agency, to seek compensation for damage to the unowned environment.

The next moves will come from both the EC and the UK Government in the form of the 1995 Environment Act. Industry, insurers and bankers will want to ensure that the new legislation is fair and that it sets strict but reasonable limits on their own liability.

5

Environmental Systems

5.1 Introduction

As Chapter 4 shows environmental risks are being taken more and more into account by investors and lenders, but companies cannot easily lay-off that risk through the insurance markets. The result is that, to keep their shareholders and lenders happy, many companies are now being forced to consider a wide range of risk-management techniques beginning with a thorough review of the relevant laws followed by practical steps to identify, monitor and maybe eliminate the environmental risks identified. Their third, longer-term task is to ensure that appropriate management systems are in place so that in future the necessary steps are taken as a matter of course to comply with the law and minimise risk.

But introducing environmental management systems is by no means straightforward. Environmental risks and concerns can cover nearly all aspects of a company's operations and therefore systems to deal with them need to be more than normally carefully structured. If the systems are sound they will also allow managements not only to implement their company's environmental policies but also to demonstrate to others that they are able to carry out their environmental promises. It is in response to this need that two relatively new standards for environmental management have been drawn up.

The first of these is British Standard (BS) 7750 on Environmental Management Systems and the second is the EC Eco-Management and Audit Regulation (EMAR). Both have a requirement for independent appraisal and in the latter case a publicly available environmental statement has to be prepared that is independently certified by an appropriately qualified environmental 'verifier' for each site covered. EMAR takes effect in the UK from April 1995.

Descriptions of both BS 7750 and EMAR make up the greater part of this chapter but a section on so-called Life Cycle Analysis (LCA) is also included. LCA is also a form of systems analysis which aims to quantify the environmental impacts of products, processes or activities from 'cradle to grave'. It is being increasingly widely used and attempts are being made to introduce consistent methodology. But claims by one manufacturer about the results of an LCA on one of its products have, from time to time, been successfully challenged by a competitor bringing the LCA concept into disrepute. The technique has the potential, however, to be of considerable importance in the not too distant future.

5.2 BS 7750

BS 7750—Environmental Management Systems was first published in March 1992 and is thought to be the world's first environmental management system standard. Being in that position brings some advantages but, equally, some disadvantages.

Perhaps the greatest advantage is that it has set the agenda for similar standards that might eventually be produced elsewhere. Others are more likely to follow within the framework it has established especially if lessons learned from its application are promptly applied. Equally, it will undoubtedly contain a number of pitfalls which might have been avoided if progress had been more measured. As it is, the first version of BS 7750 was published well ahead of the Eco-Management and Audit Regulation from the EC although it was prepared with a draft of that Regulation before it so that its approach and scope are broadly similar.

Following its launch, BS 7750 has been subject to a number of pilot studies up and down the UK and in a wide variety of industrial sectors. Some 40 sectors were involved together with seven cross-sectoral groups looking at issues such as the implications for small businesses, training and external relations. Within each sector were a number of participating companies with the largest numbers being in the chemicals, oil, construction, steel and metal finishing sectors. Most other sectors had less than 10 participants and very few financial institutions showed any interest. On the other hand, general interest was very high and in the latter part of 1992 BSI was selling approximately 1000 copies of the Standard each month.

The result of all this effort was a second edition of the Standard published in January 1994. What follows is based on this second edition but before looking in detail at its requirements a comparison with the first edition is worth making. The changes made provide some important pointers to the way in which the Standard was received and how it might be used in the future.

A key change was to make the objective of the Standard much clearer. The foreword states that:

> This Standard does not establish absolute requirements for environmental performance, beyond compliance with applicable legislation and regulations, and a commitment to continual improvement. Thus, two organisations carrying out similar activities but having different environmental performance may both comply with its requirements.

A second category of change is to emphasise the need to minimise adverse effects but also the need to maximise beneficial effects and to write an environmental policy that may make a commitment to work towards the achievement of sustainable development.

Finally, there are a number of changes in the second edition of the Standard to make its requirements compatible with those of EMAR. It is expressly stated that any industrial site certified as complying with BS 7750 should, with the agreement of the EC, be considered to have met the corresponding requirements of EMAR, although to comply fully an independently verified environmental statement will also be needed.

Attention will now be turned to BS 7750 itself, and in particular its structure and underlying philosophy, before moving onto EMAR and seeing how the two compare.

The system

The fundamental concept underlying BS 7750 is the importance of a structured management system which is integrated with a company's overall management activity and which addresses all aspects of its desired environmental performance. The Standard includes a schematic diagram of the stages in the implementation of such a system which is reproduced below. The elements within the box shown in double lines are part of the Standard's specification and are therefore assessable elements of a system.

The overall objective is to establish and maintain an environmental management system which ensures that the effects of the activities of the business concerned conform to its environmental policies, including the documentation of system procedures and instructions and their effective implementation.

Three points are worth stressing. First, environmental issues affect all aspects of business activity and therefore an environmental management system has to be capable of recognising and coping with its complexity.

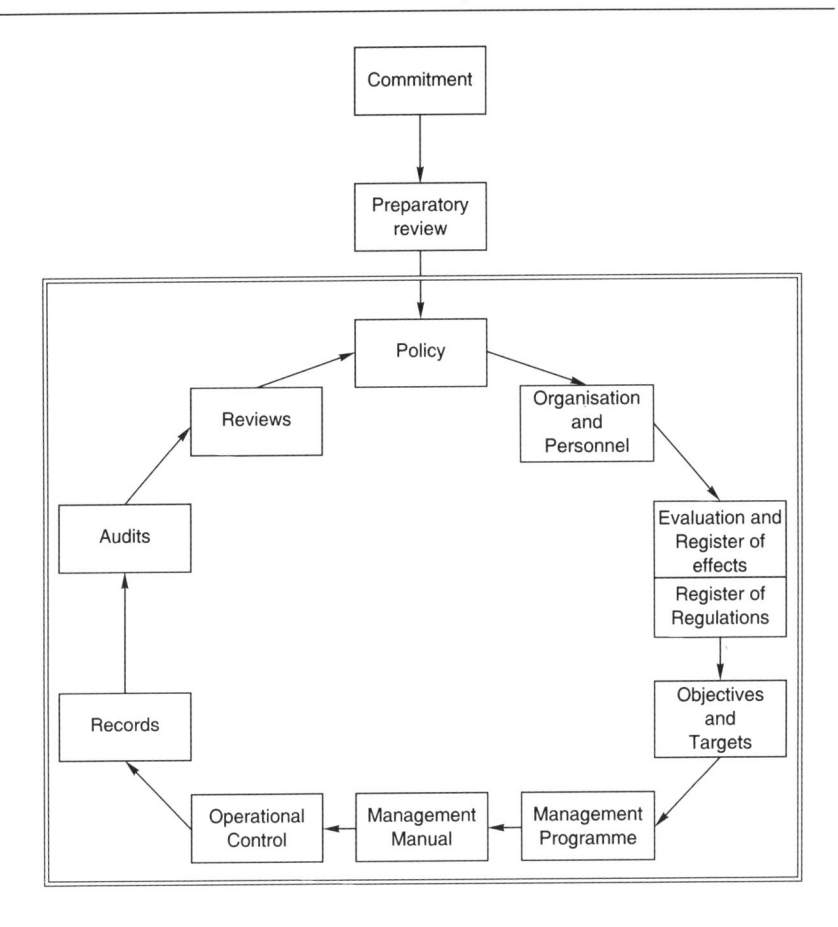

```
              ┌──────────────┐
              │  Commitment  │
              └──────┬───────┘
                     ↓
              ┌──────────────┐
              │  Preparatory │
              │    review    │
              └──────┬───────┘
                     ↓
              ┌──────────────┐        ┌──────────────┐
              │    Policy    │──────→ │ Organisation │
              └──────────────┘        │     and      │
          ↗                           │   Personnel  │
  ┌──────────┐                        └──────┬───────┘
  │ Reviews  │                               ↓
  └──────────┘                   ┌──────────────────┐
       ↑                         │  Evaluation and  │
  ┌──────────┐                   │   Register of    │
  │  Audits  │                   │      effects     │
  └──────────┘                   ├──────────────────┤
       ↑                         │   Register of    │
  ┌──────────┐                   │   Regulations    │
  │ Records  │                   └────────┬─────────┘
  └──────────┘                            ↓
       ↑                         ┌──────────────┐
  ┌────────────┐  ┌──────────┐   │  Objectives  │
  │Operational │←─│Management│   │     and      │
  │  Control   │  │  Manual  │←──│   Targets    │
  └────────────┘  └──────────┘   └──────────────┘
                       ↑     ┌──────────────┐
                       └─────│  Management  │
                             │  Programme   │
                             └──────────────┘
```

Second, the system should place emphasis on prevention rather than on detection and clean-up after the event. And, third, the system is circular—as will be seen the last stage, a review, feeds into policy making so that policies can be amended in the light of experience and changing rules and attitudes. Environmental actions are becoming increasingly important and so any management system must be able to react and amend itself as time goes by. 'Continuous improvement' are the watchwords.

Commitment

The starting point has to be the commitment of the person at the top of the organisation which, in time, has to be shared by most if not all of the senior management team. The relatively small number of British companies that seem to have taken strong environmental actions are led by people who believe in good environmental management—Anita Roddick at the Body Shop is a prominent example. To make the system work however top executives have to recognise that the emphasis has to be on prevention rather than detection and correction after the event. The aim is to be proactive not reactive.

Initial review

With this commitment in place the next step is to define the organisation's environmental policies but this cannot be done without a preliminary review—where are we now? This can take many forms but some kind of SWOT (Strengths, Weaknesses, Opportunities, Threats) analysis of the present position has to be carried out covering, BS 7750 suggests, laws and regulations, significant environmental effects of the business activities, existing practices and procedures and previous incidents. The examples given of what to include are worth reproducing here:

- areas where environmental performance could be improved;
- views of relevant interested parties;
- environmental objectives and targets beyond regulatory requirements;
- expected changes in regulations and legislation;
- adequacy of resources and environmental information;
- environmental records;
- environmental cost/benefit analysis and accounting methods;
- internal and external communication on environmental issues;
- environmental aspects of products and services;
- resource consumption (energy, fuels, materials);
- waste minimisation/recycling initiatives;
- use of hazardous processes;
- use and disposal of hazardous materials and products;
- transport policy;
- nature conservation;
- complaints and their recording and follow-up;
- visual impact, noise and odours;
- environmental probity of suppliers;
- environmental hazard and risk assessment of potential emergency situations;
- environmental aspects of emergency planning; and
- environmental effects of investment policies.

They show the enormously wide range of issues that could be addressed and, when drawn together, identifying priorities and an improvement programme to deal with them should form the basis for a company's environmental policy.

Environmental policy

The Standard requires that a company's environmental policy is defined and documented and that:

- it is relevant;
- it is communicated, implemented and maintained by everyone;
- it is publicly available;
- it is committed to continual improvement;
- it provides for the setting and publication of environmental objectives;
- it states which activities are covered; and
- it indicates how the environmental objectives will be made publicly available.

It cannot be stressed too much that getting the policy framework right is vital if the whole system is to be set up on the right lines. Without an adequate policy the system is built on sand.

Equally the commitment, visible and enthusiastically expressed, to the policy from the top is vital as is the need to make the policy relevant to individual managers by supplementing it with specialised and/or more detailed targets for particular parts of the business.

There is a lot more that could be said about environmental policies but most of what there is is dealt with elsewhere in this book. In particular, Chapter 6 looks at reporting, to anyone who is interested, on the policies themselves and compliance with them and Chapter 8 looks at their accounting implications.

Organisation and personnel

Nothing happens unless someone makes it happen and then sees that it continues to happen. Accordingly the Standard points out that a company must 'define and document the responsibility, authority and inter-relations of key personnel who manage, perform and verify activities having a significant effect, actual or potential on the environment . . .'.

In particular it stresses the importance of an appropriate 'management representative' to take the lead in making BS 7750 happen. That is not to say that other managers just leave it up to the appointed representative but it is he or she who, through them, has to make sure that everyone knows what they have to do and actually does it. The Standard is not specific about the sort of qualities such a management representative should have but experience suggests that youth, drive and enthusiasm are needed in plenty to drive forward a policy which to some may seem to be either unnecessary or, at the other extreme, far too threatening.

Also, there is the need for competent, committed people to carry out the environmental management tasks that need to be done. There may be a need for formal qualifications or, at the very least, environmental tasks will have to be built into job descriptions and performance appraisals. There is also almost certainly a need for training at all levels to ensure that everyone knows what their environmental responsibilities are as well as to motivate them or to provide them with additional technical skills.

Environmental effects

With a policy in place and the people to carry it out well briefed, the first real tasks involve the collection of data on legislation, regulations and other policy requirements that may affect the company together with the preparation of some form of register of so-called 'environmental effects' covering issues such as:

- controlled and uncontrolled emissions to atmosphere;
- controlled and uncontrolled discharges to water;
- solid and other wastes;
- contamination of land;
- use of land, water, fuels and energy, and other natural resources;
- noise, odour, dust, vibration and visual impact; and
- effects on specific parts of the environment, including ecosystems.

There is a need to keep this register up-to-date so appropriate procedures are required to review new effects continuously and to carry out ongoing examinations and assessments of the effects identified, not only under normal operating conditions, but also under abnormal conditions, in emergencies and in the past and future as well as at present. As this could be a major task, Annex A to the Standard, which gives a lot of useful guidance but is not formally a part of the Standard, suggests that risk assessment and other techniques may be used so as to compare and evaluate the effects identified.

Annex A also points out that the effects of support functions such as planning, finance, personnel and administration should not be overlooked and that both direct and indirect effects should be considered. Examples of direct effects are the disposal or release of solid, liquid and gaseous wastes arising in a production process and the use of fuels, energy and materials. Indirect effects are concerns such as the extraction of raw materials supplied by another organisation, the effects of other businesses in which the company is invested and the use, possible misuse, and disposal of the company's products.

Environmental objectives and targets

Having assessed the effects of a wide range of environmental issues the next step is to set specific environmental objectives and targets at all levels in the company. These have to be consistent with the company's environmental policy and should also quantify, wherever practicable, the commitment to continual improvement in environmental performance over defined timescales. When agreed, they should be part of a manager's personal accountability and performance appraisal.

Not all areas of activity have to make equal progress all the time and greater emphasis, Annex A suggests, should be given to those areas where improvements are necessary to reduce risks and liabilities and should be identified by cost-benefit analysis where practicable.

Environmental management programme

Each part of the environmental management system is vital but none is more vital than setting up and maintaining a formal programme to implement the company's policy by seeing that the objectives and targets are met. This programme has to designate responsibility for targets at each function and level in the company and must include information on how they are to be achieved. New projects will require their own rules and procedures and need to address the environmental effects arising at all stages of a new product life-cycle or a new service—from feasibility studies through planning and design to construction, commissioning, operation, and eventual decommissioning.

Environmental management manual and documentation

Writing all this down may be a chore but without the thought processes that lie behind formal written documentation or the ability to communicate a consistent message that the written word represents it will be almost impossible to make it work properly. So the standard requires a manual (or manuals) to be kept that:

- collate the environmental policy, objectives and targets, and programme;

- documents the key roles and responsibilities;
- describes the interaction of system elements; and
- provides direction to related documentation and describes other aspects of the management system, where appropriate.

Whilst the manual is a permanent reference point describing the implementation and maintenance of the system, the documentation describes in more detail the environmental management system itself. The more complex the organisation, the more complex will be the documentation so the Standard requires it to be clearly identified, periodically reviewed and revised, available where it is needed, and removed when it becomes obsolete.

Many of the quality-management systems introduced in the last few years have failed in this respect. Not, usually, through lack of documentation but through too much of it so that managers and staff responsible for operating the system resent it because it seems bureaucratic. There is usually a happy medium.

Operational control

The day-to-day operation of the system is the responsibility of various line managers who need to be in control and able to verify compliance with the system's requirements as well as establish and maintain records of the results. Key functions which do or may affect the environment have to be identified and then appropriate controls put in place paying particular attention to:

- documenting work instructions—how the activity should be done;
- procurement and contracting—ensuring that suppliers and contractors are complying with the required environmental policies and procedures;
- monitoring and control of such matters as effluent streams and waste disposal;
- approval of planned processes and equipment; and
- written performance criteria.

Some functions can only be properly verified by measurement. Here, too, the Standard requires the documentation of the measurements, the procedures specified, the acceptance criteria, the action needed should the results be unsatisfactory and the assessment of previous verification information when the verification systems are not working properly. More specifically, decisions have to be made about what to measure, where and at what time, quality controls, acceptance criteria, and the actions to be taken to ensure that the measuring equipment remains accurate and reliable.

If all is not well, responsibilities for investigating the problem and putting it right have to be defined and:

- the cause determined;
- a plan of action drawn up;
- appropriate preventive actions initiated;
- controls applied to ensure that preventive actions are effective; and
- changes in procedures recorded.

Environmental management records

Working the environmental management system properly is, however, not an end in itself. Proof that it has been working properly may be required at any time and to that end records demonstrating compliance over time are needed. Annex A to the Standard suggests that such records should include:

- details of any failures to comply with policy (including the results of audits and reviews) and of corrective actions taken;
- details of any incidents and follow-up actions taken;
- details of any complaints and follow-up actions taken;
- appropriate supplier and contractor information;
- inspection and maintenance reports;
- product identification and composition data; and
- monitoring data and environmental training records.

Although this sounds like a lot of information most of it should be available anyway. All that is required is that it is put into an appropriate format and made accessible, perhaps by means of signposts in the manual or other related documentation, both within the company and to interested parties.

Environmental management audits

The main purpose of an environmental management audit is to assess the extent of compliance, or non-compliance, with the company's environmental management system. In particular the Standard suggests that audit procedures should determine whether or not environmental management activities conform to the company's environmental management programme, are implemented effectively and that the environmental management system is effective in fulfilling the environmental policy. The procedures have to be carried out in accordance with an audit programme that deals with the following points:

- The specific areas and activities to be audited including organisational structures; administrative and operational procedures; work areas; operations and processes; documentation, reports and records; and environmental performance.
- The frequency of auditing of each activity or area, audits being scheduled on the basis of the contribution, both actual and potential, of the activity concerned to significant environmental effects and the results of previous audits.
- The responsibility for auditing each activity/area.
- The protocol and procedures covering personnel requirements and specifically that those carrying out the audits are independent, so far as is possible, of the specific activities or areas being audited, have expertise in relevant disciplines, and have support, where necessary, from a wider range of specialists who may be internal or external to the company.
- The protocol and procedures for conducting the audits dealing with documentation, reports and records and environmental performance as well as methodologies which may involve the use of questionnaires, checklists, interviews, measurements and direct observations depending on what is being audited.
- The reporting of audit findings to those responsible for the activity/area audited who are required to take timely action on reported deficiencies.

The guidance to this section of the Standard in Annex A makes a number of additional suggestions about environmental management auditing which are worth describing in some detail here. The parallels with financial auditing are clear, as will become clearer still in Chapter 7.

The first of these is the importance of the independence of the auditors whether that is achieved by using people from another part of the company or externally and the need for proper training to enable them to carry out the task objectively, impartially and effectively. Reference is made to the EMAR requirement for the external verification of audits and which is described more fully later in this chapter.

The second suggestion is that all parts of the company should normally undergo an audit at least every three years (especially if also seeking to comply with EMAR) and that activities having particular potential to cause environmental harm should normally be audited at least once a year.

A third comment concerns the extent to which direct observations or measurements of environmental performance itself are of value during an audit. In some cases, it is suggested, they may be of little value where there are marked variations from time to time.

A further important acknowledgement is the need for the audit team to have broad knowledge of environmental processes and effects as well as expertise in certain relevant disciplines depending on the nature of the organisation being audited. On the other hand, some organisations have limited potential to affect the environment adversely and so detailed specialist knowledge may be unnecessary.

Annex A to the Standard then talks about useful by-products of the audit process in terms familiar to most financial auditors. It stresses that whilst the primary function of environmental audits is to assess the extent of compliance and non-compliance with the environmental management system and to assess the effectiveness of previous corrective actions, auditors may also suggest remedial measures to overcome problems. Alternatively, the Standard suggests, they may simply note the nature of the problems and require that the management of the audited functions devise and implement an appropriate solution. And for all this to count, senior company management have to ensure that environmental audit personnel have the support and authority to procure the necessary information.

The section in Annex A on environmental management audits then concludes with three further points:

1. that the environmental audit report should be submitted to the company's environmental management representative for distribution and action as appropriate;
2. that self-assessment procedures carried out by line management to assess readiness for audit might be a useful addition to establishing independent environmental audit procedures; and
3. that the broad principles set out in BS 7229 dealing with quality system auditing should be applied to the auditing of environmental management systems where applicable.

Environmental management reviews

This is the final stage in the implementation of the Standard's requirements. It involves periodic reviews, which have to be documented, by management of the continuing suitability and effectiveness of the company's environmental management systems and their compliance with the Standard.

The review, however, is not just confined to existing environmental policy, objectives and targets but is also required to address the possible need for changes to them in the light of changing circumstances and the commitment to continual improvement. Annex A suggests that issues to be addressed should include:

- the findings of environmental management audit reports and whether these have been implemented;
- the continuing suitability of environmental policy in the light of new concerns, developing understanding, regulatory developments, the concerns of interested parties, market pressures, changing company activities and changes in the sensitivity of the environment; and
- the continuing suitability of the company's environmental targets and objectives.

Changes to environmental policies and the system required to implement them may be the result of the review and as a consequence the company moves on. Dealing with environmental issues is not a once-and-for-all exercise. It is an ongoing exercise and BS 7750 might play a vital central role in getting this message across in the UK.

Links to BS 5750 Quality Systems

Before leaving BS 7750 it is worth stressing the linkages between it and BS 5750: Part 1: 1987 which deals with Quality Systems. BS 7750 complements BS 5750 as both take parallel approaches to achieving and demonstrating compliance with the requirements specified. Annex B to BS 7750 explains the links between them and the introduction to the Standard says that there is an expectation that organisations operating to BS 5750 will readily be able to extend their management systems in accordance with BS 7750 but that operation to BS 5750 is not a prerequisite for operation to BS 7750.

Links to the EC Eco-Management and Audit Regulation

The other important linkage that the BSI have kept in mind in drawing up BS 7750 is with the EC Eco-Management and Audit Regulation (EMAR). The foreword to the Standard states that it was produced with the express intention that its requirements should be compatible with those of the environmental management system specified in EMAR.

The British Standard has also influenced national standards in France, Ireland and Spain and is used in Denmark and The Netherlands as a *de facto* standard. But not all EC Member States are thought to want to recognise it. Germany is believed to be particularly concerned about the absence of performance criteria from the Standard.

If and when the Standard is formally deemed to be compatible with EMAR then any industrial site certified as complying with the Standard by a certification body whose accreditation is recognised in the Member

State where the site is located will be considered to have met EMAR's requirements. The only additional requirement so as to fully comply with EMAR would be the publication of an independently verified environmental statement. This, therefore, is the time to look at EMAR itself.

5.3 EC Eco-Management and Audit Regulation

The Regulation has been a long time in coming and in its final form is very different from the original proposal, circulated to Member States in December 1990, for an EC Directive on the Environmental Auditing of Certain Industrial Activities. This proposal would have required mandatory and annual environmental audits of manufacturing sites in 58 industrial sectors and the publication of a public statement of the results. For the environmentally more significant of these sites, both internal audits and the public reports would have been subject to external verification by registered environmental auditors.

Not surprisingly these proposals brought forth numerous protests and resulted, eventually, in an amended version that was put to the EC Environment Council in December 1991 but which was also rejected. A further version published in March 1992, was put to the Environment Council meeting in December 1992 in the form of a draft Regulation rather than a Directive. A Regulation is directly binding in its entirety on Member States and therefore eliminates differences between their implementing laws. It was approved in an amended form and finally published on 10 July 1993.

The final version is radically different from its original predecessor and very different from subsequent drafts too. The most significant changes are that audits will not be mandatory, there will not be mandatory annual self-assessments for most companies which elect to participate in the scheme and company conducted internal audits will not be subject to formal verification by external auditors. Also gone are the provision for Member States to oblige specific companies to participate in the scheme as a means of improving their environmental performance and some detailed specifications for the environmental management systems which participating companies would have to establish.

So what is left in? A lot—although the amended proposals are in most respects less prescriptive than before they will still be a major challenge to most companies who are prepared to commit themselves to improving their environmental performance and to report publicly on their failings as well as achievements.

Looking first at the scheme's aims, it is clear that they are very similar to those of BS 7750. Whereas BS 7750 'is designed to enable any organisation to establish an effective management system, as a foundation for both sound environmental performance and participation in "environmental auditing" schemes', the EMAR's objective is

> to promote continuous improvements in the environmental performance of industrial activities by:
> (a) the establishment and implementation of environmental policies, programmes and management systems by companies, in relation to their sites;
> (b) the systematic, objective and periodic evaluation of the performance of such elements;
> (c) the provision of information of environmental performance to the public.

But not all commercial concerns are affected by EMAR which, in contrast to BS 7750 which is open to all forms of organisation, is open only to manufacturing industry together with electricity, gas, steam and hot water production and the recycling, treatment, destruction or disposal of solid or liquid waste.

Turning now to what EMAR involves it must first be remembered that it is voluntary. It is also open to companies to seek registration in their entirety or on a site-by-site basis. No company has to participate although once a company joins the scheme it has to observe all the rules and procedures laid down by the Regulation. There are eight steps to registration under the scheme with so-called 'competent bodies' designated by each Member State.

Step 1 Adopt a company environmental policy

The first step comprises adopting an environmental policy which, in addition to providing for compliance with all relevant regulatory requirements regarding the environment, must include commitments aimed at the reasonable continuous improvement of environmental performance, with a view to reducing environmental impacts to levels not exceeding those corresponding to economically viable application of best available technology.

Annex A to EMAR gives more detail on what is involved and includes requirements that the policy:

- is in writing;
- is periodically reviewed, in particular in the light of environmental audits, and revised as appropriate at the highest management level;
- is communicated to employees and made publicly available;
- is based upon certain principles of good environmental management practice; and
- provides for the continual improvement of environmental performance.

Step 2 Environmental review

The second step is to conduct an environmental review of the following aspects of each site:

- assessment, control and reduction of the impact of the activity concerned on the various sectors of the environment;
- energy management, savings and choice;
- raw materials management, savings, choice and transportation, water management and savings;
- waste avoidance, recycling, reuse, transportation and disposal;
- evaluation, control and reduction of noise within and outside the site;
- selection of new production processes and changes to production processes;
- product planning (design, packaging, transportation, use and disposal);
- environmental performance and practices of contractors, subcontractors and suppliers;
- prevention and limitation of environmental accidents;
- contingency procedure in cases of environmental accidents;
- staff information and training on environmental issues; and
- external information on environmental issues.

Step 3 Introduce an environmental programme and management system

The third step in implementing EMAR is to introduce, in the light of the environmental review conducted as Step (2), an environmental programme for the site and an environmental management system applicable to all activities at the site. The environmental programme must aim at achieving the policy commitments and objectives towards continuous improvement of environmental performances. Separate programmes are required for new developments or for new or modified products, services or processes. The environmental management system must be designed, implemented and maintained in such a way that a number of detailed requirements are met under the following headings:

- environmental policy, objectives and programmes;
- organisation and personnel;
- environmental effects;
- operational control;
- environmental management documentation records; and
- environmental audits.

Because of their overall importance the detailed requirements as set out in Annex 1 to EMAR are included in full in Appendix C.

Step 4 Carry out internal environmental audits

The fourth step is to carry out internal environmental audits at the site concerned. These may be carried out by either auditors belonging to the company or by external people or organisations. The issues that the audit has to address are those to be covered in the environmental review described above. Annex II to EMAR also gives the detailed requirements for the audits as follows:

- Objectives—to be defined in writing as part of each audit programme including guidance on the audit frequency for each activity, an assessment of the management systems and the determination of conformity with company policies and the site programme (including relevant environmental regulations).
- Scope—must be clearly defined for each stage of an audit cycle and must specify the subject areas covered, the activities to be audited, the environmental standards to be considered and the period covered.
- Organisation and resources—the people doing the audit work must have appropriate knowledge of the sectors and fields audited, including knowledge and experience of the relevant environmental management, technical environmental and regulatory issues, and sufficient training and proficiency in the specific skills of auditing required. Top company management must support the auditing and the auditors must be sufficiently independent to make an objective and impartial judgement.
- Planning and preparation for a site visit—must ensure that the appropriate resources are allocated, that everyone involved understands their role and responsibilities and include familiarisation with activities on the site and a review of the findings and conclusions of previous audits.
- Audit activities—will include discussions with site personnel, inspection of operating conditions and equipment and reviewing of records, written procedures and other relevant documentation, with the object of evaluating environmental performance at the site by determining whether the site meets the applicable standards and whether the system in place to manage environmental responsibilities is effective and appropriate. The audit progress will include understanding the management systems, assessing their strengths and weaknesses, gathering relevant evidence, evaluating audit findings, preparing conclusions and reporting them.

- Reporting audit findings and conclusions—in writing and in a form appropriate to ensure full, formal submission of the findings and conclusions of the audit, at the end of each audit and audit cycle, to be formally communicated to top company management. The fundamental objectives of the written audit report are to document the scope of the audit, to provide management with information on the state of compliance with the company's environmental policy and the environmental progress at the site, to provide management with information on the effectiveness and reliability of the arrangements for monitoring environmental impacts at the site and to demonstrate the need for corrective action, where appropriate.
- Audit frequency—the audit will be executed or the audit cycle will be completed at intervals of no longer than three years. The frequency of each activity at a site will be established by the top company management taking account of the potential overall environmental impact of the activities at the site, and of the site's environmental programme depending in particular, on the nature, scale and complexity of the activities, the nature and scale of emissions, waste, raw material and energy consumption and, in general, of interaction with the environment, the importance and urgency of the problems detected following the initial environmental review or the previous audit and the history of environmental problems.

Step 5   Set objectives

EMAR's fifth step is to set objectives at the highest appropriate management level aimed at the continuous improvement of environmental performance in the light of the findings of the audit and to revise the environmental programme set up as part of the third step accordingly.

Step 6   Prepare an environmental statement

Preparing an environmental statement specific to each site audited is EMAR's sixth step. A statement has to be prepared after the initial environmental review and after each subsequent audit or audit cycle in a form that is designed for the public and written in a concise, comprehensible form. Article 5 of EMAR requires the statement to include:

- a description of the company's activities at the site considered;
- an assessment of all the significant environmental issues of relevance to the activities concerned;
- a summary of the figures on pollutant emissions, waste generation, consumption of raw material, energy and water, noise and other significant environmental aspects, as appropriate;

- other factors regarding environmental performance;
- a presentation of the company's environmental policy, programme and management system implemented at the site considered;
- the deadline set for submission of the next statement; and
- the name of the accredited environmental verifier.

It must also draw attention to significant changes since the previous statement.

Article 5 requires a simplified statement to be prepared annually in the years between full audits containing, as a minimum, the figures required on pollutant emissions, etc., but without validation until the end of the audit or audit cycle. But such simplified statements are not required where either the accredited environmental verifier considers that the nature and scale of the operations on the site, particularly those of SMEs (small and medium-sized enterprises), warrants no further environmental statement until the end of the next audit or where there have been few significant changes since the last environmental statement.

The first environmental statement also has to include certain additional information set out in Annex V to EMAR.

Step 7 Conduct a verification examination

The penultimate step is the verification of the site environmental policy, programme, management system, review of audit procedures and environmental statements to ensure they meet EMAR's requirements.

Article 4 elaborates and makes it clear that someone or some organisation to be known as an accredited environmental verifier must carry out this verification and must be independent of the site's auditor. Progress with accrediting appropriately qualified organisations and individuals is described later in this chapter.

The verifier is required to check:

(a) whether the environmental policy has been established and if it meets the requirements of the eight steps described here as well as the relevant requirements in Annex I;
(b) whether an environmental management system and programme are in place and operational at the site and whether they comply with the relevant requirements in Annex I;
(c) whether the environmental review and audit are carried out in accordance with the relevant requirements in Annex I and II;
(d) whether the data and information in the environmental statement are reliable and whether the statement adequately covers all the significant environmental issues of relevance to the site.

Article 4 also imposes a confidentiality requirement on the verifier not to divulge any information or data obtained in the course of auditing or verification without authorisation from the company management.

Step 8   Register the site

Having accomplished the seven steps described in the previous paragraphs the final one is to forward the validated environmental statement to a so-called 'competent body' within the Member State where the site is located. If the competent body is satisfied that the site meets all EMAR's conditions, and once any registration fee has been paid, the site is registered, a registration number is given and site management informed.

Sites can be removed from the register if no validated environmental statement and registration fee is received when due but, more significantly, if a 'competent enforcement authority', such as HMIP or the NRA in the UK, tells the competent body of a breach at the site of relevant regulatory requirements. The site can go back on the register once satisfactory assurances have been received from the competent enforcement authority that the breach has been rectified and that satisfactory arrangements are in place to ensure that it does not recur.

Every year a list of all the registered sites in the EC is to be published in the Official Journal of the European Communities. Companies may also use for their registered sites a prescribed logo and one of four forms of 'statements of participation' which must always accompany the logo. EMAR's Article 10 specifically states, however, that the logo and statement may not be used to advertise products, or appear on the products themselves or on their packaging.

That concludes the description of EMAR. Its longer term impact in the EC in general and the UK in particular can only be guessed at. But the UK accounting profession is beginning to show interest with a growing recognition that the audit procedures described in EMAR and the external verification process have a lot in common with financial auditing. The profession is also waking up to the commercial opportunities that being an accredited environmental verifier (or an 'eco-auditor') may bring. Registration as eco-auditors by some financial auditors with the UK competent body, when it is established, may follow. The next few years will be critical. If the accounting profession wants to be involved it will have to make a concerted effort immediately to get recognition of its expertise across and then sustain that effort so as to influence the way in which the new eco-auditing profession develops.

The final section of this chapter describes arrangements for accrediting eco-auditors in the UK, but, before looking at what is happening, a further form of environmental system—which may also need some form of eco-audit procedures in the future—is worth considering. This is known as Life Cycle Analysis.

5.4 Life Cycle Analysis

Life Cycle Analysis (LCA) is, put simply, a form of systems analysis which can be used to quantify the environmental impacts of any products, process or activity from 'cradle-to-grave'.

The basis of an LCA is to identify and quantify flows of material and energy through industrial systems and to use the findings to compare each system with others or find ways to optimise them with environmental considerations in mind. The system, when applied to a product, begins with raw material extraction and processing, through manufacture and distribution, to use and final disposal. For each of these states inputs such as energy and raw materials and outputs of solids, liquids and gaseous wastes are quantified and perhaps summarised for each parameter across the life-cycle to give an overall profile of the resource intensity and polluting capacity of the system.

It all sounds very simple and logical but the reality of conducting LCAs and, more importantly, interpreting the results is fraught with problems. Perhaps four stages can be recognised in a typical LCA. A few words about each should give some insights into the methodology and the problems:

1. The first stage involves a clear definition of the goals and scope of the study. The approach might be different if the study is used as a management tool or as part of a marketing strategy, or if socio-economic or aesthetic issues are to be included or excluded. The basis unit to be evaluated is also of vital importance as LCAs are normally carried out to allow comparisons to be made per unit weight of material or, in the case of detergents, weight per unit washed, for example.
2. The second stage is also a matter of definition and involves decisions about the life cycle stages to be addressed and the system's boundaries themselves. Ideally, all life-cycle stages should be covered but it is often particularly difficult, for example, to trace materials back to the natural environment from where they actually began.
3. The third stage is developing an inventory of results and is much the most time-consuming. It is therefore vital that data is collected in as open and straightforward a manner as possible—that it is transparent—and that it is aggregated as little as possible. For example, sulphur dioxide should not be added to other airborne emissions to give a

single value for total airborne emissions as different emissions have different levels of impact on the environment.
4. The fourth stage can be where it all goes wrong because this stage involves making judgements about the information collected and there are, as yet, very few generally accepted guidelines on how to go about this. A typical difficulty might be to decide how to weight a product's impact on the ozone layer against its contribution to global warming.

There is obviously a lot more to an LCA than these few words can get over not least the matter of cost and return on that cost—that is, what use can be made of the results. There are a few published costings available but some estimates given in the *Financial Times* on 19 February 1992 suggest that a simple inventory to compare the performance of, say, three types of packaging would cost between £15 000 and £25 000. More complex analysis could cost £120 000—not cheap. There is scope, however, for some sharing of data. Companies producing commodity products such as glass and cardboard could spread the cost of LCAs through pooling arrangements organised by trade associations but natural competitors may mean that not everyone is prepared to join in.

Which is why the final points about LCAs must concern the use made of them, now and in the future. Perhaps the best way of concluding is to use the words of the European Head of Environment for Procter & Gamble who, according to *ENDS Report 198*, July 1991, said that:

> Simple comparisons can be done now and used in marketing—for example, comparison of packaging materials. And if a company is prepared to stand up in public and defend its conclusions then it should be allowed to do so.

On the other hand he goes on to say that:

> ... where products being prepared produce wastes which are very different in nature then it is difficult to use LCA in marketing at the moment.

The way forward, and most people believe there is a way forward, that will see LCAs playing a central environmental role in years to come, seems to be through co-operation. The Confederation of British Industry is currently co-ordinating an effort to bring environmentalists, academics and business people together to develop independent evaluation techniques whilst companies such as Shell, Unilever, BASF, Procter & Gamble and Enichem are behind the Society for the Promotion of Lifecycle Development. Perhaps they will also play an important part in the development of an eco-audit profession?

5.5 Accreditation

For an eco-audit profession to develop, however, formal recognition of the skills required is probably needed. EMAR requires each Member State to have formally recognised a competent body. This has given an impetus in the UK and Europe that might otherwise have taken years to bring about. The UK accounting profession, as will be seen, is getting involved but is by no means taking a leading role. This in contrast to Denmark where the national financial auditing body, Foreningen of Statsautoriserede Revisorer (FSR), took the initiative as long ago as 1991. FSR emphasises that publication of an annual environmental statement fits comfortably alongside annual financial statements and, therefore, has sought a prominent role in forming a new eco-auditing profession in Denmark.

Although the UK accounting profession may not be closely involved, the UK has taken a leading role throughout in the development of environmental management systems and latterly in plans for recognition of accredited environmental certification bodies (BS 7750) and accredited environmental verifiers (EMAR). It has been doing this through the National Accreditation Council for Certification Bodies (NACCB) which was appointed by the UK Government in October 1993 to accredit organisations seeking to certify/verify companies for compliance with BS 7750 and EMAR. The UK Department of the Environment has however decided to act itself as the 'competent body' required by EMAR to maintain a register of sites participating in that scheme.

This appointment has forced some changes onto NACCB which had previously been mainly involved with approving organisations to certify quality management systems and not with the environmental credentials of prospective environmental certification bodies. NACCB, however, has established a separate Environmental Accreditation Panel which published Environmental Accreditation Criteria in January 1995. These criteria were tested on a number of organisations, although not on an accounting/financial auditing firm. NACCB is also playing a trading role in developing European-wide guidelines for the criteria.

What follows is a brief description of some of these criteria with comment on their likely importance for accounting and financial auditing firms. This chapter then concludes with some remarks about the qualifications of individuals as eco-auditors and the rival schemes currently being set up.

The NACCB Panel has, perhaps not surprisingly, placed considerable emphasis on the links between quality management and environmental management. Almost certainly too much so, given the EMAR requirement for an independently verified environmental statement, which demands different auditing skills and an awareness of standards of evidence and potential liabilities on the part of those depending on the verified statements of which quality assessors have had little experience so far. Indeed, the NACCB suggest that, if a company wishes, quality and environmental system certification should be done at the same time as in effect there are two standards but only one integrated system.

The NACCB Panel also wants to encourage the bodies they certify to give special attention to small and medium-sized enterprises by developing a simple certification service. They say they will encourage the development of sector application guides to assist smaller companies in those industrial sectors where processes give rise to 'relatively standard' environmental effects. Audits of accredited certification bodies will be carried out by the NACCB at least once every twelve months and NACCB plan to perform a complete reassessment every fourth year.

A key point is that there is nothing in the criteria to stop accounting and auditing firms from carrying out the work whether for smaller or larger organisations. It had been thought that firms engaging in activities 'which might compromise their impartiality'—such as consultancy—would be prohibited but this is not now the case thereby removing what might have been a barrier for accounting and auditing firms. Individuals involved in the certification process will however be required to declare any connections with the company being certified.

The NACCB also recognises that few organisations will have the expertise to certify companies across all sectors and so will accredit firms according to the scope of their activity. So there is nothing to stop accounting and auditing firms seeking accreditation even if it is limited.

As far as individuals are concerned the NACCB criteria might also work to the accountant/auditor's advantage. They recognise the difference between expertise at 'management' level and at 'assessor' level.

Whilst everyone involved has to have an adequate understanding of BS7750 and EMAR 'management' will need to know only enough to be able to assemble an assessment team with the competencies needed for a particular assignment within their firm's accredited scope. Senior members of accounting and auditing firms are therefore likely to be able to carry out this 'management' function with limited additional training.

Whether or not individual 'assessors' will be found in accounting and auditing firms will depend on future recruitment policies but many graduates joining the profession have science-based degrees that may be relevant and allow them to meet the criteria set by NACCB or bodies awarding appropriate environmental qualifications as well as, in due course, a professional accounting body.

NACCB have listed four organisations giving qualifications which, may be judged to be relevant as measures of environmental competence. No accounting body is, so far, included. The list is as follows:

- Registration Board for Assessors
- Environmental Auditors Registration Association
- Register of Eco-Audit Specialists (Royal Society of Chemistry)
- Institution of Chemical Engineers Register of Environmental Professionals

If more of the professional accounting bodies take up the challenge, the Environmental Auditors Registration Scheme promoted by the Environmental Auditors Registration Association (EARA) may be a way forward for individual accountants wanting to work as some form of eco-auditor.

EARA was launched in July 1992 and by January 1994 had 505 individuals registered with it. Of this total, 23 meet the highest standard of 'Principal Environmental Auditor'. A further 300 applications were being processed at that time (*ENDS Report No. 228*, January 1994).

EARA's stated aims are to:

- independently assess and verify the relevant experience of individual environmental auditors;
- publish a comprehensive register of environmental auditors;
- provide an auditor referral service to industry;
- promote good standards of practice in environmental auditing; and
- provide individuals, from a range of occupational disciplines, with a structured route of entry to this emerging profession.

Registration is at one of three levels based on a points system awarded for matters such as training, qualifications, and field experience. The three levels, together with EARA's publicly stated requirements, are as follows:

1. Associate Environmental Auditor: requiring a combination of either appropriate qualifications and experience or through qualifications and training alone. Training points are only awarded for attendance at EARA accredited courses. Persons registered as Associated Environmental Auditors are expected to have a basic knowledge of environmental auditing and to be active as 'trainee' environmental auditors or active (sometimes in a senior capacity) in areas closely related to this field (e.g. environmental audit commissioning or training roles).
2. Environmental Auditor: requiring a minimum of 100 days environmental auditing experience and passing a written exam. Environmental Auditors are expected to have a good appreciation of

environmental issues and environmental auditing techniques and to be competent environmental auditors in the areas in which they operate. However, their experience may be confined to a limited number of environmental audit types and sectors. Environmental Auditors will typically be regular and full members of environmental audit teams.
3. Principal Environmental Auditor: requiring a minimum of 200 days environmental auditing experience, a thesis of up to 5000 words and an oral exam conducted by a peer group. Principal Environmental Auditors are expected to have a wealth of environmental auditing expertise and will typically lead/manage audit teams and liaise with senior management, both on a regular basis. They are expected to take on greater responsibilities than Environmental Auditors and to have an excellent appreciation of issues relating to environmental auditing.

Perhaps the professional accounting bodies can work with EARA to enable their members' experience and qualifications to be appropriately recognised by either side. In any case, it should not be overlooked that, so far as BS 7750 is concerned, NACCB cannot stop firms it has not accredited offering certification under the Standard. As both BS 7750 and EMAR are voluntary if the ground rules are too restrictive for the accounting/financial auditing profession (and EARA too is left out) separate forms of accreditation may be developed which might, in time, acquire an equivalent status to the UK government approved scheme. It is by no means clear at present which direction a UK eco-audit profession will take.

6

Environmental Reporting

6.1 Introduction

There is a growing demand for environmental information. All kinds are wanted and, it often seems, the more the better with little regard for its relevance, the cost-effectiveness of obtaining it or, most importantly, its reliability and quality.

The loudest demands come from pressure groups and lobbyists, but increasingly consumers want to believe the claims that advertisers make about the green credentials of their products. They also want reliable information to support the claims made on the labels of the products they buy. So this chapter begins with a look at these issues and the slow development of advertising standards and eco-labels to meet the public demand.

It then turns more directly to the world of business and looks at what employees want of the organisation they work for. Recruiting and motivating the people who work in companies is becoming more and more affected by soft issues such as corporate ethics and environmental policies. Pay and conditions of work remain of equal importance but they are not an end in themselves.

The information needs of shareholders and, in particular, the role of Annual Reports in meeting those needs are considered next. This is the longest part of the chapter, because Annual Reports fall squarely in the lap of the company finance director and auditor, but in many ways it is the least complete because environmental reporting to shareholders is very much in its infancy.

The chapter concludes with some recommendations on the disclosure of information on environmental performance that were published in February 1993 by the Financial Sector Working Group of the Advisory Committee on

Business and the Environment. The list is long. There is much to be done, particularly when considering the reliability of all this information and the role of independent verification in giving it credibility.

The importance of the Environmental Information Regulations 1992 also must not be forgotten. These regulations implement an EC Directive on the Freedom of Access to Information on the Environment and oblige various public bodies, including government ministers and their departments, to make environmental information available. As ever there are exceptions allowing information to be treated as confidential if it:

- relates to matters affecting international relations, national defence or public security;
- is, or has been, the subject-matter of legal or other proceedings (whether actual or prospective);
- relates to confidential deliberations or the contents of any internal communications;
- is contained in a document or other record which is still in the course of completion; or
- relates to matters to which any commercial or industrial confidentiality attaches or which affect any intellectual property.

On the other hand the Regulations state that information must be treated as confidential if disclosure would contravene any statutory provision or rule of law or would involve a breach of any enforceable agreement, if the information was supplied voluntarily by someone who has not consented to its disclosure, or if the disclosure would increase the likelihood of damage to the environment.

The Regulations have not yet been in place long enough to make it clear how local authorities or regulatory bodies will deal with the uncertainties inherent in the exceptions but lawyers and pressure groups are already using them to try to elicit otherwise unavailable information.

The Government has, however, issued guidance to local authorities on their implementation covering the following issues:

- environmental information—what information is covered;
- practical arrangements—publicity, published reports, public registers, personal requests, timeliness, charging and monitoring;
- who may apply—it matters not who the applicant is or why the information is required;
- grounds for refusing a request—a review of the various categories of confidential information; and
- appeals—how an applicant refused access to information can seek a remedy.

6.2 Pressure groups

The most obvious and immediate demand for reporting and information from business which the Environmental Information Regulations encourage comes from increasingly sophisticated and well-organised pressure groups. This not only reflects their greater experience as persuaders, influencers and lobbyists, but also their much greater resources.

Friends of the Earth, for example, only started in the UK in 1970 but, by 1991, claimed 230 000 members operating through 330 groups nationwide. The worldwide Friends of the Earth organisation began a year earlier in the United States and is now found in 47 countries. With formidable growth like this and their grassroots appeal it is not surprising that they are getting their views across. No business can afford to ignore them.

The other major thorn in the side of some UK businesses is Greenpeace. That too has grown from a tiny group that in 1972 sailed to and around Mororua in the South Pacific protesting about French nuclear tests to a worldwide organisation with a membership in the UK alone approaching 400 000. It differs from Friends of the Earth and other perhaps more genteel organisations in that it specialises in direct action and doing the unthinkable or impossible. Images of protesters wearing gas masks and anti-pollution suits blocking waste-discharge pipes or abseiling from a chimney emitting noxious fumes are familiar to most of us. What was once seen as a cranky minority is now a force with which to be reckoned.

The more genteel organisations referred to in the previous paragraph number amongst them the National Trust (2 million members), the Royal Society for the Protection of Birds (860 000 members) and the Royal Society for Nature Conservation (250 000 members), all of which have also seen a huge recent rise in their paid-up members. Last, but by no means least, is the Worldwide Fund for Nature (WWF) whose panda motif is universally known and which has made a particular effort to work with and not against business. It is blessed by high profile royal patronage (Prince Philip), as well as by some big corporate leaders, which enables it to have an impact that is arguably rather greater than its 230 000 UK members might otherwise have been able to support.

For many years, all of these organisations have to a greater or lesser extent demanded information from, and lobbied, business and industry. Often the protests were very specific—preventing the destruction of a site of special scientific interest threatened by a motorway, for example—or directed at a particular industry, most notably the nuclear power sector. But there have also been highly successful campaigns attracting attention to issues that may draw many more companies into their net.

In 1988, for example, thousands of common seals died in the North Sea and the Baltic, and scientists concluded that the disease affecting them so widely was a result of their reduced immunity. The reason for this reduced immunity was thought to lie in the millions of tonnes of toxic chemicals discharged into these seas each day. They contain polychlorinated biphenyls, dioxins and other persistent organic compounds which accumulate in seals and can reduce immunity to disease. Any UK company discharging waste into the North Sea became a target for protestors, although none suffered the fate of the Kemira group of companies' headquarters in Helsinki where Greenpeace Germany dumped 20 tonnes of blinded fish, covered with sores, on their doorstep.

A more recent trend has been pressure-group action to draw attention to the application of the law and permits that some might judge to be set in too lenient a way. In Autumn 1992, Greenpeace UK launched a 'No legal pollution' campaign based on a National Rivers Authority report showing that licensed discharges of industrial effluent have resulted in nine 'pollution hotspots' around the UK. It is mainly chemical companies, and larger ones too, who are identified as the culprits. Many of these companies claim high environmental standards for all their activities and spend large sums on telling the world about them. Yet they still find themselves accused of perhaps discharging heavy metals and organochlorines, or discharging cancer-causing chemicals, or discharging chemicals that are blacklisted or greylisted by the Paris Convention in 1974 requiring them to be banned 'as a matter of urgency' from marine discharges. Greenpeace also claim that some discharges actually break the law at six of the nine spots.

The purpose of this example is to show how, when information is published or obtained by a pressure group, the spotlight can be turned on a regulator (the NRA) and a number of major companies. Most people, whilst not necessarily accepting every Greenpeace claim, will probably think that in the absence of reliable reports to the contrary 'there's no smoke without fire' thereby creating a climate in which government, regulators and industry will be forced to take some action and certainly step up their already costly public relations efforts.

Indeed, the goalposts might actually be moved as a result of a campaign such as this. At present natural marine processes are relied on to break down these chemical discharges, quite legally, yet Greenpeace has drawn attention to the Royal Commission on Environmental Pollution's finding that 'progressively less reliance should be placed on the environment as a mechanism for processing wastes'. They quote Eberhard Lebin, a director of Du Pont, as saying 'Hazardous waste disposal in any form will eventually be impossible—prevention is the great chemical industry challenge for the nineties'. He could have gone on to say—and maybe he did but he is not quoted as doing so—that it will be one of the chemical industries' greatest costs too. Publicly available information about chemical discharges will play a central part in these changes.

6.3 Advertising

Pressure groups have people, many millions, behind them and those people are also customers. An obvious point but one that industry cannot ignore. Regulation and government policy may set an operational framework from the top but in a free-market economy the factors affecting small day-to-day buying transactions are what makes the economy tick. In aggregate they account for the sales of our companies.

Recognition of this is what the advertising industry is all about and it survives, even in times of recession. Environmental influences on people as customers, therefore, have to be considered very carefully: like it or not the consumer is king. But there are risks in making any claims or giving reports about the 'greenness' of a product whether it be about the raw materials it uses, the production process itself or its biodegradability. Some claims have been shown, in an embarrassingly high-profile way, to be exaggerated or false whilst others are simply hard to prove one-way or another. This aspect of environmental 'reporting' cannot be ignored.

There are an increasing number of environmental awards. Some, such as the European Better Environment Awards for Industry, organised by the European Commission and supported by the United Nations Environment Programme, seem to do a company nothing but good. In 1992, two of the five runners up were parts of BP—BP Exploration for the good management of its on-shore oil field at Wytch Farm, Dorset and BP Chemicals for a new liquid airfield runway de-icer which is easily biodegradable and, unlike most existing products, does not pollute groundwater or harm animal and plant life. Others, such as the Friends of the Earth Green Con Awards, not surprisingly have the opposite effect. Eastern Electricity was the winner of this award in 1990 with its letter, sent to more than 1000 of its customers, urging them to use more electricity as a way of combating global warming. The company claimed that using electricity instead of burning fossil fuels such as gas, coal or oil in the home would produce less carbon dioxide, the most important of the so-called greenhouse gases. Friends of the Earth pointed out in the citation accompanying the award that most power stations give out carbon dioxide in producing electricity!

Perhaps the advertising world has woken up now to the dangers of making claims such as that made by Eastern Electricity. In the late 1980s they were not alone as advertisements claimed variously that dishwashers save fish (AEG), aerosols could be 'ozone friendly', Tesco was the 'green grocer', Procter & Gamble's Ariel Ultra 'washed greener' and Varta's batteries were 'green'.

Apart from the impact of the Green Con Award the Advertising Standards Authority (ASA) has had an influence through the voluntary scheme which controls all advertising appearing in print as has the Committee on Advertising Practice (CAP) and the Independent Broadcasting Authority (IBA). All these, however, have wrestled with a seemingly intractable problem—there are no absolutes and the importance of hard science to the evaluation of many claims means that watchdog bodies such as these or pressure groups find it difficult to assess the validity of claims made.

Some claims are simply irrelevant. At one time Austin Rover claimed that its cars, when running on lead-free petrol, would be 'ozone-friendly'. The ASA took the sensible view that this was an irrelevant claim because leaded petrol was not 'ozone-unfriendly' to begin with. Other claims are misleading. Citroen had an advertisement in the late 1980s that boasted 'while you're looking after the pennies you're looking after the planet, diesel is lead-free'. The implication here, quite wrongly, is that lead emissions are the motor industry's only environmental impact. And, finally, certain claims are inaccurate. In 1990, for example, BP claimed that cars running on its unleaded petrol cause 'no pollution of the environment'. The ASA criticised BP for this claim pointing out that whether they run on leaded or unleaded fuel, vehicles still pollute the air. They also recognised that such a claim was absolute and, in order to stand up, needed detailed support. Equally the claim, even if substantiated, might really be of no consequence if the product, such as a 'biodegradable adhesive tape', was unlikely ever to have much of an environmental impact.

There is probably no last word on what is or is not a fair environmental claim—the debate will continue and standards will evolve to meet changing circumstances. A summary of the position published by the Incorporated Society of British Advertisers (ISBA) in December 1991, however, is worth referring to. The ISBA, which incorporated the views of the ASA and others in its guidelines, has tried to produce clear and positive guidance on just how far advertisers and their agencies can go in making environmental claims. For example the guidance from the ASA and the Committee of Advertising Practice is that:

- Claims should not be absolute unless there is convincing evidence that a product will have no adverse effect upon the environment.
- The basis of any claim should, if possible, be clearly explained.
- The cloaking of claims in extravagant language should be avoided; this will cause consumer confusion.

- Spurious claims should not be made.
- Advertisers must hold substantiation for all factual advertisement claims.

The guide goes on to explain that terms such as 'environmentally friendly' suggest an absolute quality which may be unattainable in practice. It states that in the rare instances where an absolute claim is capable of substantiation consumer understanding will be aided by making the basis of the claim clear, for example, 'environmentally friendly—wholly biodegradable' would be acceptable for a fully biodegradable product which did not harm the environment during the course of its use or disposal.

The guide also suggests that less absolute claims—'greener', 'friendlier'—may be acceptable where a genuine improvement in use in environmental terms can be demonstrated, but the basis of the claim should be explained. It is, the guide points out, acceptable to claim 'ozone friendly' for products which may previously have caused damage to the ozone layer but no longer do so because of the removal of CFCs. The key problem is establishing the reliability of such claims using publicly available information. It is also where labelling schemes, either specific to an industry as in the case of the timber trade or more generally, come in.

6.4 Eco-labelling

The name given to such schemes is 'eco-labelling' and the forerunner of the present European Community Scheme began in Germany in 1977 using a 'Blue Angel' to identify environment-friendly consumer goods. All manner of claims have been made about the success of the German scheme including the rise from 1% at the end of 1970 to 50% presently of the DIY market accounted for by paint, lacquers and varnishes that are low in dangerous substances. It obviously has been a success, even after discounting some of the exaggerated claims made for it, so it is a good place to start.

The Blue Angel award is not given to particular products but to categories of products that meet certain criteria—including publicly reported, environmentally relevant information. Currently there are 66 product groups and about 3600 products that carry the sign. Product groups include retread tyres, returnable bottles, low-noise mopeds or solar-energy products and mechanical watches. Groups can include anything from one product (re-usable crates for food products) to 891 (low pollutant coatings).

There are three main bodies involved in the selection and testing for the new product groups: the Environment Label Jury, The German Institute for Quality Control and Labelling (RAL) and the Federal Environment Agency (UBA). In theory, anybody can propose a product or product-group to the

UBA for Blue Angel status but in practice it is almost always the manufacturer. The UBA usually receives between 150 and 200 applications a year which are then passed on to the Jury, which meets twice a year, for initial examination. Only between 5 and 15 product groups pass this initial examination each year.

If a product group passes the initial examination the UBA lays down precise qualifying criteria and the RAL organises public listings for interested parties. The UBA then sends a report and recommendation back to the Jury for a final decision. When the Jury has decided in favour of a particular product group the RAL tests to see that individual products in the group meet the newly established product group criteria and then, if the product passes, a civil law contract between the RAL and the manufacturer is signed and the product is entitled to carry the Blue Angel sign for the next three years. After the three years have passed, the product has to be re-assessed and if, in the meantime, the product group criteria have been tightened the product may lose its award. This has happened with CFC-free hairsprays, shaving foam and deodorants.

Setting the criteria is based on an assessment of all aspects of environmental risk—hazardous substances, emissions, noise and waste—and through the entire life-cycle of a product. So an otherwise promising candidate may fail because of the high levels of energy needed to produce it or the problems it creates when it comes to disposal. The UBA, which carries out this assessment process, accepts, however, that there is no such thing as a wholly environmentally friendly product, which is a reason behind the change in slogan from 'environmentally friendly' to 'environment label because. . .'. Nevertheless, the Blue Angel sign is now greatly respected and is familiar to 80% of German households according to a 1988 survey. It is also increasingly used as a condition for public procurement.

The scheme is not without its problems: companies complain that they often have to wait more than a year to discover if their product has been accepted and consumer groups continue to complain that the criteria for selection remain obscure. More fundamentally there are no clear criteria for weighing the importance of the environmental factors to be assessed when deciding what is required of a Blue Angel lawn-mower or vacuum cleaner. But in many ways these matters are less important than the vision that the Blue Angel scheme represents—a genuine and practical attempt to assess publicly and recognise good environmental performance.

Not surprisingly others are now trying to catch up with the Germans and there is a danger that too many such schemes of varying qualities around the world will discredit the concept. This is perhaps where the European Commission comes in—for the UK and most other European states at any rate. Although it took some time to draw up the Council of Environment Ministers adopted an EC Regulation in March 1992 for a scheme by which a European eco-label is awarded to those products which have the best environmental performance within particular product categories. For each product category criteria are set on the basis of a Life Cycle Analysis of environmental performance and only those products which meet the criteria are awarded a label. Other key features of the scheme are that it is voluntary, self-financing and does not include food, drink or pharmaceuticals.

The EC Regulation sets out how the scheme works and specifies that each Member State designates a Competent Body to administer it. The Competent Bodies are to:

- propose product groups for inclusion in the scheme;
- assist in the development of criteria for the products;
- assess individual's applications for a label; and
- conclude contracts with successful applicants.

An Eco-Labelling Board was set up in the UK on 1 July 1992 with a small staff of civil servants and an independent group of members representing a broad range of interests and expertise.

One of the Board's main tasks is to work up proposals of product group criteria for adoption at Community level. They are expected to last for about three years but the period may be shorter or longer depending on the rate of technological development in a particular category. An application for a label for a particular UK product will pass through the Board to the EC Regulatory Committee which then has to inform the other Member States. An award can be made if no objection has been raised within 30 days.

It all sounds fine in theory but in practise the European scheme has given rise to all manner of problems and delays. It was launched in June 1993, with labelling criteria agreed for only two product groups, instead of a launch in December 1992 and agreed criteria for up to twelve groups. The UK Board has made public its criticisms of the EC for failing to back the project with sufficient resources and some Member States for neglecting to make arrangements for participating in the scheme.

Washing machines and dishwashers were the first two product groups for which agreed criteria have been published. They were joined by soil improvers and toilet and kitchen tissues when they were approved by the EC's Regulatory Committee in March 1994. Criteria for light bulbs and hairsprays are likely to come next. The first EC ecolabels were actually awarded to three Hoover New Wave washing machines at the beginning of 1994.

Developing criteria and getting them accepted is not without controversy. The basic methodology used is Life Cycle Analysis, as described in Section 5.4, but a study to look at ways of drawing up a common approach was only commissioned in October 1993. Until the results of this study have been agreed and adopted there are likely to be further delays in approving criteria for more product groups. Even then all may not be well. Powerful vested interests are at work. In the case of lightbulbs, for example, the consultants recommended that energy-efficiency should be the sole primary eco-labelling criteria because their work showed that energy consumption during use is the overriding cause of environmental impacts associated with light bulbs. As a consequence the most energy-efficient compact fluorescent bulbs would receive eco-labels, whereas the more conventional incandescent bulbs, which have a European market share of more than 90%, would not. Perhaps not surprisingly the European Lighting Council, which is dominated by the four main producers, told the Commission that it did not support the scheme.

The scheme is also being criticised by some manufacturers for the level of bureaucracy it creates and even environmental pressure groups are not always happy. They want the scheme to exclude products tested on animals but the EC's Regulatory Committee argued that animal testing was covered by other EC legislation. The Body Shop, which makes personal care products and campaigns against animal testing, is included.

All the signs are that progress in the EC will continue to be slow. Maybe a United Nations plan, announced in February 1994, to draw up a certification scheme for environmentally sound products from developing countries that might be adversely affected by the EC scheme, will act as an incentive.

6.5 Employees

We have looked at the way environmental reporting and information pressures affect people as customers but we have not looked specifically at their effect on people as employees. Yet this is an aspect of employment policy, internal motivation and morale, as well as long-term corporate goodwill and image that cannot be ignored. Young people, in particular, are asking companies about their environmental policies and records before they sign up. If they do not like the answers, even in recessionary times, there is a real danger that they will go elsewhere.

Research conducted by the Henley Centre for Forecasting and published in May 1991 looked at the sort of society that British children of today will live in as adults. They concluded that when considering what the world will be like in the year 2025 the fate of the environment is the overwhelming issue for the children of today.

These points were also forcibly made in a 1990 survey by KPH Marketing which concluded that the next generation of senior managers is likely to be considerably more environmentally conscious than at present, and a large minority would take a drop in salary to work for an environmentally responsible firm. Some of the survey's key findings were that:

- a company's socially responsible image is important and environmental policies ranked third behind personnel and marketing policies, but well ahead of industrial democracy, community concern, etc.;
- more than half of those marketing, personnel and administration managers interviewed, especially women, considered their personal interest in the environment to be strong; and
- of the environmental factors considered important when selecting an employer, the record on industrial disasters ranked highest followed by recycling initiatives and the existence of an environmental policy.

The Trades Unions as well are increasingly aware of the importance of information on environmental issues to their members. In March 1991 for example the GMB, Britain's second biggest union with 920 000 members, launched a green bargaining initiative they dubbed 'Green Works'. They want employees to sign a **GMB Model Environment Agreement** which emphasises the need for companies to develop a strategic approach to environmental issues and contains sections on environmental audits, training for GMB and employer representatives and the provision of information to employees, the local community and the media.

The GMB 'Green Works' initiative was followed in July 1991 by a guide from a 21-union environmental working group of the TUC. It recommended that:

- unions should negotiate 'green' agreements setting out general environmental principles and supplemented by a joint policy together with provision for joint union/employer examination of environmental issues;
- unions should seek full disclosure of all but truly confidential information contained in environmental audits and impact assessments to themselves, local councils, environmental groups and local communities; and
- environmental training should be provided at the employer's expense for both union members and employers.

Employers have not been rushing to sign such agreements but by raising the profile of environmental issues in this way unions will discourage employees from working on sites with bad records or where there are environmental hazards. Pressures are mounting from all sides.

It has to be said by way of conclusion, however, that at present real responses from businesses to these sorts of issues only really happen when there is commitment to them by top management either from the Chairman or Chief Executive or through a senior director charged with the environment as a key business responsibility. This is a recurrent theme because recent experience suggests that without such a commitment change happens slowly if at all. Perhaps employee and union pressure from the bottom will reach the top eventually but there is a danger that the changes described in the attitudes of children and young employees will get there too late and such businesses will then find themselves at a competitive disadvantage.

6.6 Shareholders

Introduction

There are signs that business in general and the accountancy profession in particular are waking up to the possibilities offered by annual reports as a means of passing on environmental information to shareholders and, at the same time, to the wider world. The general idea is not new although if you go back to the mid-1970s when the Corporate Report was published in the UK the emphasis was at least as much on the wider aspects of so-called 'social reporting' as it was on 'the environment'. Since then discussion of social reporting dropped down the average UK finance director's reporting agenda before beginning to reappear in the early 1990s.

The same cannot be said of other countries, the USA in particular, nor of UK accounting academics who have continued to look at social reporting concepts and ideas throughout the 1980s. But it has been the general rise in environmental awareness during the late 1980s and early 1990s that has given social reporting in general and environmental reporting in particular a firm shove forward.

International

It is doubtful that in the day-to-day world of UK financial reporting United Nations recommendations have a profound influence but international pressures do increasingly affect all aspects of UK business and multinationals in particular. So it is worth beginning with a brief mention of two reports by the UN Intergovernmental Working Group of Experts on International Standards of Accounting and Reporting in 1990 and 1991 and an international survey of corporate environmental disclosures published in August 1992. Although this Group has now been disbanded, its work has been widely considered, particularly at governmental level, and, in its second report reviewing the implementation of its previous recommendations for disclosure in annual reports, it concluded that accounting for environmental expenditure was feasible although definitions used were rather arbitrary.

The main recommendation in its first report was that enterprises should disclose their environmental policies and programmes in their annual reports. All but one of the governments that responded agreed. Comments from industry were by no means as supportive although the International Chamber of Commerce, which has taken corporate environmental issues very much to its heart in recent years, was very positive in its response, agreeing that one format for reporting the environmental effects of companies' activities was an annual performance report presented as an integral part of a corporate annual report.

In the light of the comments it received, the UN has revised its recommendations which, because they are from the UN and therefore are as close to a genuine 'world view' as can realistically be achieved, are summarised here as a starting point. It recommends that the annual report should:

1. include discussion about the type of environmental issues relevant to the business and its industry;
2. state what formal policies and programmes have been adopted and what improvements they have achieved;
3. give information about emission targets and performance;
4. report on the extent to which measures are being taken as a result of government legislation and how far the requirements are being achieved;
5. refer to any material legal proceedings and known potentially significant environmental problems;
6. disclose the financial or operational effect of environmental protection measures on the capital expenditure and earnings of the business for the current period as well as for future periods;
7. disclose, where material, the amounts charged to operations in the current period and the current and accumulated amounts capitalised relating to environmental protection; and
8. in notes to the financial statements, include the company's policies for accounting for environmental protection measures such as

    - recording liabilities and provisions
    - setting up catastrophe reserves out of retained earnings, and
    - disclosing contingent liabilities.

Although these recommendations are hardly a fully comprehensive programme for environmental disclosure they are a first-class starting point. They are practical and, whilst in need of amplifying in guidance notes, they are capable of more or less immediate introduction.

The UN's recommendations are not the only ones calling for more environmental information in annual reports. The EC Eco-Management and Audit Regulation described in Chapter 5 also requires voluntary disclosure in a statement, written for the public in a concise non-technical form, of certain environmental data. It could be included in a company's annual report but as statements are required for each site audited it seems unlikely that this will happen unless perhaps the company operates from one site only.

Another call for an environmental annual report is found in *Business Strategy for Sustainable Development: Leadership and Accountability for the '90s*, published in Canada in 1992 by the International Institute for Sustainable Development/Deloitte & Touche, with the Business Council for Sustainable Development. This publication does not suggest that the environmental annual report is necessarily included with the existing annual report but obviously it could be. Its emphasis would have to be to give information on sustainable development or operating in such a way so as to 'meet the needs of the present without compromising the ability of future generations to meet their own needs'—a concept that not all companies would sign up to in detail although most would in principle.

What is actually happening around the world as opposed to what some people would like to happen was the subject of the survey of international corporate disclosures, published by the UN Working Group of Experts in August 1992 (and referred to earlier). This was based on the 1990 reports and accounts of 222 transnational corporations, particularly those domiciled in the USA, Japan and Germany, operating in six major global industries, namely: chemicals; forestry and forestry products; metals; motors; petroleum and petrochemicals; and pharmaceuticals, soaps and cosmetics.

Overall, the survey results showed that 191 corporations or some 86% of the sample reported at least some information on their environmental impacts. On the other hand whilst 100% of the forestry corporations reported at least some information and the level of disclosure was also particularly high in petrochemicals (95%), chemicals (90%) and metals (87%), disclosure levels were significantly lower in pharmaceuticals (79%) and motors (76%).

The environmental information disclosed, the survey showed, tended to be descriptive or qualitative, especially in respect of environmental policies, programmes undertaken and major areas of concern. While information of this kind was provided by a total of 155 corporations (70%), there were significant industry differences ranging from a high of 94% for the forestry industry to only 35% for the motor industry—the only industry for which environmental policies and programmes were not the most commonly found item of information. For the motor industry, the most commonly found item was a description of key or major environmental improvements provided by around half of the motor corporations (49%). Again, the motor industry figure was lower than that found across all industries (62%). The only other item disclosed in the majority of reports across all industries was information on the financial impacts of environmental measures undertaken, although more often than not this was qualitative rather than quantitative. However, at least some information on the financial impacts of environmental actions was found in the reports of the majority of corporations (68%), and especially those of petrochemicals corporations (76%) and chemicals corporations (82%). While many did not break down financial impact into its constituent parts, a significant number provided information on capital expenditures (45%) and research and development expenditures (39%). Disclosures of operating expenditures and remedial expenditures were far less common (16% and 11% respectively). Other areas where a relatively low level of disclosure was evident were emission levels, governmental legislation, legal proceedings and information in notes to the accounts.

Although this survey is now a few years old it is of interest because of the emphasis it places on industrial sectors that have a significant global impact. A more recent survey published in October 1993 by the KPMG International Environmental Network did not have this emphasis but covered 690 annual reports, a much larger number than the UN survey. The reports requested were those of the leading companies, based on market capitalisation or revenue, in 10 countries: 100 from each of Belgium, Canada, France, The Netherlands, UK and USA together with 79 from Ireland, 56 from Denmark, 45 from Portugal and 30 from Germany. The overall response rate was 85%.

The main findings were:

- 105 companies (15%) produce a separate environmental report. Companies in the USA, UK, Canada and Germany and in certain industrial sectors, such as oil and gas and chemicals, provide the most environmental reports.
- 400 companies (58%) referred to environmental issues somewhere in their annual report. These comments were most commonly in the message from the chairman and/or president or operational review sections. There were also references in the financial statements, the notes to the financial statements, the directors' report or management's discussion and analysis.
- 45 companies (7%) included environmental costs in the financial statements or notes to the financial statements. These were predominantly in the USA where there are accounting requirements to disclose such information but a number of companies in Germany, Belgium

and the UK also provided information on environmental expenditures.
- 183 companies (27%) referred to environmental issues in the directors' report or management's discussion and analysis. Of these, 72% were accounted for by the USA, Canada, UK and The Netherlands. In the UK, the directors' report has to be reviewed by the financial auditors to ensure that any information disclosed is consistent with that contained in the financial accounts.
- 287 companies (42%) published an environmental policy statement. UK companies produced the highest number (70), with France producing around 50, but with only 18 from the USA. Of the policy statements, 85% also set specific plans and targets for implementing their policy, but only 83 companies (29%) also set quantitative targets.
- 128 companies (19%) provided some quantitative data on their environmental performance but the majority use just brief references to the cost of environmental investments or fines incurred. In particular the mining sector concentrated heavily on cost data. No companies in the retail, engineering or business services sector gave any data.
- 63 companies (9%) gave bad news about their environmental performance such as prosecutions or lack of progress. Companies in the UK and Canada (15%) did so most often. Of those (12%) who did give some bad news, 35% in Belgium and 100% in The Netherlands also disclosed their plans for remedying the situation.
- 63 companies (9%) disclosed the fact that they had performed an internal environmental audit and 33 (5%) disclosed that they had had an environmental audit carried out by external consultants. The highest incidence of either form of audit was in the UK.

Overall, when comparing these findings with those of a similar survey on companies in the USA, UK and Canada a year before, KPMG conclude that there have been few significant changes. Those companies that produced good reports in the previous year continued to do so. A few more had started to report on environmental issues and many more were found to be putting a brief statement into the annual report.

KPMG suggest that a reason for this slow progress is the high standard of reporting now required. Reports can no longer be just glossy magazines but are expected to be logical, honest and full of quantifiable data. Few companies, it is pointed out, have environmental management systems that allow them to produce this kind of data. Nor has the role of the financial auditor in dealing with and verifying environmental statements been sorted out. KPMG say that the increasing number of references to environmental matters in directors' reports and management's discussion and analysis will fuel this debate.

Before leaving the international scene, a word of caution is required before drawing too firm conclusions about what these surveys show is happening. Clearly they are both drawn on relatively small samples and are perhaps biased in favour of good reporting because they rely on respondents to a survey who might not have replied had they nothing favourable to report. But, more importantly, it must not be forgotten that these results are based on some of the world's largest companies. Smaller public companies and private companies have been left out altogether. Further surveys are needed to target these companies; a very different picture might emerge.

United Kingdom

There are many recent UK accounts surveys with some form of emphasis on environmental disclosures. A large one published in late 1993 is thought to be reasonably representative and is worth describing here. It appears in the journal *Company Reporting*, No 38, August 1993 and is based on 570 UK annual reports published in the previous 12 month period.

The raw data showed that only 26% of the 570 companies were addressing environmental issues, however briefly, in their annual reports. A low figure perhaps, but a similar review carried out 12 months previously, also by *Company Reporting*, showed that 23% of the sample companies were referring to environmental issues in their annual reports. There is a small upward trend which, given the increasing interest in public reporting on the environment, seems likely to continue for a year or two yet.

But the method of such reporting varies widely. Of the 26% of annual reports with some form of environmental protection statement *Company Reporting* showed disclosure to be as follows:

	%	
	1993	*1992*
Environmental information mentioned in a supplementary publication	5	2
Environmental information mentioned in a separate statement:		
• Environmental issues statement	11	5
• Within operations review	8	14
Environmental information mentioned within another statement:		
• Chairman's statement	20	30
• Within operations review	21	25
• Directors' report	35	27
• Other	7	9

Company Reporting stress that for the purpose of their survey supplementary publications are only included if they are routinely mailed to shareholders with the annual report. As a result the National Westminster Bank, which publishes a separate comprehensive environmental review which it does not distribute along with its annual report, is excluded other than for the brief environmental comments it does make in that report. This approach is justified in the survey on the grounds that where environmental information is relegated to a separate statement there is a danger that it will not be available to the public on a systematic basis.

But whilst any disclosure is perhaps better than none the nature of that disclosure makes all the difference and here *Company Reporting* found that of the 148 companies (26%) disclosing something:

- 84 companies (57%) disclosed information on their environmental policies with 19% quantifying their targets in some way. In the 1992 survey, 39% disclosed information on their environmental policies.
- 55 companies (37%) described their environmental achievements with 33% quantifying what they had done. Only 13% talked about their achievements in the 1992 survey.
- 6 companies (4%) gave information about remedial costs.
- 4 companies (3%) disclosed information about their environmental liabilities and contingent liabilities.
- 30 companies (20%) said something about carrying out an environmental audit but of this total 17% gave the fact a mention only with just 3% giving the results or findings of the audit.
- Finally 50 companies (29%) put in some form of general statement on the environment but nothing more specific.

The whole question of formulating and disseminating corporate environmental policies is also discussed by the *Company Reporting* survey. Again there should be reflection on the trend, which is upward: 5% of the companies in the 1991 survey disclosed environmental policies in their annual reports, 9% in the 1992 survey and 15% in the 1993 survey. But what may be a 'policy' to one company may be a 'generality' to another. At one end of the spectrum perhaps is a policy statement that 'the Group seeks to conserve scarce and non-renewable resources, such as energy, in all its operations', and at the other is ICI's 20 page booklet detailing policies, objectives and achievements.

Another vexed question is the nature and extent of disclosure of the results of environmental audit procedures. The *Company Reporting* survey has picked up references in annual reports to the word 'audit' whenever and however used in an environmental context. References in this way appeared in 5% of the 1993 companies surveyed and 3% in 1992—hardly a significant change! In very, very few cases are the results of environmental audits actually published, but in one or two they can be obtained by writing to the company. In its annual report British Gas states that:

> Recent initiatives include a company-wide environmental audit to ensure that our operations comply with stated environmental policy and publication of our first report on environmental performance. Copies are available from the Shareholder Enquiry Office . . .

Similarly Coats Viyella notes in its 1991 Directors' Report that:

> The Group Environmental Policy established in 1990 required each of our business units to accept responsibility for the environmental issues affecting them. Audit procedures have been put in place to establish the current position, to identify goals and to ensure that action is taken to achieve them . . . A copy of the Group Environmental Policy may be obtained from the Company Secretary.

References such as these suggest that some companies are prepared to chance their arm and be more open, but at present they are the exception rather than the general rule. What is said in public audit reports perhaps lacks real credibility unless it is independently reviewed. This question is dealt with more fully in Chapter 7.

And what of the 55 companies (10%) surveyed who made reference to their environmental achievements in their latest annual reports? *Company Reporting* found considerable variability in form, content and the extent of quantification. They quote, amongst others, from the SmithKline Beecham annual report which says that in the USA a reduction of air emissions of more than 75% has been achieved since 1987, that '35 000 trees have been planted to soften the impact of noise at SB's production plant at Rixenstart, Belgium'; and that by increasing the size of toothpaste tubes Netherlands SB have 'saved 35 tonnes in packaging materials in one year'.

Company Reporting also praise ICI's comprehensive environmental reports, both the examples of achievements in the annual report and the 20 page environmental booklet which accompanies it. But the unanswered question, prompted by the survey, remains—exactly what achievements warrant inclusion? Big ones, unusual ones, technically innovative ones, cost-saving ones? (This will be investigated later when the issues surrounding independent verification are discussed.)

Finally *Company Reporting* found that only 6 companies (1%) of its 570 strong sample made any reference to the costs incurred in carrying out environmental protection measures. Undoubtedly the problem is knowing what to put in without a proper framework for such disclosure. The environmental cost disclosures of three of the companies the survey identified illustrate the point very well:

- British Gas made a special provision of £125 million to meet legal obligations associated with remedial actions for old gas sites.
- ICI had remedial costs of £148 million which were taken to the profit and loss account as exceptional items.
- Powergen included the investment of £400 million used to reduce emissions at its power stations as a result of the provisions of the Environmental Protection Act 1990 as a contingent liability.

Company Reporting also observe that the extent of these cost disclosures, and the others relating to policies, auditing and achievements appear to bear no relationship to the extent of environmental impact. Their survey and others like it show that many (although by no means all) companies in manufacturing and heavy industries which impact heavily on the environment say little, if anything at all, about environmental matters whilst a number of companies in the services industry address the issue in some detail.

Overall, whilst the various interest groups who want hard environmental information on which to judge a company's environmental performance might find these survey findings disappointing—even *very* disappointing—any such disclosure is voluntary unless, in accounting terms, the effects are material to the company's financial position or reported results. A prevalent attitude, particularly in financial reporting, is that it is better to give the minimum information required by law so as to provide as little scope for critical questioning as possible. In the light of such attitudes the level of existing disclosure should be seen as positive and encouraging rather than disappointing.

6.7 The future

There are clear signs, therefore, that the climate is changing. Environmental reporting by companies is increasing in all manner of ways. The challenge now is to ensure that the right form of reporting is encouraged and that potential users of the reports justify what they are calling for. Information for its own sake does no-one any good.

One important initiative promoting good sense in this area is the CBI Environment Business Forum which promotes voluntary action by business and aims to influence public and political debate on issues such as contaminated land, environmental liability and recycling. Signing up to the Forum involves commitments to preparing an environmental action plan, producing an environmental policy and producing a public report on progress every 12 months.

On the financial reporting front the Chartered Association of Certified Accountants sponsors an annual Environmental Reporting Award which is helping raise the profile of annual reports as a means of reporting environmental information. But probably the most influential statements on the way forward came from the environmental working party of the Hundred Group of finance directors which issued a 'Statement of good practice—environmental reporting in annual reports' (June 1992), and in September 1992 the Environment Research Group of the ICAEW produced a research paper entitled 'Business, Accountancy and the Environment: a policy and research agenda'. Both make recommendations on good practice which is well in advance of legislative or regulatory requirements.

The Hundred Group's Good Practice recommendations look at operational reporting, comments on environmental policy and organisation and the use of the Chairman's or Chief Executive's report. Taking each in turn:

- Operational reporting. The Hundred Group believe that because environmental impacts and risks vary from business to business segmental reports should give sufficient information to permit major environmental impacts and costs to be identified. They say that good practice is to comment on environmental impacts, risks and targets within operational reports for segments and to identify the major countries of operation.
- Environmental policy and organisation. Good reporting practice is said to include disclosure of the group environmental policy which should establish guiding principles, identify priorities and key environmental issues for individual areas of operations, identify realistic and where possible measurable targets for prospective improvements against substantial environmental issues and, finally, be based on careful analysis of the current position and capabilities, and of the changes necessary to make the policy achievable. In particular the Hundred Group's statement recognises that ensuring compliance with regulatory requirements provides a minimum starting point and that all claims made should be capable of being substantiated.
- Chairman's/Chief Executive's report. The Group recommends that commitment to the corporate group's environmental policy at the highest level should be reinforced by appropriate comments in the signed Chairman's or Chief Executive's report.

The Hundred Group's Statement then goes on to look at what it calls 'The Way Forward'. It begins by recognising that once an Environmental Policy Statement has been published it will inevitably attract attention and questions will focus on whether or not performance measures up to the promises. In particular, as the natural successor to disclosure of environmental policy and targets is to report on progress against targets, then this should happen in relation to key environmental issues and report good as well as bad news. In conclusion, the Hundred Group announce that they have little doubt that such reporting 'will develop as the norm' and recommend that companies consider the implications of this for their businesses as well as work to develop relevant 'meaningful and practical measures'.

The ICAEW research paper takes a similar line. It recognises that whilst some environmental factors affecting a company's polices and activities will need to be dealt with in accordance with existing accounting requirements, it is also advisable that as far as possible environmental targets and performance are reported in quantified terms either of a technical or financial nature. It lists a number of points that it would like to see companies publish as part of their annual reporting cycle. These are:

- The company's environmental policy.
- The identity of the director with overall responsibility for environmental issues.
- The company's environmental objectives expressed in a way that enables performance against them to be measured.
- Information on actions taken, including details of the nature and amounts of expenditure incurred, in pursuit of the identified environmental objective.
- The key impacts of the business on the environment and, if practicable, related measures of environmental performance.
- The extent of compliance with regulations and any industry guidelines including, if applicable, whether the company's sites are registered under the EC Eco-Management and Audit Regulation and the details relating to applications and approvals for registration under BS 7750—Environmental Management Systems.
- Significant environmental risks not required to be disclosed as contingent liabilities.
- Key features of external audit reports on the enterprise's environmental activities, including those relating to particular sites.

Another list addressing a wider range of financial issues was published by the Financial Sector Working Group of the Advisory Committee on Business and the Environment in February 1993. It sets out a disclosure agenda for UK companies in a wider sense than just company annual reports. It recognises that standards will be required, that verification may be appropriate and that legislation may also be necessary. The nine-point agenda is as follows:

1. Data currently available on public registers should be made more easily accessible to users. In particular it should be available from a centralised source and in electronic form. Registration requirements should be such that information about parent companies is available in addition to the operational companies in question.
2. A guide to current and forthcoming UK/EC legislation pertaining to environmental disclosure should be produced (and subsequently updated) in simple, summary form, by the Government.
3. Institutional investors, it is suggested, could greatly assist in raising the standards of environmental performance by calling for systematic and regular reporting procedures which adopt the proposals recommended by the Hundred Group, described above.
4. The London Stock Exchange should consider adopting standards of environmental disclosure as one of the requirements of its listing particulars.
5. The recently formed Securities Institute and the Institute of Investment Management and Research should establish standards of environmental awareness amongst their membership.
6. The accountancy and insolvency professional bodies should provide guidance, both for those in practice and those in industry, as well as providing input to the development of legislation and regulation, on environmental issues affecting accounting matters, financial statements, audit, due diligence and other opinion work and insolvency matters.
7. The Government should take the lead in the formation of a UK-wide professional body for environmental auditors and the development of associated professional standards.
8. Professional bodies in the financial sector should include a coverage of environmental standards, as they affect listed companies, in their examination syllabi. Examination on this subject should become compulsory for student members wishing to become associates.
9. The Government should promote and publicise research which seeks to demonstrate the relationship between environmental management and financial performance and the effects of disclosure on standards of environmental practice.

This is certainly the most comprehensive list of issues and tasks currently confronting environmental reporting in the UK. The emphasis on the links with financial reporting is one of the main themes of this book and the recommendations about developing standards and professional training are discussed further in the remaining chapters.

7

Environmental Auditing

7.1 Introduction

The environmental issues currently affecting British business are enormously wide-ranging in their scope and impact. So much so that most facets of business activity are affected to a greater or lesser extent. They pose a major difficulty to the management of all businesses who need systems and procedures in place to develop policy, implement that policy and then monitor it. There is no such thing as a quick environmental fix.

In particular, top management, in the form of Chairman, Chief Executive or Managing Director, is as likely nowadays to be challenged by environmental lobbyists as by any other external group. How can they develop the knowledge base which then gives them the confidence to answer criticisms with hard, factual, supportable information? Whether or not they can refute all criticism is not the issue. Without knowledge, without reliable quantified information top management cannot either answer questions or bring about changes if they are needed. Nor, indeed, can they demonstrate the integrity of the information and opinions they provide. This is where environmental auditing comes in and this is what this chapter is all about.

To begin, there is an overview of the way in which environmental auditing has developed, firstly in the USA and then, more recently, in the UK and Europe. Some definitions are called for because the words 'environmental auditing' are widely used but do not always mean the same thing to different groups of people. Next, there is a discussion of the wide range of different audit types and, in particular, the relationship of environmental auditing to financial auditing—familiar ground to many accountants.

There then follows a description of a suggested audit routine modelled on and tied in to financial audit procedures as an illustration of what the accounting profession might turn its hand to—always recognising the need to work with technical specialists in a way that financial auditors have done for many years. Vital issues of recording and documentation are referred to, as is the equally vital issue of quality control. Some of this has already been described in Chapter 5 which looked at environmental systems, but it is also a much wider issue of professionalism and ethics as well as formal reporting on environmental performance for external consumption.

Finally, environmental due diligence is covered: the enquiries that need to be made of any business being acquired or sold about its environmental track record and future prospects. Again accountants, it is suggested, can play a central role in that they may already be reviewing and checking other aspects of the business and its financial records. Extending this process of review and checking to environmental issues will require additional expertise but as an extension of existing business and financial skills and not as something completely separate.

7.2 History

The words 'environmental audit' have only arrived in the vocabulary of British business over the last few years and it is only very recently that most managers will admit to having heard them. Most do not know what they really mean and many are sceptical, not least about their value in the real world of the recession-hit 1990s. Those that are best informed have either worked in the USA or have some experience of modern business practices there because environmental auditing in one form or another has been around for at least 10 years.

Environmental auditing began its life as a distinct management tool in the USA during the late 1970s and early 1980s in response to the introduction of increasingly tough environmental laws and regulations. There was, and there remains, a need to ensure and to assure at least minimum compliance with them at all company locations, as well as to monitor good management practices, corporate environmental policies and procedures.

Perhaps the real stimulus, for large corporations at any rate, was action by the Securities and Exchange Commission (SEC) against three major multinationals: US Steel (1977), Allied Chemical (1979) and Occidental Petroleum (1980). In each case the SEC required the company to undertake company-wide audits to determine accurately the extent of their real environmental liabilities. In essence, the SEC seems to have believed that each company was seriously under-stating its environmental liabilities in its annual report to stockholders. Since then each company has had an effective environmental audit programme in place. But the SEC remains concerned and has again, in general terms, raised the issue. It believes that many companies may not be portraying their potential Superfund liabilities properly. This issue shall be returned to as part of the discussion on environmental accounting in Chapter 8.

The other big stimulus in the USA was the 1980s implementation of the rules concerning hazardous waste, etc., introduced during the late 1970s. As discussed in Chapter 2, many of these rules were comprehensive, administratively complex and potentially costly if not adhered to. The chemical companies in particular responded quickly and introduced various forms of environmental audit programme.

By the early 1990s, environmental auditing in the USA has reached a certain level of maturity. Its application has spread well beyond chemical companies to all types of industry and government agencies. Even simple property transactions are now the subject of audits or assessments before sale and most generators of hazardous waste are auditing the sites to which their wastes are being brought for handling and disposal by third parties.

Not surprisingly there has been a major growth in the number of specialised environmental consultancies formed to carry out this work but in the USA, as in the UK so far, the accounting profession has not been much involved and has certainly not taken a lead. Architects, planners, civil engineers as well as scientists and conservationists have done so, however, and there are now a number of major environmental consultancies which are well on their way to having not only offices throughout the USA but around the world as well.

Some of these firms have set up in Europe and the UK and are beginning to position themselves in such a way as to be able to meet any increase in demand for independent environmental audits should the need arise. Whether this need will be the result of legislation and regulation has already been touched on in Chapters 5 and 6. What is presently happening in the UK and Europe is a greatly enhanced awareness of what environmental management and environmental audits are all about.

Chemical companies and European subsidiaries of US owned multinationals have been at the forefront in Europe in carrying out various forms of environmental auditing routines. But in the past these were largely internal and the results, good or bad, were seldom made known outside the companies themselves. It is only with the rise in the 'green' movement during the late 1980s and the growing number of associated laws, both at EC and local levels, that the idea of some kind of formal review of a company's environmental position has become more accepted.

In the UK, the Confederation of British Industry (CBI) has been particularly innovative and proactive in urging business to respond positively to environmental matters. It launched its environmental programme, under the banner 'Environment Means Business', in April 1989 and since then has published a wide range of books and pamphlets and organised many conferences, a number of which have promoted the role of environmental auditing. It hopes to forestall demands for tough environmental legislation by demonstrating that voluntary environmental action is effective. As a part of this process it is actively promoting the use of environmental audits as a positive management tool.

As a result of experience overseas, the CBI's efforts and the green movement in general there has been a surge in interest in all forms of environmental consulting in the UK and, most recently, in environmental auditing specifically. Environmental Data Services publishes annually a Directory of Environmental Consultancies which in 1988 had 125 entries and in 1992/93 had 339 entries. Similarly one of the embryonic professional associations for environmental consultants, the Institute of Environmental Assessment, has seen its membership grow from nothing in 1989, when it was formed, to more than 500 in late 1994. Many of these consultancies offer an environmental auditing service and almost as many are now looking at the EC Eco-Management and Audit Regulation, BS 7750 and Life Cycle Analysis which require or may require some form of auditing service. Details of the UK's embryonic system of accreditation for environmental auditors are to be found in Section 5.5.

7.3 Types of audit

In spite of resistance from some quarters, the words 'environmental auditing' now seem to be well established as part of the business vocabulary of the 1990s. No attempt is made here, therefore, to re-define the words or suggest alternatives. Rather, the links with financial auditing are emphasised as the process of financial auditing requires a wide and thorough understanding of a business—and not just its accounting routines—in much the same way as environmental effects on a business do. It is worthwhile repeating here, however, what is now the most widely accepted definition as published in 1989 by the International Chamber of Commerce (ICC). This describes environmental auditing as:

> A management tool comprising a systematic, documented, periodic and objective evaluation of how well environmental organisation, management and equipment are performing with the aim of helping to safeguard the environment by:
>
> (i) facilitating management control of environmental practices;
> (ii) assessing compliance with company policies, which would include meeting regulatory requirements.

Although helpful in general terms, such a definition is so far-reaching that it almost ceases to have a practical value. A few words of further description of some of the more well-known sub-sets of the overall environmental audit umbrella are called for.

Corporate audits—A corporate environmental audit is nearest to the ICC definition in that it aims to cover every aspect of a company's operations against pre-determined environmental standards.

Compliance audits—Environmental compliance audits are restricted to ensuring that a company is complying with all laws, by-laws, regulations, standards, etc., that might affect it. Such is the growth in environmental laws that this is not as easy as it might at first seem: deciding what rules apply has to precede testing compliance with them.

Site audits—Environmental site audits also cover every aspect of operations against pre-determined environmental standards but are specific to a particular site, office or factory unit.

Activity audits—Environmental activity audits concentrate on particular corporate activities such as purchasing, distribution or transportation. Purchasing audits, involving questions about environmental policies and procedures of suppliers up the supply chain, are becoming increasingly common as companies want the comfort of knowing that important providers of components or sub-assemblies conform to acceptable environmental standards too.

Issues audits—Environmental issues audits cut across business units and activities and concentrate on reviewing performance in relation to particular issues such as energy efficiency, waste management or paper usage.

Due diligence reviews—Environmental due diligence reviews are carried out at the time a company is bought or sold. Such is their importance to accountants and finance directors that a separate section at the end of this chapter describes what might be involved more fully.

Life cycle analysis—Life cycle analysis (or eco-profiling as it is sometimes called) is described in Chapter 5 but, as it involves the quantification of environmental impacts of any product, process or activity from 'cradle to grave', this list of types of environmental audits would not be complete without it.

Environmental Impact Assessments—Environmental Impact Assessments (EIAs) have a legal definition as well as a wider meaning. Basically an EIA is the drawing together and assessment of the environmental effects of a major project and, in the form of an Environmental Statement, the findings may be submitted to a UK planning authority together with a planning application.

There could be other types of environmental audit but it is believed that these are the main ones which when listed show the wide range of subjects that could be covered when discussion first turns to the relevance of 'environmental auditing' to a business. But in the minds of many general managers, auditing is also a financial process and they question the relationship between the two. It is to this question that attention is now given.

7.4 Financial auditing

Financial auditing in the world's developed economies in general and the UK in particular is a well established, well regulated and reasonably clearly understood process. The need for financial audits is based on legal requirements, in the Companies Acts in the UK, and the standards of work and procedures to be adopted are set out in comprehensive Auditing Standards and Auditing Guidelines approved collectively by all the major UK accountancy bodies.

Environmental auditing in contrast is, in the UK at any rate, almost none of these things. The process is relatively new, there are virtually no regulations in place that are enforceable in law and the business world, let alone the world at large, has a very poor understanding of what might be involved.

It therefore seems fair to ask whether environmental auditing has anything to learn from financial auditing and, in particular, whether financial auditors should take a lead and extend their remit to cover most major environmental business exposures. Some businesses would welcome this. In spite of moves by the UK government in recent years to lessen the 'burdens on business' many remain and adding a further environmental audit requirement organised and controlled by completely separate people would not be welcomed.

Mandatory environmental auditing is not yet in force in the UK but the growing popularity of BS 7750, which as we have seen includes an audit component, is seen by some businessmen as the thin end of an environmental audit wedge. And there is also a real possibility of a new breed of environmental verifier emerging as the EC Eco-Management and Audit Regulation comes into force. Could financial auditors be a part of this new breed?

If the existing financial auditing routines are modified to meet most if not all the environmental audit requirements under BS 7750 and EMAR then the answer is probably 'Yes'. But some changes will be needed and new professional guidance prepared although there is a lot of help available already in the UK through the Auditing Practices Board (APB) and a series of Statements of Auditing Standards. A full list is given in Appendix D. Clearly many of these have specific financial connotations but many do not or could, with a minimum amount of modification, be made to apply to environmental auditing procedures as well. Several key questions, however, are raised in the mind of the environmental auditor after reading the Introductory Statement covering the Scope and Authority of APB Pronouncements. These questions together with suggested answers are:

What is an environmental audit auditing?—There are two answers to this question. The first is that the audit is about compliance with the company's environmental management procedures. And the second is some form of company Environmental Statement if one is prepared.

When is an environmental audit needed?—There is no legally enforceable environmental audit requirement so at present such audits are only carried out with company management's agreement or at their specific request. As has been stressed in Chapter 5, EMAR is voluntary but if it is adopted for a particular site an independent accredited environmental verifier is required to verify that its requirements have been met.

What is an 'environmental auditor'?—Either an individual or a firm can call themselves environmental auditors but such is the wide range of areas of expertise needed that firms are much better placed to do this job than are individuals.

Who has the responsibility for preparing an environmental statement?—If the example of the financial accounting, auditing and reporting process is followed the environmental statement is akin to the company's financial statements. As such management prepare the statement and auditors audit it.

Accepting these answers the environmental auditor, then, would do well to turn to the list of Statements of Financial Auditing Standards set out in Appendix D. All these Statements are the responsibility of the Auditing Practices Board and in most cases were, at the time of writing, in the form of Exposure Drafts (EDs) issued for consultation. They reflect current thinking about the way financial audits should be conducted and are based on a well tried and tested list of Standards, Guidelines and Statements which they are gradually replacing. Although some may be modified as a result of a period of wide consultation the list is unlikely to change much and the main recommendations in each Statement will also probably stand relatively unaltered.

Those that are most likely to be relevant to the environmental auditor are:

   100   Objectives and general principles
   110   Fraud and error

120 Consideration of law and regulations
140 Engagement letters
160 Other information in documents containing audited financial statements
170 Comparative figures

200 Planning
210 Knowledge of the business
220 Audit materiality
230 Documentation
240 Quality control for audit work

300 Audit risk assessment
310 Auditing in an EDP environment

400 Audit evidence
410 Analytical procedures
430 Audit sampling
440 Management representations

500 Considering the work of internal auditors
510 The relationship between principal auditors and other auditors
520 Using the work of an expert

600 The auditors' report on financial statements
610 Reports to directors or management
620 The auditors' right and duty to report to regulators in the financial sector

Most of the issues raised in these Standards are referred to in the sections that follow on the conduct, documentation and quality control of an environmental audit when carried out as a part of, or extension to, the external financial audit process.

Before leaving these brief general comments about the links between financial and environmental auditing, a word or two is needed regarding some concerns recently expressed about financial auditing and some of the ideas about its future direction. These have been set out in a paper 'to provide public debate' called *The Future Development of Auditing*, published by the APB in November 1992. Whatever the eventual response to the debate the issues are of wide interest and require careful consideration by the infant environmental auditing profession too. They cover the role and scope of an audit, the independence of the auditor, the audit report, competition between audit firms, the threat of litigation for bad work, the regulatory framework and finally the training and skills required of an auditor. Each of these is dealt with in what follows:

Role and scope—The APB says that there is a gap between the role expected of financial auditors and that performed by them today. They also say that there is a demand for auditors to recognise the interests of a wider group than shareholders alone.

Both of these comments apply equally well to the environmental audit process where there is a real danger that carrying out some form of environmental audit procedures will be seen as laying bare all major environmental business risks. However the scope of the work is defined by the auditor with management this perception may be hard to live down. Similarly company management, and possibly shareholders if the reports go to them too, may not consider that information about the environmental performance of their business—as revealed by the environmental audit—is of relevance to anyone other than themselves. The general public may not share this view.

Independence—The greatest concern, according to the APB, is a perception that financial auditors are not sufficiently independent from the companies they audit with the result that auditors have not taken a tough enough stand on the appropriateness of the accounting policies used by companies. Financial auditors' judgements may, some suggest, be unduly influenced by the extent and nature of the commercial relationship they have with the company.

Very similar considerations apply to environmental auditors. Whilst, for example, there are no generally accepted environmental policy standards equivalent to accounting standards there must be a danger that by lending their name and reputation to a report on a company's environmental systems and policies environmental auditors give these systems and policies credibility whether or not they are excellent or only barely acceptable.

Equally environmental auditors are paid by the company they audit—there is no independent regulator similar to the local government Audit Commission, for example—and there must be a risk of a similar charge of undue influence of company management on judgements being made by the environmental auditor.

The audit report—The APB points out that there is a public demand for greater disclosure by financial auditors which, they say, stems in part from inadequate disclosure by directors in financial statements.

As there are no mandatory environmental audit reporting requirements this is not yet an issue but the wide variability in the information given in voluntary audit reports, discussed in Chapter 6, suggests that it may become an issue for environmental auditors too in the future.

Competition—Excessive competition combined with directors' desires to reduce financial audit costs may, according to the APB, have lowered the quality and rigour of financial audits to unacceptable levels.

The considerable growth in the number of environmental consultancies claiming to offer environmental auditing services suggests that there may be competitive pressure on environmental audit fees too. In the absence of generally acceptable and enforceable standards of work, lower fees may also lower the quality and rigour of audit work for environmental auditors.

Litigation—The APB maintains that financial auditors are constrained by the prospect and scale of potential litigation which, they also say, is a barrier to proactivity and change.

Here too there is a strong parallel for environmental auditors who undoubtedly face large claims for professional negligence should a clean environmental audit report be found to have been incorrectly given. Much depends, however, on the form and content of the report. It would be a rash environmental auditor who did not qualify his report by reference to the work done (and, just as important, not done) and the purpose of the report itself. So far no significant claims have been made against environmental consultants for bad work or a failure to report an environmental problem.

Governance and regulation—The APB refers to the concerns of some who believe the present system of financial audit regulation is ineffective and, in particular, to the suggestion that the regulatory framework lacks the necessary independence, objectivity and impact. They note that there is some demand for an independent body to oversee financial audits.

So far as environmental auditing is concerned the effectiveness of a regulatory framework is a matter for the future: at present there is no environmental audit regulatory framework at all. The key question to which environmental consultants now have to address themselves is whether they favour self-regulation of environmental auditing or whether an independent (possibly government appointed) body should do the job. At present the Institute of Environmental Assessment is setting up a register of qualified environmental auditors which is a starting point (see Section 5.5). The need for this is brought about by the requirement in EMAR that company environmental statements should be subjected to external verification.

Skills—Finally the APB notes that the necessary changes to financial audit both now and over the longer term require considerable investment in training and development of auditors.

An identical issue faces the burgeoning world of environmental consultants and auditors. There is a real need for training and development in the widest of senses. There is a great deal of technical expertise available but knowledge and experience of the rigour and discipline of the audit process is in many cases lacking. This is where the trained financial auditor has a part to play.

As to the future, the APB has a number of specific financial audit proposals which do not warrant repeating here. What do warrant repetition, however, are eight Enduring Principles of Auditing which apply, each and every one, just as much to environmental auditing as to financial auditing. They are:

1	Integrity	Auditors should observe high standards of integrity.
2	Independence	Auditors should at all times be objective, expressing opinions which are free from influence, independent of the company and its directors and unaffected by commercial conflict of interest.
3	Competence	Auditors should act with a high degree of professional skill.
4	Rigour	Auditors should apply a high degree of rigour to the audit process, maintaining a stance of professional scepticism in their assessment of evidence.
5	Accountability	Auditors should act in the best interests of shareholders whilst having regard to the wider public interest.
6	Judgement	Auditors should apply sound professional judgement.
7	Communication	Auditors should openly disclose all matters necessary for a full understanding of the opinion they express. Auditors may make disclosure in the public interest to the appropriate authorities when they become aware of matters indicative of fraud or a breach of law or regulation with which the business is required to comply and consider it necessary to do so.
8	Providing value	In providing their service, auditors should ensure that they provide value to shareholders.

7.5 Environmental and financial auditing

So, drawing on the skills and experience of financial auditing, how should a corporate environmental audit be conducted? It is here that the Statements of Financial Auditing Standards referred to earlier in the chapter come into their own. They have considerable weight behind them in that the UK's accountancy bodies have undertaken to adopt them all and apparent failures to apply them by financial auditors are liable to enquiry by the appropriate committee of the accountancy body to which the auditor belongs. Disciplinary or regulatory action may follow. It is also worth noting that to be eligible for appointment as a company auditor an individual or a firm must be registered with a Recognised Supervisory Body (RSB) under the Companies Act 1989. Each of the major professional accountancy bodies is an RSB.

There are clearly parallels here with the UK's environmental audit accreditation plans described in Section 5.5 whereby the National Accreditation Council for Certification Bodies will accredit firms (or individuals) to act as environmental certification bodies under BS 7750 and accredited environmental verifiers under EMAR. There are however, as yet, no generally accepted and supported environmental auditing principles by which the work of accredited firms can be judged. Most of what is needed can be found in Financial Auditing Standards, which suggests that most aspects of an environmental audit, especially verification of a public statement, could be conducted by a financial auditor who had received some additional training and was prepared to bring in other special scientific and technical skills where necessary.

What follows, therefore, describes briefly what each relevant standard covers and comments on how the principles might be amended, where necessary, to cover a financial auditor carrying out environmental work too.

SAS 100 Objectives and general principles

This is the first Statement covering an auditor's responsibilities. Its full title is 'Objectives and general principles governing an audit of financial statements' which makes it clear that financial auditing is primarily directed at forming an opinion on financial statements rather than systems. Environmental auditing at present is more likely to be biased to systems but the call for more and better factual information on companies' environmental performance, described in Chapter 6, and the requirement for an independently verified publicly available environmental statement suggest that this may not be so for long.

The main principles behind this Statement, therefore, are the need to get enough evidence to report that an audited statement has been drawn up in accordance with whatever regulations or laws (if any) apply and to give a clear opinion to this effect. The Statement makes clear that doing so is a matter of judgement and that an auditor's opinion enhances the credibility of the statement by providing reasonable assurance from an independent source. The words 'reasonable assurance' are vital because while an auditor can provide a level of assurance that is reasonable in the context of an environmental statement it cannot be absolute. There is clearly a risk that an inappropriate opinion might be given and therefore the Statement requires auditors to perform their work with an attitude of professional scepticism.

The other key principle in this Statement, equally applicable to environmental audit work, is the need to apply the ethical principles which the accounting profession bodies have in force. These give a qualified accountant an advantage over other consultants in that he can demonstrate that his professional status is governed by defined responsibilities covering his integrity, objectivity, independence, professional competence and due care, professional behaviour and confidentiality.

SAS 110   Fraud and error

In some respects fraud and error in the preparation of environmental information seem rather less likely than for financial information. Direct financial benefit is unlikely to be the result. Nevertheless, the possibility of fines or criminal penalties as a result of breaching legislation as well as public disapproval may be sufficient to tempt company management to act fraudulently. Many of the principles in this Statement, therefore, are relevant also to the work of an environmental auditor.

The starting point is to plan the audit with the possibility of fraud or error in mind and then, if it is found to any extent, consider its impact and do more work if necessary. The main likely difficulty arises if it is confirmed that the fraud or error, such as unreported leaks or breaches of licensing requirements, is serious and company management is informed. Given the voluntary nature of environmental auditing, and externally reporting its results especially, it may be that at this point the work will be redirected and plans to say anything externally cancelled. And no-one need know.

A more difficult problem for the auditor, if the fraud or error is important and thought to be in the public interest, therefore, is whether the matter should be reported to a 'proper authority' and the extent to which he or she can any longer have confidence in the integrity of the company's directors by whom he or she has been employed. Resignation may be the only course open.

SAS 120   Consideration of law and regulations

Similar judgements face the auditor if he is faced with company failures to comply with laws or regulations. This Statement is prepared with the aim of setting a standard for financial auditors who may find that such failures have a material impact on the financial statements. But, as has been seen already, laws and rules are probably the main factors driving companies to improve their environmental performance and those that want publicly to claim high environmental standards also have to show that they know what is needed and that they have complied with a very wide range of them.

The financial auditor, therefore, has a responsibility, in carrying out his audit work on a company's financial statements, to have a general understanding of the environmental legal and regulatory framework in which that company is operating. If he or she was carrying out an environmental auditing assignment, in parallel, there would clearly be efficiencies and cost savings.

The Statement, in the explanatory material presented alongside the basic principles and essential procedures, sets out some ways in which directors may discharge their legal and regulatory responsibilities which may also help environmental auditors. It is suggested that a company:

- maintains an up-to-date register of significant laws and regulations with which it has to comply;
- monitors legal requirements and any changes to them and ensures that operating procedures are designed to meet them;
- institutes and operates appropriate systems of internal control;
- develops, publicises and follows a Code of Conduct;
- ensures employees are properly trained and understand the Code of Conduct;
- monitors compliance with the Code of Conduct and acts appropriately to discipline employees who fail to comply with it;
- engages legal advisers to assist in monitoring legal requirements; and
- maintains a record of complaints.

The similarities to the requirements of both BS 7750 and EMAR are clear.

SAS 140   Engagement letters

There is certainly nothing unique to financial auditing in the requirement to obtain an appropriate engagement letter. This Statement stresses not only the need to set out in writing the terms agreed for each new audit engagement but also the need for regular reviews and updates if needed.

More specifically it is part of the Standard to include in the letter the respective responsibilities of the directors and the auditors, the scope of the engagement and the form of any reports. For many companies environmental audits are relatively new. Defining what is required avoids misunderstandings and possible disappointment. The Statement also suggests that some other matters might be dealt with in the letter. They include arrangements with previous auditors, a proposed timetable and, of particular importance to environmental auditors, fees and billing arrangements, arrangements with other auditors, experts and internal auditors and any restrictions of the auditors' liabilities to the client company.

The need for most of these is fairly obvious but, given widely differing perceptions of what environmental audit is and entails, it is probably even more necessary to agree fees formally up-front for an environmental audit assignment.

Given the wide range of technical and scientific skills, as well as organisational and financial abilities, that some environmental audits require, arrangements for the use of other auditors and technical experts can also be of particular importance. Clarity over which firm or individual has the lead role is vital.

Finally, there is the possibility of limiting liabilities: not for financial auditors who, by virtue of Section 310 of the Companies Act 1985, are unable to come to any arrangement with their company clients to exempt or indemnify them from liability arising from the role as auditors, but possibly for environmental auditors who are not subject to such a restriction. There is scope, therefore, for agreeing a cap to any liability arising from environmental auditing procedures. The engagement letter is one place for setting out the precise terms.

SAS 160   Other information in documents containing audited financial statements

As in the case of SAS 120 dealing with law and regulations, SAS 160 is also of direct relevance to both financial auditors who have to consider some environmental information in reaching their opinion on the financial statements and to environmental auditors who may now find reference to their work, voluntarily given by the company, in the annual report or some other publicly available financial document.

The introduction to this Statement makes it clear that the 'other information' referred to in its title is that found in a directors' report required by statute, a Chairman's statement or operating and financial review, financial summaries, employment data, planned capital expenditures, financial ratios and selected quarterly data. Recent surveys of environmental reporting (as described in Chapter 6) have shown that these are the very places where companies are increasingly putting comments and reports on their environmental policies and performance.

As a result, financial auditors, whether they like it or not, are now being drawn in to more active consideration of environmental information, because SAS 160 requires financial auditors to read the 'other information' to determine whether there are any material inconsistencies with the audited financial statements. If they find inconsistencies they are required to 'perform appropriate procedures'. In the case of a UK company's directors' report, the Companies Acts require a reference in the audit opinion if the inconsistency remains unresolved but in the case of the remaining types of 'other information' the position is less clear. If the inconsistency is sufficiently serious and cannot be resolved through discussion, the Statement suggests that the auditor may have to resign from the appointment. The environmental auditor could find himself in the same sort of position too. His only remedy might also be to resign the appointment.

SAS 200   Planning

This Statement's simply stated overall requirement, just as applicable to environmental audit work as to financial audit work, is to plan the audit work so that 'an effective audit is performed in an efficient and timely manner'. The overall plan has to be documented, as does an audit programme, providing a set of detailed instructions to assistants, which set out the nature, timing and extent of planned audit procedures. Both have to be revised as necessary during the course of the audit.

For both forms of audit, a knowledge of the type of business is required including general economic factors, financial performance, the competence of management, legislation and regulations. The level of audit risk and judgements about what is material will differ but there will be similarities between the types of work to be done and considerable scope for co-ordinating between work at subsidiaries, branches and divisions, the use of experts and the numbers and type of field staff needed.

SAS 210   Knowledge of the business

This is the second of the five Statements covering audit planning, controlling and recording. As has been shown with SAS 200 on planning, this Statement is just as applicable to environmental audit work as to financial audit work.

The overall requirement is to have or obtain a sufficient knowledge of the business to be audited to enable the auditor to understand the events, transactions and practices that may affect his work. Other requirements cover the need to know something about the business before taking on the work, acquiring more knowledge so as to be able to plan it successfully once an appointment has been accepted and then keeping up to date.

The Appendix to the Statement, which is nearly four pages in length, lists 'matters to consider in relation to knowledge of the business'. It includes: general economic factors, such as interest rates, inflation, government policies; the industrial sector covering areas such as the market, product technology, business risk, energy supply and cost; and the company itself including its management and ownership, its products, markets, suppliers, warehouses and offices, and its financial performance. There are many references to policies, laws and regulations and even a specific reference to 'environmental requirements and problems'.

All of this is relevant for the environmental auditor, too, but it may also suggest that in some cases the complex scientific and/or technical background to a particular business may make financial auditors less able to acquire the level of knowledge needed to carry out an environmental audit as well as a financial audit. So long as this is recognised, however, specialist help can be called in and the work can proceed as a team effort.

SAS 220   Audit materiality

The word 'materiality' is well known to financial auditors but probably not familiar to many others, including environmental auditors from non-financial backgrounds. The concept, however, is of fundamental importance if any form of audit work is to be directed in an efficient and cost effective manner. Put simply, it is about deciding what is 'important'. Put more formally, as SAS 220 does, materiality

> is an expression of the relative significance or importance of a particular matter in the context of [financial] statements as a whole. A matter is material if its omission or misstatement would reasonably influence the decisions of a user of the [financial] statements. Materiality may also be considered in the context of any individual primary statement within the [financial] statements of individual items included in them. Materiality is not capable of general mathematical definition as it has both qualitative and quantitative aspects.

The relevance of this concept for environmental auditing is clear. If environmental information is being produced and presented as being audited, the auditor will have had to consider the extent and risk of misstatement. If a system is being reported on, the misstatement will be of a qualitative nature and will need to be judged by the likelihood that a user of the environmental statement could be misled by the description.

SAS 230 Documentation

The auditing process, be it financial or environmental, involves planning, risk assessment, testing, evaluating, concluding and reporting. It is an 'art' not a mechanical performance of pre-determined procedures because at each stage judgements are required born of skill and experience. But whilst it may be hard to do much about the judgements, after the audit is complete—be they right or wrong—the basis on which they were made can be set down. Without this information no independent assessment on the audit process can be carried out, other members of the audit team cannot put their work in context and there is no means of accumulating experience to inform subsequent audit assignments.

Whilst most of this may seem relatively self-evident, the experience of the regulation of financial auditors is that inadequate documentation of audit work is one of the most common failings. Similarly, it seems likely that it will be a common failing for environmental auditors.

SAS 230 therefore makes it clear that auditors should document matters which are important in providing evidence to support the audit opinion and evidence that the work was carried out in accordance with auditing standards. It also states that working papers, which are confidential and are to be kept safely, should

- record the auditors' planning, the nature, timing and extent of the auditing procedures performed, and the conclusions drawn from the evidence obtained; and
- include the auditors' reasoning on all significant matters which require the exercise of judgement, together with the auditors' conclusions.

What to put down is a matter, again, of judgement and experience. The lessons learned by the financial auditing profession are clearly of relevance.

SAS 240 Quality control for audit work

The contents of this Statement, almost word for word, apply to both environmental and financial audits and auditors. The overall requirement is for quality control policies and procedures to be implemented both at the level of the audit firm and on individual audits.

At the level of the firm, policies and procedures are needed to ensure compliance with auditing standards and the regulations issued by the relevant Recognised Supervisory Body. As yet, there are no recognised environmental auditing standards and, as described in Section 5.5, formal accreditation procedures are not yet in place. Perhaps, with regard to the former, some of the financial auditing standards being described here should be adopted?

Such is the importance of firm-wide quality control procedures, however, it is worth setting out here in full the Statement's list of policies normally required. These are:

(a) Professional requirements—personnel to adhere to the principles of independence, integrity, objectivity, confidentiality and professional behaviour;

(b) Skills and competence—personnel to have attained and maintain the technical standards and professional competence required to enable them to fulfil their responsibilities with due care;

(c) Acceptance and retention of clients—an evaluation of prospective clients and a review, on an ongoing basis, of existing clients to be conducted. In making a decision to accept or retain a client, the auditors' independence and ability to serve the client properly and the integrity of the client's management are to be considered;

(d) Assignment—audit work to be assigned to personnel who have the degree of technical training and proficiency required in the circumstances;

(e) Delegation (direction, supervision and review)—sufficient direction, supervision and review of work at all levels to provide confidence that the work performed meets appropriate standards of quality;

(f) Consultation—consultation, whenever necessary, within or outside the audit firm to occur with those who have appropriate expertise;

(g) Monitoring—the continued adequacy and operational effectiveness of quality control policies and procedures to be monitored.

The remaining parts of the Statement deal with quality control procedures for individual audits and cover such things as the overall direction, in accordance with a plan, of each assignment, supervision of staff and review of their work.

SAS 300   Audit risk assessment

The concept of audit 'risk' is superficially straightforward to understand but as this Statement makes clear there is more to it than first meets the eye. The Statement also covers the auditor's approach to understanding internal control systems. Both can be applied directly to environmental audits.

The main requirement of the Statement is for the auditor to understand the internal control systems well enough to develop an effective audit approach and to use professional judgement to assess audit risk so as to perform the audit in such a way that it is reduced to an acceptably low level.

Audit risk is said to mean the risk of giving an inappropriate audit opinion on the financial statements but it could equally well apply to opinions of environmental statements or reports on systems. These components to audit risk are identified as:

1. Inherent risk—susceptibility to material misstatement while assuming no related internal controls;
2. Control risk—the risk that material misstatement could occur and not be prevented or detected on a timely basis by the internal control systems;
3. Detection risk—the risk that auditors' procedures do not detect a material misstatement.

All can be applied to environmental audit risk, as can the definition of an internal control system which, modified slightly, the Statement states:

> comprises the company's control environment and control procedures. It includes all the policies and procedures (internal controls) adopted by the management to assist in achieving management's objective of ensuring, as far as practicable, the orderly and efficient conduct of its business, including adherence to management policies, the safeguarding of assets, the prevention and detection of fraud and error, the accuracy and completeness of the environmental/accounting records, and the timely preparation of reliable environmental/financial information. Internal controls may be incorporated within computerised systems.

The Statement is longer than many of the others and describes how tests need to be designed to cover the types of risk identified in the light of the auditor's assessment of the internal control system. A short section also stresses the limitations of an approach relying on control systems for many small businesses which numerically, if not economically, are the main type of business entity in the UK.

SAS 400 Audit evidence

This Statement requires auditors to 'obtain sufficient appropriate audit evidence to be able to draw reasonable conclusions on which to base the audit opinion'. Put another way it might be said to require auditors to do enough work.

Again the concepts described have a lot of relevance to environmental as well as financial audit work. The Statement, for example, says that audit evidence is obtained from an appropriate mix of tests of control and substantive procedures—in some cases entirely from the latter. Tests of control are tests to obtain evidence about the suitability of design and effective operation of internal control systems. Substantive procedures are obtaining audit evidence by tests of details of transactions and balances and analytical procedures. Transactions and balances would be taken to be most items of environmental data (such as average emission levels). Analytical procedures consist of

> the analysis of significant ratios and trends including the resulting investigation of fluctuations and relationships that are inconsistent with other relevant information or which deviate from predictable patterns.

The final concept that is worth a reference is that of 'assertions' in the public statement produced by company management embodied in that statement. In the case of an auditors' report on a company's environmental statement, therefore, audit evidence would be needed to ensure that the assertions made could be supported. The company statement might, for example, refer to the occurrence of a particular event—the number of times a certain level of contamination had been exceeded—for which evidence would be needed in the form of an examination of the relevant records and tests to ensure that they are reliably put together.

SAS 410   Analytical procedures

Analytical procedures have already been defined in the paragraphs describing the relevance of SAS 400 to environmental audits. This Statement covers not only their use as a substantive test but also as a part of the planning and overall review stages of the audit as well.

But what really are analytical procedures? Some examples are called for. Whether in respect of financial or environmental information, they might involve comparing the company's information that is the subject of the audit with:

- comparable information for prior periods;
- anticipated results from budgets or forecasts; and
- similar industry information, such as comparisons with industry averages or with other entities of comparable size in the same industry.

The Statement's first requirement is that procedures such as these should be used at the planning stage to help understand the business and the areas of potential risk. A second requirement is their use as a substantive procedure which can be very efficient, provided the auditors are satisfied that the data they propose to use have been properly prepared. The final requirement is to use such procedures at or near the end of the audit when forming an overall conclusion about the environmental statement or other company-prepared environmental report.

At each stage, the aim is to identify significant fluctuations or relationships that are inconsistent with other relevant information or that deviate from predictable patterns. If they find such fluctuations or relationships, the Statement requires the auditor to investigate and obtain adequate explanations and appropriate corroborative evidence.

SAS 430   Audit sampling

Both financial and environmental auditors would not normally expect to examine all the information available to them. It is generally impractical to do so and, as this Statement makes clear, valid conclusions can be reached using audit sampling techniques.

Audit sampling means the application of audit procedures to less than 100% of the items involved but, nevertheless, enough to have the evidence to form a conclusion on the population as a whole. This Statement provides guidance on defining audit objectives to be met by sampling, the population from which to sample, and sample size. Nearly all of it is relevant to sampling for environmental as well as financial auditing ends.

Similarly, there is a helpful section on the evaluation of sample results involving analysing any errors detected in the sample, projecting the errors found to the population as a whole and re-assessing the sampling risk. These may be particularly relevant in assessing levels of company management's claims about the overall impact of certain types of emissions over time. To what extent is a particular period representative of a longer period? One major unrecorded incident may account for more than many small recorded ones. Financial auditing experience is undoubtedly relevant and helpful in addressing these sorts of environmental concerns.

SAS 440   Management representations

At the time of writing, there are eight draft Statements, prefixed 400, etc., dealing with various aspects of audit evidence. SAS 440 is the remaining one of relevance to both financial and environmental auditors and their work in equal measure. In fact, it could be argued that this Statement dealing with management representations is of even more relevance for environmental auditors. In the absence of an accepted framework for publicly reporting environmental information, independent auditors may have particular difficulties in knowing how to recognise and deal with problems arising from their work. What company management tells them might be all they have to go on.

This Statement, therefore, deals with such management representations as audit evidence. It sets out the procedures to be applied in evaluating and documenting those representations and the action to be taken if company management refuses to provide confirmation. The key requirements of the Statement are that:

- auditors should obtain written confirmation of appropriate management representations particularly on material matters;
- the auditors should get evidence that company directors acknowledge their responsibility for the environmental statements or reports; and
- where management representations appear to contradict other audit evidence the circumstances should be investigated and consideration given to whether it casts doubt on other management representations.

The required written representations may be in the form of a letter from management but there could also be a letter from the auditors outlining their understanding of management's representations, duly acknowledged and confirmed by management or minutes of meetings of the board of directors, or similar body, at which such representations are approved.

None of this is unusual, or unreasonable, to the financial auditor. At present, it is doubtful that more than a small number of firms and individuals holding themselves out to be environmental auditors would recognise the need for such procedures.

SAS 500 Considering the work of internal auditors

This is the first of three Statements of Financial Auditing Standards on the subject of 'using the work of others'. All three are likely to be of critical importance to a financial auditor extending his work to cover environmental reporting requirements as well as to the environmental auditor looking at financial auditing standards for guidance on what to do.

Clearly an internal audit function can benefit either a financial or environmental auditor if the work they do is of relevance. Indeed, in the case of environmental audits most work to date has been carried out internally. It is only with the arrival of BS 7750 and EMAR, with their requirement for third-party accreditation and verification procedures, that external auditors have come onto the scene.

The Statement contains a useful section on the scope and objectives of internal audits, which, it makes clear, can vary widely. Appropriately amended to make them of more general application, rather than geared only to financial matters, the Statement says that they normally include one or more of the following:

- Review of the environmental, accounting and internal control systems: the establishment of adequate systems is a responsibility of management which demands proper attention on a continuous basis. Often, internal audit is assigned specific responsibility by management for reviewing these systems, monitoring their operation and recommending improvements.
- Examination of environmental, financial and operating information: this may include review of the means used to identify, measure, classify and report such information and specific enquiry into individual items including detailed testing of transactions, balances and procedures.
- Review of the economy, efficiency and effectiveness of operations including non-financial controls of an organisation.
- Review of compliance with laws, regulations and other external requirements and with management policies and directives and other internal requirements including appropriate authorisation of transactions.

The main part of the Statement deals with the way in which an external auditor should develop an understanding of internal audit activities to assist in planning and developing an effective audit approach. If the work of the internal auditor is important there will be a need to assess his activities so as to confirm how much they can be relied on.

SAS 510   The relationship between principal auditors and other auditors

Financial audits on large diversified organisations often involve more than one external audit firm, although normally one firm signs an audit opinion on the financial statements of the entire group. It is very probable that similar situations will arise with large-scale environmental audits so that the main requirement of this Statement—that the principal auditors should obtain sufficient appropriate evidence that such work is adequate for the purposes of their audit—will apply too.

Other considerations dealt with by the Statement cover such things as the extent of the principal auditor's own participation. Is it enough to allow him to carry the principal auditor's burden? Similarly are the other auditors professionally competent and have they done enough work of the right sort? Given the recent arrival of environmental auditors on the scene, there is no guarantee that there are competent auditors to be found in many locations around the world. Perhaps specialists will have to be brought in from outside, which may give rise to further problems of language, culture and an understanding of the local legislation and regulatory background.

SAS 520   Using the work of an expert

This is the third Statement on 'using the work of others' and requires that when an expert is engaged to provide specialist advice:

- sufficient evidence should be obtained that the work is adequate for the purposes of the audit;
- the objectivity and professional competence of the expert should be assessed; and
- appropriate evidence is obtained that the expert's scope of work is adequate and appropriate.

The Statement gives detailed guidance on how to use and control an expert, when to use one and how to assess his work. Perhaps, from the point of view of a financial auditor using expert help to enable him to carry out environmental auditing and reporting procedures too, the most important thing is the objectivity and professional competence of the expert.

To assess this, the Statement suggests that the auditor should consider the expert's professional certification or licensing by, or membership of, an appropriate professional body and experience and reputation in the field. It points out that the risk that the expert's objectivity is impaired increases when the expert is employed by the company being audited or is related in some other way by, for example, being financially dependent upon it or having an investment in it.

SAS 600   Auditors' reports on financial statements

Much of this Statement is not relevant to the environmental auditor but there is one aspect of it that is worth highlighting—Example 4 in Appendix 2 to the Statement. This Example is of an unqualified audit opinion on a company's financial statements with an explanatory paragraph describing a fundamental uncertainty. That uncertainty relates to an alleged breach of environmental regulations.

The relevant extract from the opinion reads as follows:

Fundamental uncertainty

In forming our opinion, we have considered the adequacy of the disclosures made in the financial statements concerning the possible outcome to litigation against B Limited, a subsidiary undertaking of the company, for an alleged breach of environmental regulations. The future settlement of this litigation could result in additional liabilities and the closure of B Limited's business, whose net assets included in the consolidated balance sheet total £... and whose profit before tax for the year is £... Details of the circumstances relating to this fundamental uncertainty are described in note ... Our opinion is not qualified in this respect.

Here is an example, if one was needed, of the coming together of the roles of financial and environmental auditor.

SAS 610 Reports to directors or management

This Statement covers situations where an auditor reports to directors, including an audit committee, or to management weaknesses in control systems and errors found during the course of an audit. Reports such as these are in addition to, not instead of, formal external audit reports where these are required. As external environmental reporting is entirely voluntary and in its infancy, this form of reporting is particularly relevant at the conclusion of environmental audit work.

The Statement, amended slightly, says the principal purposes of such reports to directors or management are:

- to enable the auditors to comment on the design and operation of the internal control systems examined during the course of the audit and make suggestions for their improvement;
- to provide other constructive advice, for example comments on potential economies or improvements in efficiency identified during the audit; and
- to communicate other matters that have come to the auditors' attention during the audit, for example comments on adjusted and unadjusted errors or on particular policies and practices.

It goes on to provide helpful guidance on what could be included and concludes with an important section on the interest of third parties in such reports. It stresses that such reports are confidential and that the auditor cannot show them to a third party without the consent of the directors or management. Similar considerations apply the other way round but in practice auditors have little control over what happens to a report once it has been despatched. They are advised, therefore, to state in their report that it has been prepared for the sole use of the company, that it must not be disclosed to a third party without the written consent of the auditors and that no responsibility is assumed by the auditors to any other person. Good advice to environmental auditors too.

SAS 620 The auditors' right and duty to report to regulators in the financial sector

On the face of it this is an unlikely Statement to include in this review. It is relevant however in that the imposition of a duty to report to regulators such as Her Majesty's Inspectorate of Pollution and the National Rivers Authority may be placed on environmental auditors too at some time in the future. When it is, environmental auditing will have to move from being a voluntary exercise to being imposed by statute.

Although some pressure groups might advocate such a course of action, there is a case for leaving well alone. So long as an auditor/client company relationship is a confidential one, with only a limited form of audit report being made publicly available, problems are likely to be more freely shared and the auditors may be part of a process of progressive improvement and not its policeman. The careful wording of SAS 620, and the Statement's length, demonstrate the change that comes about when the auditor not only has a right but also a duty to report to regulators.

7.6 Due diligence

Introduction

It has become accepted practice in the UK, and elsewhere too, to instruct independent accountants to carry out a business and financial review before many corporate deals are done. This is particularly true when buying or selling private companies, whereas public companies with a Stock Exchange listing cannot make price-sensitive information available to one group or interested party without making it generally available to the Market. Investigating accountants in such circumstances have a much more limited role and have to rely largely on published or publicly available sources of information.

With the greatly increased importance, or threat, of environmental matters this sort of review now needs to be extended. In some cases specialised environmental auditors or engineers are brought in to look at technical problems if they are believed to exist. But there is no reason why the accountant's job should not be enlarged if he or she knows what to do and where to look.

The purpose of this section is to suggest a framework for going about this task. Clearly it cannot be done in isolation. Close co-operation with lawyers is essential and in some cases with technical environmental auditors, engineers and scientists to carry out sampling of waste streams, put down test bore holes, etc.

We begin by looking at the overall framework of a typical corporate acquisition of a private company. Clearly a seller will see the process from the other side of the negotiating table, but he or she too will need to know about any environmental risks which may affect the strength of the negotiating position. Then a look is taken at the sort of environmental research that could be done by the investigating accountant and it is suggested when and how specialist help might need to be brought in, perhaps on a subcontract basis. Particular emphasis is placed on the availability of information from public registers, etc., and consideration is given to trends in corporate disclosures, whether brought about by changing UK laws or from the European Community.

Further parts of this section then look at the negotiation itself, ways of laying-off environmental risk and the attitudes of lenders who might be behind the buyer. The aim will be to show how a well-briefed investigating accountant can play a vital role in dealing with the environmental aspects of the transaction. It should also suggest to finance directors that environmental matters are for them, too, and not just for their engineering or more technically minded colleagues.

Acquisition framework

There is no such thing as a typical acquisition but there are certain common features to a deal which are repeated time and time again. Set out below is a model which shows seven main stages and where environmental issues must be addressed.

Stage 1—Evaluation of target
- Any land involved can be surveyed visually, if not technically, and desk research on its history carried out.
- The overall environmental impact of the business activity can be evaluated and the apparent success of any known environmental management programmes assessed.

- The environmental market profile and associated packaging issues can be investigated.

Stage 2—Formulate and negotiate the proposal
Stage 3—Exchange Letters of Intent
Stage 4—Conduct due diligence

- Assess legal compliance with environmental laws and regulations.
- Conduct a financial audit including an evaluation of any clean-up costs or process changes in the pipeline.
- Carry out site surveys and consider the company's environmental policies and management systems (if any).

Stage 5—Review findings and decide options

- Renegotiate if environmental problems are greater than originally envisaged.
- Exclude certain problem assets or processes/products.
- Consider the availability of some form of environmental risk insurance.
- Insist on certain environmental problems being remedied before purchase.

Stage 6—Obtain lender approval (if required)
Stage 7—Negotiate final terms of contract and complete

As the model shows there are certain key points where environmental concerns feature prominently. The first of these is well before anything other than a very informal approach to the target company has been made. It involves a wide range of strategic issues such as fit with the buyer's own manufacturing facilities, product-range, management team, etc., but should also include a careful assessment of the visible condition of the target's assets, the environmental profile of the business and the scope for material environmentally related costs, whether they be for clean-ups or product liability. The second point is when, after exchanging letters of intent, a full due-diligence review is being carried out. Lawyers, accountants and in some cases environmental specialists will need to liaise closely. The final point is the evaluation of the findings of the due-diligence process together with consideration of the options reflecting environmental issues, such as fines, clean-up costs, asset values, etc. These will need to be appropriately reflected in the final contract.

The first level of investigation is prior to any firm approach being made to the target and, therefore, necessarily relies on publicly disclosed environmental information. What follows is a wide-ranging review that is just as applicable to a listed company as a private company, whereas the second level of investigation—full due diligence after letters of intent have been exchanged—will normally be very different for a private company.

The normal starting point, particularly for an investigating accountant, will be the annual directors' report and statutory accounts of the company. But, as has already been made clear in Chapter 6, there is still a long way to go before anything other than the most material of environmental events or liabilities is fully reflected in the report or accounts. There is no specific obligation in UK law or accounting standards to disclose anything about environmental matters and only a handful of companies—honourable exceptions such as British Airways, ICI and the Bodyshop—say anything meaningful voluntarily.

Nevertheless, a review of any set of accounts, paying particular attention to the nature of any extraordinary or exceptional items and the contingent liability note, is an obvious starting point. In both cases, however, disclosure will only be necessary if the items are material in the context of the results or the assets of the company or group. Some of the more obvious examples of things that might appear are:

- substantial clean-up costs, not necessarily only those arising from civil or criminal proceedings;
- the costs of improving industrial and commercial practices, particularly as a result of the licensing requirements under the Environmental Protection Act 1990 in applying integrated pollution control (IPC) procedures using best available techniques not entailing excessive cost (BATNEEC);
- additional depreciation charges as a result of the re-assessment of asset lives in the light of changes in environmental legislation or best practice;
- the write down of asset values, and land values in particular, should they be adversely affected by long-term environmental factors; and
- the impact or existence of litigation including fines, damages and costs arising from the existence of environmental legislation, product liability claims or from breaches of occupational health and safety legislation.

In some cases it will be very difficult to predict the outcome of, for example, environmental litigation or costs associated with the introduction of IPC. Such contingent losses have to be provided in the accounts where they can be estimated with reasonable accuracy or noted if not.

In due course, the report and accounts may become a better source of environmental as well as much other relevant but non-financial information. In May 1992, the UK Accounting Standards Board published a discussion paper on the contents of a voluntary 'Operating and Financial Review' (OFR) which it hopes to see adopted by all major UK companies. The idea behind OFRs is to give company directors the opportunity to discuss in a structured way the main factors underlying the company's operating as well as financial performance. Indeed specific reference to the need for comment arising from uncertainties such as environmental risk is made in the discussion paper.

As so often happens in the world of company reporting, the USA has already adopted this concept. Companies listed on the US Stock Exchanges and governed by the rules of the SEC are required to include in their annual filing a section called 'Management's Discussion and Analysis of Financial Condition and Results of Operations' (MDA). But the requirement goes further than envisaged in the UK's OFR because disclosure is required of uncertainties—including environmental ones—that are 'reasonably likely to have a material effect' unless that effect 'is not reasonably likely to occur'. UK companies listed in the USA, or UK subsidiaries of US parents, need to be mindful of this requirement and any investigation should study the US MDA carefully: it could be the start of an important environmental trail.

Once the accounts (and any relevant US SEC accounts-related filings) have been looked at UK company investigations would turn to public registers and publicly available planning information as well as the attitudes of customers, suppliers, and employees to the target's operations. This information would be available for both quoted and private companies too, but there might also be environmental information available in a quoted company's listing particulars, circulars to shareholders drawn up under the provisions of the Stock Exchange Yellow Book, or material produced if the company has made or has been the subject of a takeover bid in recent times.

Public registers can provide a lot of relevant environmental information if you know where to look and what to ask for. These registers normally contain permits under legislation and, subject to exceptions for commercial confidentiality, are usually available for inspection by the public. Some of the more obvious permits that it might be worth looking at are:

1. Water discharge consents under Section 10 of the Water Resources Act 1991 granted by the National Rivers Authority.
2. Trade effluent consents under Chapter III of Part IV of the Water Industry Act 1991 dealing with the discharge of trade effluent to public sewers.
3. Waste disposal licences under Section 5 of the Control of Pollution Act 1974 which become waste management licences (granted by Waste Regulation Authorities) under Part II of the Environmental Protection Act 1990.
4. Authorisations under Part I of the Environmental Protection Act 1990 covering Integrated Pollution Control (through HMIP) and Air Pollution Control (through local authorities).

5. Registration and authorisation (with HMIP) to keep, use and dispose of radioactive material under the Radioactive Substances Act 1960.
6. Licences under the Food and Environment Protection Act 1985 from the Ministry of Agriculture, Fisheries and Food to dump at sea.
7. Consents (from June 1992) from the local planning authority to store and use hazardous substances in prescribed quantities under the Planning (Hazardous Substances) Act 1990.

In addition, there are various reporting obligations, mainly arising from health and safety legislation, covering such things as injuries, diseases, dangerous occurrences, new and dangerous substances, installations handling hazardous substances and 'industrial major accident hazards'. These too may be worth enquiring about if the target company's activities are at all dangerous.

Turning to the planning system, here too there may be very useful information about current or proposed major projects by the target. The Town and Country Planning (Assessment of Environmental Effects) Regulations 1988 introduced the requirement for Environmental Impact Assessments, some of which have to be carried out and some of which the Secretary of State can require to be carried out. These are available for public inspection and should allow the effect of, for example, a new motorway on a company's operations to be properly assessed. In due course a register of contaminated land may also be a vital source of information. As originally proposed, the register would have included all land that at any time in its history had been put to certain defined kinds of 'contaminative use'.

At European Community level two developments strengthen the hand of those wanting access to environmental information. The first of these is an EC Directive on freedom of access to information held by public authorities which has been implemented in the UK through the Environmental Information Regulations 1992 that strengthen the rights of public access to the sources of information described above. The second is the EC Eco-Audit Management Regulation which, although voluntary, will involve an externally verified public environmental statement.

Once these sources of information have been explored, investigation of a quoted company can be extended to cover listing particulars, circulars to shareholders and any recent takeover bid documentation. Given the general state of environmental awareness when the rules governing these documents were drawn up, notably the Financial Services Act 1986 (FSA), there is little direct reference to environmental matters within them. Reliance, therefore, has to be placed on, for example, the general duty of disclosure imposed by the FSA requiring that listing particulars and circulars give details 'of all such information as investors and their professional advisers would reasonably require and expect in order to make an informed assessment of the financial position of the company'.

Disclosure is also required of litigation, material contracts and prospects all of which might contain something that is environmentally relevant. In particular, the Yellow Book requires a statement on any environmental factors which may affect the commercial viability of a mining project.

When all these public sources of information have been examined and conclusions have been drawn about the overall environmental rating of the target company decisions about the nature of any offer will have to be made. On the assumption that an offer is made and is accepted in principle, letters of intent may be exchanged and provision made for further due diligence, including environmental due-diligence which can go much further than that using public information sources alone. At this point, an investigating accountant may have relatively free reign and is in an excellent position to co-ordinate environmental experts as well as make appropriate environmental enquiries of his own—as has been shown earlier in this chapter.

A financial auditor can be an environmental auditor as well if he wishes and if both the market-place and the emerging environmental auditing regulatory bodies will allow.

8

Environmental Accounting

8.1 Introduction

Accounting in the widest sense of the word is all about measurement and then reporting what has been measured so that the parameter being measured is better understood. Applying this apparently simple concept, however, to something as unfocused as the 'environment' is not at all easy. All too quickly there is confusion over what to measure, what criteria to use, whether the basis is comparable, how much to say (good and bad or just good?), where to say it and what commitments should be made for the future.

This chapter will try to avoid this potential confusion and will look, almost exclusively, at environmental accounting from a company's point of view. It will begin by considering the way in which environmental information already has to be reported under existing accounting conventions, principally in the UK but also with references to the USA and elsewhere in the world. This is much the longest section of the chapter reflecting, as it does, the practical day-to-day issues affecting company financial management in the mid-1990s.

The next section is almost as important. It looks at the problems of measurement of environmental information and the relevance of money values in reporting what has been measured. It is only when relevant data has been obtained and expressed in financial terms that conventional accounting principles and practices can be applied to it. But it would be a mistake to think that accountants and business managers can simply stop at that point. New concepts and ideas are emerging and there are signs that in the next few years more and more companies will be looking at them. Two of the more prominent are the practical application of the principles of sustainable development and the use of a system of environmental bookkeeping that quantifies, in money terms, damage to the environment caused by a company's activities.

For many company managers the last two items will be too theoretical but the concepts are increasingly widely discussed and, particularly in the case of sustainable development, form the basis for a lot of management thinking in the 1990s.

8.2 Existing conventions

Whilst much has been written about the wider aspects of environmental reporting, little attention seems to have been given—so far—to the way in which existing accounting conventions can or should be modified to reflect changes in environmental laws, business practice and public interest. This is particularly true in the UK where there is a well-developed series of accounting standards and a mechanism for updating them and issuing new ones as the need arises, but, as yet, there is no wish (or time) to put environmental accounting onto the agenda.

A full list of Accounting Standards (including Statements of Standard Accounting Practice, Financial Reporting Standards, Consensus Pronouncements, Accounting Recommendations and Statements of Recommended Practice) is set out in Appendix E. Those which may have environmental consequences and to which some amendment may be required to reflect more fully current and future environmental developments are listed below:

Accounting Recommendation	The interpretation of 'material' in relation to accounts
SSAP 2	Disclosure of accounting policies
SSAP 9	Stocks and long-term contracts
SSAP 12	Accounting for depreciation
SSAP 15 and SSAP 15A	Accounting for deferred tax
SSAP 17	Accounting for post-balance sheet events
SSAP 18	Accounting for contingencies
SSAP 19	Accounting for investment properties
SSAP 23	Accounting for acquisitions and mergers
SSAP 25	Segmental reporting
FRS 2	Accounting for subsidiary undertakings

FRS 3   Reporting financial performance
ASB Statement   Operating and financial review

The interpretation of 'material' in relation to accounts (Accounting Recommendation)

Guidance on the interpretation of 'material' is given in an Accounting Recommendation published by the Institute of Chartered Accountants in England and Wales (ICAEW). The Recommendation stresses that materiality has to be judged in the context of accounts that are required to give a true and fair view. But the meaning of the words 'a true and fair view' is constant, whereas the content of accounts required to give a true and fair view can only be judged in the particular circumstances of that item and the accounts to which it relates. Developing environmental awareness might be part of these changing circumstances.

The Recommendation also makes the distinction between two classes of question relating to materiality: first, whether an item needs to be disclosed; and second, what margin of error (if any) is acceptable in the amount attributed to an item. Both of these questions can be of particular importance in looking at some types of environmental liability/risk where certainty about the consequences of contamination, process licensing, technical obsolescence, etc., may be impossible. An item of small amount (for example, a fine for pollution) may not be material in itself but may be material in the context of a company's particular circumstances (public image), especially if that context would lead the user to expect the item to be a substantial amount.

Disclosure of accounting policies (SSAP 2)

This Standard requires that accounting policies which are judged material or critical in determining profit or loss for the year and in stating the financial position should be disclosed by way of note to the accounts.

With the growing significance of the environmental issues affecting many businesses, it is now more likely that some reference to the way in which environmental costs, investments, liabilities, etc., have been accounted for, will be needed. Indeed, the absence of a stated policy for some companies operating in environmentally sensitive fields such as the chemicals industry or holding large land banks may be a cause for comment or criticism.

Stocks and long-term contracts (SSAP 9)

The environmental interest in SSAP 9 is likely to lie in the area of long-term contracts particularly in respect of construction projects where environmental impact assessments may be required or contaminated land require clean-up. In particular, guidance on the recognition of foreseeable losses from contamination might be helpful, particularly if there is uncertainty over who is liable to pay the clean-up costs and the existence of insurance cover.

Accounting for depreciation (SSAP 12)

SSAP 12 is probably one of the accounting standards most in need of some reference to and guidance on environmental effects on depreciation. The key paragraph in the Standard requires that provision for fixed assets having a finite useful economic life should be made by allocating the cost (or revalued amount), less the estimated residual value of the asset, as fairly as possible to the periods expected to benefit from their use.

The key issues here relate to estimating residual values and the periods expected to benefit from the assets use in the light of changing technologies and environmental standards. In the UK, the integrated pollution control (IPC) regime introduced by the Environmental Protection Act 1990 requires certain significant industrial processes to be licensed by Her Majesty's Inspectorate of Pollution (HMIP). In evaluating the acceptability of the process, HMIP may require modifications that might either be capitalised and then depreciated or written off as a period cost: without a licence, operation of the process has to stop.

Furthermore, IPC requires the application of best available techniques not entailing excessive cost (BATNEEC). It may be that HMIP's and company management's view of what are best available techniques differ and that the costs are thought by company management to be prohibitive. It may follow, therefore, that an existing process has to halt in a much shorter time scale than originally envisaged and that the period over which the related assets are written down has to be shortened with a consequent increase in the annual depreciation charge to the profit and loss account.

Indeed, if the investment required to license a process is thought by company management to be unacceptably high and if that process is central to the operation of a plant or factory, premature closure may be required with what might be a material one-off write-off as a result.

Accounting for deferred tax (SSAP 15 and SSAP 15A)

Although SSAP 15 is relatively simple in terms of its requirements, it is a Standard that requires a high level of judgement which might be significantly affected by environmental developments. The basic requirements are that deferred tax should be computed under the liability method and that tax deferred or accelerated by the effect of timing differences should (or should not) be accounted for to the extent that it is probable that a liability or asset will (or will not) crystallise. The assessment of whether deferred tax liabilities or assets will or will not crystallise should be based upon 'reasonable assumptions'.

Assessing what are reasonable assumptions requires a review of financial forecasts or projections covering a period of years sufficient to enable an assessment to be made of the likely pattern of future tax liabilities. In the UK, the main category of timing difference arises from the differing rates of fixed-asset depreciation for accounting and taxation purposes, and because of this capital expenditure forecasts are of critical importance. They may be affected profoundly by changing environmental standards, process licensing or consumer pressures. The main environmental factors affecting corporate depreciation have already been described, but future governments may also increase the tax-allowable rates of depreciation for certain types of environmental protection equipment so as to encourage its use. Assessing the reasonableness of any assumptions made is clearly going to require a proper understanding of environmental issues on the long-range plans of business.

Accounting for post-balance sheet events (SSAP 17)

Major accidents such as spills, leaks or explosions can have catastrophic and expensive environmental effects. They can also happen at any time and, therefore, if such an accident has happened it may need to be included or referred to in a set of financial statements for a particular period.

SSAP 17 requires that financial statements are prepared on the basis of conditions existing at the balance sheet date and that material post-balance sheet events require changes in the amounts included if the events are 'adjusting events' or if the outcome of the event suggests that application of the going concern concept to a whole or a material part of the company is not appropriate. An adjusting event is defined in the standard as one which provides additional evidence of conditions existing at the balance sheet date.

Adjusting events arising from environmentally related matters might be the result of product defects existing but not known about at the balance sheet date or contamination of land that was either unknown or the extent of which was not appreciated at that date. An explosion or leak after the period end that closes a plant might need to be reflected in the financial statements if it results in the closure of all or a major part of a plant and thereby puts the long-term future of the plant in question.

The Standard then goes on to talk about the circumstances in which a non-adjusting event nevertheless requires disclosure in notes to the financial statements. The most important category in this context is when the event is of such materiality that its non-disclosure would affect the ability of the users of financial statements to reach a proper understanding of the financial position of the company. The threat posed by a newly introduced or recently announced environmental regulation or licensing requirement might come under this heading.

Accounting for contingencies (SSAP 18)

This Standard describes a contingency as being a condition which exists at the balance sheet date where the outcome will be confirmed only on the occurrence or non-occurrence of one or more uncertain future events. It requires that a material contingent loss should be accrued for where it is probable that a future event will confirm a loss which can be estimated with reasonable accuracy when the financial statements are formally approved. If it is not accrued, the Standard points out that the existence of the material contingent loss should be disclosed except where the possibility of loss is remote.

This is a particularly difficult area for environmental liabilities, most of which are long term, and difficult to both determine and calculate because of uncertainties about the ways in which future legislation might develop, as well as the technological changes and the extent of the clean-up that might be required. Given these sorts of uncertainties, an accrual is often unlikely to be made. In such cases, the Standard requires the following information to be given instead by way of note:

- the nature of the contingency;
- the uncertainties which are expected to affect the ultimate outcome; and
- a statement that it is not practicable to make such an estimate.

As shall be shown, practice in this respect in the USA is more advanced than in the UK, where such disclosure of environmental liabilities is very much the exception. ICI is such an exception. The company noted the following in its 1992 accounts under a heading 'Environmental Liabilities':

> The Group is exposed to environmental liabilities relating to its past operations, principally in respect of soil and groundwater remediation costs.

Provisions for these costs are made when expenditure on remedial work is probable and the cost can be estimated within a reasonable range of possible outcomes.

Accounting for investment properties (SSAP 19)

The main requirement of this Standard is that properties held for their investment potential should not normally be subject to periodic charges for depreciation but should be included in the balance sheet at their open-market value. Although establishing open-market value is a job for a professionally qualified valuer, the effects of contamination of the land itself or that of immediately adjacent land may need to be taken into account. The possible arrival in the UK of registers of contaminated land (see Chapter 3) has brought this issue much more into focus and may well, in the short term at any rate, give rise to a downward revaluation of some investment properties.

Accounting for acquisitions and mergers (SSAP 23)
Accounting for subsidiary undertakings (FRS2)

These two Standards are dealt with together because the most direct environmental factor affecting the companies and groups to which they apply is the question of the fair value applied to the assets acquired as a result of a business combination.

The main thrust of SSAP 23 is to define the circumstances when a business combination should be accounted for as a merger or as an acquisition. Most UK combinations are accounted for as acquisitions when the fair value of the purchase consideration, for the purpose of consolidated financial statements, has to be allocated between the underlying net tangible and intangible assets other than goodwill on the basis of the fair value to the acquiring company in accordance with what was SSAP 14 and is now FRS 2. This fair value requirement is also a matter of law, being required by Schedule 4A, Paragraph 8 of the Companies Act 1989. Any difference between the fair value of the consideration and the aggregate of the fair value of the separable net assets represents goodwill.

Here again the environmental issues can affect asset values whether they be proven or potential contamination of land, problems over process licensing, legislative changes in the pipeline or developing customer and consumer preferences. A proper understanding of the strategic as well as practical importance of these issues is needed by all company directors and the finance director in particular.

Segmental reporting (SSAP 25)

This Standard states that if a company has two or more classes of business, or operates in two or more geographical segments which differ substantially from each other, it should define its classes of business and geographical segments in its financial statements, and it should report with respect to each class of business and geographical segment the following financial information:

- turnover;
- result before accounting for taxation, etc.; and
- net assets.

A separate class of business is, the Standard points out, a distinguishable component of a company that provides a separate product or service or a separate group of related products or services.

In all but a few special cases, environmental activities will not constitute a separate class of business. What might emerge is the voluntary grouping of certain products and services using environmental criteria to give a summary of financial information of environmental relevance. Whether this could be expanded to cover environmental expenditures, environmental capital assets and environmental operating expenditure needs further consideration. The report of The Environment Research Group of the ICAEW, published in late 1992, recommends that explicit guidelines are developed for classifying environmental expenditure as well as assessing the appropriateness of present accounting standards for distinguishing environmental capital assets and operating expenditure.

Reporting financial performance (FRS 3)

FRS 3 was published in 1992. It represented a major change to a number of aspects of UK companies' financial statements and, in particular, the format of the profit and loss account. The profit and loss account requirements it introduced are that:

(i) There should be an analysis of turnover and operating profit between continuing operations, acquisitions (as a component of continuing operations) and discontinued operations.
(ii) All exceptional items, other than in (iii) below, should be included under the statutory format headings to which they relate and be separately disclosed by way of note or on the face of the profit and loss account.

(iii) Three items should be shown separately on the face of the profit and loss account after operating profit and before interest:

- profits or losses on the sale or termination of an operation;
- costs of a fundamental reorganisation or restructuring; and
- profits or losses on the disposal of fixed assets.

(iv) Extraordinary items should be disclosed.

No specific reference to environmental matters is made anywhere in the Standard, although the scope for doing so is considerable. Part of a company's business may stop operating as a result of environmental factors. The disclosure of exceptional items could include various types of environmental costs including clean-up expenses, fines, damages, etc., if they are material in amount. A further category of items could be shown separately on the face of the profit and loss account: environmental costs—either in their own right or, possibly, as a subset of the 'costs of fundamental reorganisation or restructuring'. But as in the case of SSAP 25 disclosure, research is needed into how to define what should be included as an environmental cost.

Operating and financial review (ASB Statement)

Before leaving this section looking at the existing UK accounting conventions and how they can be made to relate to environmental matters, it is worth examining, briefly, a recent Statement published by the Accounting Standards Board in which the contents of a voluntary operating and financial review (OFR) are described. The ASB hopes that such a review will be carried out by many UK companies. If this hope is realised OFRs may become the natural place to disclose information about a company's environmental performance, both operating and financial. Specific reference to the need for comment arising from risks and uncertainties, such as environmental protection costs and potential environmental liabilities, is made in the Statement.

On that hopeful note, this examination of the relevance of the existing UK accounting conventions to environmental matters ends. There is clearly a lot that is directly relevant to all manner of environmental concerns. What may be missing amongst the preparers and auditors of accounts is a proper understanding of strategic and practical environmental developments. This can be bridged, perhaps, by refreshing existing accounting standards and ensuring that they contain environmental references and examples.

Also missing are many definitions for classifying environmental income, costs and assets, and a clear vision of how such financial information should be presented. Perhaps there is a case for a separate environmental report expressed in financial terms, but this may mean that environmental issues continue to be seen as separate from mainstream business life, which this book aims to show is very far from the truth. If tax incentives and other pricing mechanisms are introduced to effect national environment priorities (reduce carbon dioxide emissions, for example) and if these are related to defined environmental costs this separation will not last long.

Is the UK behind the rest of the world in dealing with these issues? A general answer is an emphatic 'no' but there are some important pointers to be found elsewhere and, in particular, in the USA.

There has been long-standing interest in the development of reporting models for evaluating corporate social performance in North America. Some of them, such as the 1973 report of the American Accounting Association's Committee on Environmental Effects of Organizational Behavior, are environmentally related. This report analysed in some depth a number of reporting alternatives. These alternatives ranged from separate classification of environmental control expenses and the use of accrual accounting for environmental liabilities to verbal description of organisational activities centring on identification of specific problem areas and disclosure of pollution abatement goals and information relating to their attainment. Other matters covered included disclosure of material environmental effects on the financial position, earnings and business activities of the organisation.

To what extent have these ideas been reflected in the development of US accounting standards? A review of the 106 standards produced by the Financial Accounting Standards Board (FASB—established by the American Institute of Certified Public Accountants (AICPA)) since it was formed—also in 1973—shows that there is not one that specifically deals with environmental accounting. The FASB has also published 38 Interpretations, various technical bulletins and six Statements of Financial Accounting Concepts none of which deals specifically with environmental issues. Fortunately the AICPA recognised the need to react promptly to emerging accounting issues in the 1980s and, in 1984, established the Emerging Issues Task Force which published, in 1990, a Statement on the Capitalisation of Costs to Treat Environmental Contamination—in response to the need for consistent treatment of the sort of Superfund clean-up costs described in Chapter 2.

The precedent set in the USA seems to have prompted an accounting standard on capital assets from the Canadian Institute of Chartered Accountants, which requires provision to be made for removal and site restoration costs and a reference in the International Accounting Standards Committee's Exposure Draft 43 on Property, Plant and Equipment (May 1992) to the extent to which expenditure on property, plant and equipment for safety or environmental reasons may be capitalised. Nothing similar has yet emerged from the UK Accounting Standards Board.

In the US, therefore, the pace of environmental accounting disclosure has not been set by the accounting professionals but by the Securities and Exchange Commission (SEC) which, beginning in 1971, has issued a series of releases stipulating certain environmental disclosures that are to be made in the narrative portions of corporate SEC filings. The current requirements are outlined in:

- Regulation S-K 101, which requires disclosure of the material effect that compliance with federal, state and local environmental laws may have on its capital expenditures, earnings and competitive position. Additionally, disclosure is required of existing estimates of current and future environmental expenditure.
- Regulation S-K 103, which requires disclosure of significant environmental, administrative or judicial proceedings, both contemplated by government and pending, that will have an impact on the company.

Of particular importance is SEC Release 6835 (May 1989) which requires company management to disclose any environmental problem of known potential significance unless it is able objectively to conclude that the problem is not reasonably likely to occur or, should it occur, the effect is not likely to be material. It is the existence of this Release that probably lies behind the recent increase in US company disclosure of Superfund liabilities. Another contributor is the SEC requirement that environmental liabilities be disclosed in the 'Management Discussion and Analysis of Financial Condition and Results of Operations' section of corporate filings.

But, in practice, what exactly is disclosed in US financial statements—particularly in respect of 'hazardous waste remediation' or clean-up? A Price Waterhouse survey of 125 major US corporations published in 1991 found that:

- There are many areas of uncertainty and evolution. A changing regulatory and legal framework and advances in remediation technology complicate the accounting.
- There is strong corporate interest in environmental accounting issues.
- Only 11% of the respondents had prepared written manuals that specifically address environmental accounting matters.
- Only 4% of respondents reported their environmental accounting policies in the footnotes to published financial statements.
- Measurement can often be difficult and practice mixed with regard to the timing of recording of environmental clean-up liabilities.

- Estimating the magnitude of liabilities relating to environmental remediation involves many variables.
- Recording liabilities net of anticipated recoveries from insurers and other third parties is a common practice.
- Post-remediation monitoring costs at closed sites are not always considered when establishing accruals for environmental clean-up obligations.
- Only certain extractive industries and the nuclear power industry have broadly instituted the practice of accruing for future site restoration obligations over the life of operating facilities.
- Nearly 79% of the survey's respondents indicated that provisions for clean-up liabilities were classified as operating items.
- Nearly all respondents noted that they included environmental costs in measurements of net gains (loss) upon disposal of a site using the same recognition and measurement criteria as in accounting for such matters at ongoing facilities.
- The majority of respondents disclosed significant environmental matters upon initial notification by a regulatory agency. Nearly half use their Annual Form 10-K as the vehicle for initial public disclosure.

This same survey then formed the basis of an article in the US *Journal of Accountancy* in March 1992 which set out several broad guidelines to be considered in accounting for environmental exposures. Adapting them slightly to give them a direct application to many UK situations they form a useful framework which demonstrates, again, the need for some specific guidance from the Accounting Standards Board on accounting for the environment. They might read as follows:

Cash basis accounting—The pay-as-you-go approach for environmental clean-up obligations is inconsistent with accrual accounting and should be questioned unless the amounts involved clearly are immaterial.

Amortisation of costs—No conceptual or practical support exists for amortising environmental clean-up costs related to past activities through periodic charges to future income.

Expense recognition—For major environmental clean-up costs (brought about in the USA by the Superfund and related legislation) a strong presumption should exist for recognition no later than completion of the remedial investigation and feasibility study phase. Other variables, such as participant share and third-party recovery, should also be assessed to determine if there is a basis for delayed recognition or recording less than the gross estimated liability.

Net versus gross—Recording an environmental liability net of expected recoveries may be acceptable depending on the likelihood of recovery.

Plant shutdowns and other disposals—Environmental clean-up and other site restoration obligations should be considered in measuring sale, abandonment or other disposal transaction results.

Business combination liabilities—To the extent that they are reasonably estimable environmental obligations assumed on the purchase of a business should be treated like any other assumed obligation in recording assets acquired and liabilities assumed.

Present value approach—Accruing remediation costs at present value should be approached cautiously and restricted to times when future cash flows are highly predictable.

8.3 Measurement

Naturally the accountant thinks most readily of money as a common standard of measurement allowing relative values to be judged. As business success or failure is also generally judged in financial terms this way of looking at environmental issues may be no bad thing. Indeed, it might be a means of persuading sceptical business people that sound environmental management practices can be not only morally but also financially beneficial. But not everything can be measured financially.

The practical problem is knowing what to try to measure and how to present the results so as to give a picture of corporate environmental performance consistent with, if not the same as, the company profit and loss account and balance sheet. Only when the end product has been decided can the company's management systems be adapted to produce what is required although as this will need a combination of accounting, scientific and technical co-operation it might be difficult to achieve.

Perhaps a simple starting point would be to look at regulatory requirements and the information needed to ensure that a company is complying with, for example, its process licence from HMIP and that the cost of so doing is measured and understood in financial terms as well. When this has been done, other costs and benefits may be identified to suit particular aspects of corporate environmental policy in areas such as energy saving or waste management. These too need to be built into a company's environmental management systems and their financial consequences calculated and presented in a meaningful way.

Until recently there has been little available guidance on how this sort of approach might be put into practice. But, in September 1992, a start was made in the form of a useful booklet called *A measure of commitment—guidelines for measuring environmental performance*, published by Business in the Environment and KPMG. In the booklet guidance is given on how companies can adapt general principles of measurement of environmental performance and experience elsewhere (including outside their own sector) to their own situation. Fourteen companies co-operated in the project to produce a guidebook illustrated by case studies from each company.

The guidelines and cases, the authors suggest, illustrate five key points:

1. That performance measurement needs to be developed within the context of environmental policy, objectives and management systems.
2. That developing environmental performance measures cannot be a quick fix but should be part of a continuing process requiring trial and error and further development.
3. That it is important to recognise different types of measure particularly those suitable for external reporting, where direct impacts on the environment are likely to be emphasised, as opposed to those for internal reporting which may impact less directly but just as importantly.
4. That participation in the development of performance measures of other managers and staff gives results.
5. That there are a range of resulting benefits, such as a sharper focus on the possible effects of an area like waste disposal leading to new objectives, performance monitoring and early signs of waste reduction.

The booklet is 86-pages long and contains a wealth of material to which, short of repeating its contents word for word, this chapter cannot hope to do justice. An overall observation, however, is that few of the measures described include money values. That is not to say that money values cannot be ascribed to, say, energy savings but the fact that the booklet tends to see things in relative terms and not financial terms suggests that accountants may not yet be sufficiently engaged in the process of devising performance measures.

The booklet proposes an outline methodology for the development of performance criteria which has five stages—on the assumption that an overall corporate environmental review has been carried out and policies already set.

The first stage is to decide on performance area and objectives drawing on already established environmental policies but requires a decision to be made about priorities reflecting what is environmentally important rather than what is relatively easily measurable. At the same time, realistic and attainable objectives need to be set so that the information needed to judge the extent of their attainment is available. Measurement can cover any aspect of the company or its product life cycle (processes or operations, suppliers, product use and disposal), any area of performance which has potential direct environmental impact (emissions to air and effluent to water, waste taken away for disposal, energy use, natural resources), contributors (infrastructure and equipment, management systems) and external relations.

The second stage is to review a so-called performance hierarchy which begins by looking at 'contributors' to processes that have an environmental 'impact' which, when aggregated, represent the overall company environmental 'impact'. Contributors include plant efficiency, the effectiveness of operational procedures and related training, plant efficiency, materials quality and the recyclability of materials. These all contribute to processes such as metal manufacture, finishing and coating and product packaging where policy objectives might be to reduce waste by 10% (90 tonnes), 75% (5 tonnes) and 15% (5 tonnes) respectively at each stage. The overall company environmental 'impact' therefore becomes a 100 tonnes or 25% reduction in waste which could then be evaluated financially. Each company will have its own performance hierarchy which should help identify where performance measurement is most likely to have an effect.

The third stage is to select performance measures in accordance with a number of basic principles that the guidelines identify as being consistent with policy and corporate objectives, not too many, simple and understandable, appropriate for users, providing a track record of performance against objectives, measurable and transparent. Choices then have to be made as to whether each performance indicator should look at impacts (which may relate to processes, suppliers or products and will normally be at company level) or at contributors. Impact measures are likely to be of external interest whilst contributor measures could be of more internal concern. Risk and/or external relations may also be considered as a basis for a performance indicator.

The fourth stage is to set up a pilot project. This process is said to be especially useful in gathering information, testing ideas and examining the feasibility of using particular types of performance measure and gaining wider commitment to improving environmental performance.

Finally, the guidelines stress the important principle that environmental management should be an integral part of other aspects of good management. As such a successful pilot project should lead to the performance measures becoming part of the company's management systems. This may not always be straightforward as it might affect several different parts of an organisation and may need to overcome resistance to changing deep-rooted practices. The key management systems affected will be in the area of assessing and rewarding performance and in the information systems that support different business functions. Integration with accounting and financial systems is vital although not mentioned in the guidelines.

These five stages are drawn from fourteen company case studies which are also described in some detail in the booklet. They cover issues which include effluent management within a process company (Bluecrest Convenience Foods), supplier performance within a major procurer (BT), energy management in a process environment (Hydro Aluminium Metals Ltd) and measuring store waste in the retail sector (Safeway Stores). Each case study is different but Hydro Aluminium is described in more detail below to show the sort of approach adopted and the benefits flowing from it.

Hydro Aluminium is one of fifteen manufacturing subsidiaries in the UK of Norsk Hydro AS, Norway's largest industrial company. It provides a recycling service primarily for UK manufacturers of aluminium extrusions. Recyclable material is remelted and returned in the form of prime quality billet ready for the manufacture of more extrusions.

Part of Hydro Aluminium's overall strategy for business decisions on the environment has been the objective of 'competitive energy efficiency'. This objective combined with the company's annual budgeting process, which has in the past called for 5% saving in energy costs per unit of output, makes the consideration of energy performance measures critical so the aim was to develop a system of measuring more accurately the use of energy.

A major part of the company's environmental strategy is identical with its operational strategy which is to ensure continued competitive energy efficiency. As a consequence of an independent study into the company's energy utilisation, it was clear that more direct measures of gas and electricity consumption were required for each of the key areas of the process. Before the study, the only measure of consumption levels was based on suppliers' invoices. The company now uses two measures—gas and electricity consumption per tonne of aluminium processed and the percentage of waste heat re-utilised.

Energy monitoring now involves the weekly reading of meters and processing the information to provide gas and electricity consumption per tonne of aluminium processed as measures of performance. These showed that the main contributor to the current level of energy consumption in the process stage was the melting furnace with much underused energy disappearing up the chimney stack. The company therefore concentrated on the possibility of capturing and utilising waste heat in the stack emissions. Engineering studies suggested that it may be possible to save up to 10% of total gas consumption, yielding a payback period on the expenditure involved of less than two years. A future measure of performance, therefore, became the percentage of waste heat re-utilised from the stack gases.

The end result was a rapid financial payback and real long-term financial benefit to the company. The challenge for the accountant is to put the systems in place to ensure that the information needed to monitor ongoing performance in ways such as this is available internally and externally too if required.

8.4 Sustainable development

Much is heard nowadays about sustainable development in international, national, corporate and personal terms. Much less is heard about the real measurement and accounting issues behind the concept and, in particular, what companies can actually do to contribute to the development of sustainable business practices.

The concept and the importance of environmental protection in the pursuit of sustainable development was first prominently emphasised in the 1987 report entitled 'Our common Future' from the World Commission on Environment and Development (the Brundtland Commission). In that report sustainable development was defined as involving meeting the needs of the present without compromising the ability of future generations to meet their own needs.

The International Chamber of Commerce (ICC) has picked up and endorsed the concept on behalf of the world's business community and launched its Business Charter for Sustainable Development at the Second World Industry Conference on Environmental Management in April 1991. The principles set out in the Charter are included as Appendix F. In the introduction to these principles, the ICC makes the important point that it believes that 'economic growth provides the conditions in which protection of the environment can best be achieved, and environmental protection, in balance with other human goals, is necessary to achieve growth that is sustainable'.

Most business leaders would have little difficulty in agreeing with this concept but turning agreement into policies that can then be implemented, measured and reported objectively and financially is much harder. As a result there have, so far, been few attempts to do so although one published in 1992, is worth a mention. This is a Canadian report entitled *Business Strategy for Sustainable Development: Leadership and Accountability for the '90's*, and was prepared jointly by the International Institute for Sustainable Development, Deloitte & Touche and the Business Council for Sustainable Development. The report suggests augmenting a company's annual report by including a separate report on sustainable development objectives and performance measures. It suggests what the contents of this report should be, which include statements of policy and objectives, as well as confirmation that laws and regulations have been complied with. So far as performance is concerned it suggests that 'a comparison of actual performance against each of the sustainable development objectives using financial, operational, scientific and other relevant statistics and data' should be given. It does not suggest that such information be integrated into existing accounting routines and reporting conventions.

On the other hand a number of suggestions are made about how to strengthen the existing accounting processes to capture elements of environmental impact. This is well short of a proper accounting framework for measuring accountability but it is a starting point as has been argued already in this chapter. The suggestions involve:

- improving the classification of environmental expenditures in financial statements to reflect more clearly the results of sustainable programmes;
- assessing whether present accounting standards for distinguishing between capital assets and expenses are appropriate for environmental and sustainable development programmes.
- strengthening accounting standards for estimating and allocating the costs of restoration programmes and other related environmental commitments over the useful life of the business operation; and
- re-examining the measurement and accounting issues for contingent liabilities that relate to environmental problems.

The validity of these suggestions has already emerged from the earlier review of the existing framework of accountancy conventions. So far, therefore, the concept of sustainability does not appear to have contributed much in the way of new thinking on environmental accounting within the existing framework.

8.5 Environmental bookkeeping

Perhaps what is needed is a new framework along the lines described by David Pearce and others in the influential Blueprint for a Green Economy published in 1989. Pearce suggested that sustainable development depends on the identification of both man-made capital and environmental capital. Additions to man-made capital frequently involve diminution in environmental capital which is not recognised by our existing accounting systems. We can therefore impoverish the natural world in our pursuit of accretions to man-made capital, but not recognise or measure the extent to which we have done so.

Dr James Lovelock, the originator of the Gaia theory, gives an interesting example of how a value might be put on one particular form of environmental capital—the Amazon rain forest and its role as a giant air-conditioner helping to keep the Earth cool and moist. In a recent lecture he stated:

> One way to value the forest as an air-conditioner would be to assess the annual energy cost of achieving the same amount of cooling mechanically. If the clouds made by the forests reduce the heat flux of sunlight received within their canopies by only 1% then their cooling effect would require a refrigerator with a cooling power of fourteen kilowatts per acre. The energy needed, assuming complete efficiency and no capital outlay, would cost annually £2000 per acre . . . On this basis, an accurate but imprecise estimate of the worth of the refrigeration system that is the whole of Amazonia is about £100 trillion.

Ideas like these form the basis for Professor Rob Gray's suggestions in his booklet, published in 1990 by the Association of Certified Accountants, *The Greening of Accountancy*. Gray suggested that there was a need for a redefinition of assets and capital maintenance with the disclosure of:

(a) man-made, natural and critical capital assets (critical capital assets being life-supporting resources such as the ozone layer and tropical rain forests);
(b) transfers between categories of assets; and
(c) data on the maintenance of critical and other natural assets.

Gray argued that much of the world's critical capital is not owned but is treated as a free good by traditional accounting systems and that ownership of natural capital seemingly confers the right to abuse and deplete these assets. Accordingly current concepts of property ownership need to be amended towards a recognition that ownership involves stewardship, entailing a responsibility to care for and maintain the assets owned on behalf of this and future generations. Similar concepts of capital maintenance have also to be applied to non-owned critical assets.

More recently (1992) Gray has developed these ideas further in a book, entitled *Accounting and Environmentalism: An Exploration of the Challenge of Gently Accounting for Accountability, Transparency and Sustainability*, where he explores the possibility of employing sustainable-cost analysis as a shadow of current price-driven accounting information. The proposed system would be based on calculations of what inputs to an organisation's activities would cost if it were not to leave the planet worse off. This calculated cost could then be used to attach a 'value' to natural capital used in the production process. In the case of critical capital, sustainable cost is infinite. Gray suggests that these calculations are carried out in parallel to the existing accounting systems and reports, and the resulting costs are deducted from the conventional accounting profit to be expended in restoration of the biosphere.

An example of the application of these sorts of concepts is to be found in the recent annual accounts of the Dutch management consultancy company BSO/Origin, where an attempt has been made to quantify the damage to the environment in financial terms based on a theoretical calculation of the costs that would be incurred in repairing the damage back to a level where the natural eco-system is able to eliminate the residual effects. The 'net value withdrawn' calculated in this way gives an indication of the costs not taken into account in the financial statements but which are passed on to the next generation.

BSO/Origin's 1991 environmental accounts are effectively a form of value-added statement which show that the company added value of 377.3 million Dutch guilders but withdrew environmental value of 3.4 million Dutch guilders offset by some environmental expenditure (0.3 million Dutch guilders). Value added is a combination of personnel costs, depreciation, provisions, financial expenses, taxation and net profit/loss. Environmental value withdrawn came from natural gas consumption, electricity consumption, traffic by road, traffic by air, waste incineration, waste water and other waste. Because the company is a consultancy with its workforce highly mobile in their cars, the main adverse environmental effect is in respect of NO_x and CO_2 emissions from these cars costing an estimated 2.94 million Dutch guilders

The most crude aspect of the preparation of these accounts is the estimation of unit costs of energy consumption, transport, incineration of wastes and solid waste. BSO/Origin say they have adopted a pragmatic approach based on the marginal costs of the emission reduction measures in 'optimal' environmental circumstances. The assumption is that society takes environmental measures to the point where the marginal cost of those measures equals the marginal benefits. The accounts also only recognise the direct effects of the company's own activities and do not include indirect effects caused by third parties in the production of purchased raw materials.

With fundamental reservations like these the accounts are at best of academic interest only and are unlikely to be widely copied.

9

Taxation

9.1 Introduction

Business people like a stable operating environment. Whilst change is inevitable, and a whole new area of consultancy and training is growing rapidly to deal with what is now called change-management, they are not happy with recurring alterations to the rules of the business game. And nowhere is this more true than with respect to taxation. So the increasing likelihood of the use of various forms of fiscal and other economic instruments to help bring about environmental policy objectives may give company directors in general, and finance directors in particular, cause for concern.

The way in which taxation, levies, duties, etc., may be used in future, however, is by no means certain. The apparent political attractions of both raising revenue and cleaning up the environment that seemed so compelling in the early 1990s are now being looked at more sceptically. But the fact remains that by the end of the 1990s, and maybe sooner, there will be a number of green taxes in the UK, some of which may have a profound influence on business decisions. Indeed, it has been suggested that over the next few years there will be a gradual shift from taxing income and profits to taxing environmentally unsound products and processes as the main source of government income.

The reasons for this shift lie in the theoretical attractions of environmental taxation and other economic instruments. Whilst one of the main aims of this book is to be not only relevant but also practical, some words of theory are nevertheless required before turning to what is actually happening and what may happen in the future.

The main issues and developments will then be dealt with in a UK context but that necessarily includes Europe and the European Commission where there is probably more enthusiasm for the use of environmental taxation than anywhere else in the world. It should also not be overlooked that environmental taxes in the UK may affect the operation of free-market forces that can have knock-on effects with the UK's trading partners and the global economy generally.

9.2 In theory

The principal theoretical justification for taxing pollution is that it is an attempt to put a cost on what economists call the 'externalities' of pollution. By this they mean the otherwise unmeasured or unrecognised costs that a polluter imposes on other members of society by using, for example, the atmosphere and the world's water systems as a free means of disposing of unwanted waste products. Taxing this free use puts a cost on it that is then recognised in a company's product prices, etc., and which can be used by government to control the pollution. The economists argue that the objective of environmental tax policy is this cost recognition and the optimal policy is when the costs of pollution and the costs of controlling pollution are in balance.

The Institute of Fiscal Studies (IFS) (*Commentary* No 19, January 1990) recognises three key advantages of environmental taxes provided they are set at the right level. The first of these is that such taxes will often be more economically efficient than stopping polluting behaviour by direct regulation. The IFS uses the example of a farmer who finds using fertilizer on one field worthwhile in terms of higher crop yields even though the price reflects the cost of removing excess fertilizers from the water system raised by means of a tax or levy. Using fertilizer on another field is not worthwhile because lower yields do not justify it. The alternative approach of direct regulation might allow the farmer to use only a specified amount of fertilizer per acre which would mean that one field would have less fertilizer than the farmer needed and the other too much. As long as the tax was set at a level which made the price of the fertilizer reflect the economic costs of using it, therefore, it would allow more food to be grown than direct regulation and have the same consequences for the environment.

The second advantage identified is that environmental taxes are potentially an important revenue source and yet at the same time they improve economic efficiency. The economy benefits not only when government spends the money raised but also because the tax payer may change his polluting practices.

And the third advantage is that environmental taxes provide a continuous incentive for innovation to develop less polluting products or processes. Regulation on the other hand merely encourages the minimum necessary compliance.

The major disadvantage is that it is rarely feasible administratively to tax pollution directly. The purchase or use of inputs to the process generating the pollution might be the only possible tax points but the relationship between inputs and pollution is not always precise. Diesel engines are thought to be quite clean when well maintained but dirty when badly maintained. A tax on diesel fuel, therefore, would fail to discriminate between the two types of engines. A second major disadvantage is the need for the uniform application of environmental taxes across Europe or the World. Otherwise consumers may buy cheaper 'undesirable' imports in preference to more expensive local products. Serious trade distortions could result.

Taxation, however, is only one form of economic investment. Whilst it is the one that is probably best understood by most finance directors and company managers there are a wide range of other 'economic' or 'market-based' instruments that are being used increasingly. Their overall aim is to allow producers and consumers rather than regulators to decide how best to alter their demands in order to meet government-set environmental priorities. They include charges, subsidies, deposit/refund schemes, market creation and enforcement incentives. The most widely used at present are some form of charge, the proceeds of which are used to finance environmental expenditures. Most UK government priorities, however, are presently effected by using direct regulations and administrative controls.

9.3 In practice

So much for the general theory. What is happening in practice that UK businessmen should be aware of? There are not many examples around yet but those that there are warrant a mention before looking at the much wider range of environmental taxes and other economic instruments that have been proposed but not yet implemented.

In the UK, the most obvious use of green tax principles that would be immediately identified by the average consumer is the differential rate in the tax on hydrocarbon oils (petrol and diesel fuel) in favour of unleaded petrol. The differential was first introduced in 1987 and has been increased at subsequent budgets. Now that all new UK cars have to be capable of being run on lead-free petrol the switch away from lead-based petrol is almost complete. The effectiveness of a real price difference and a straightforward choice that is easy to explain and understand shows what can be done.

The second relatively recent example of the proposed 'green' use of taxation could be said to have been the plan to impose VAT on domestic fuel at the rate of 8% for 1994/1995 rising to the full standard rate of 17.5% for 1995/1996. The UK government argued that the increase would encourage every householder to look to the energy efficiency of his or her home and reduce fuel bills wherever possible. The full validity of this argument will not now be tested following the defeat of the Government's proposals for the second stage of the increase in November 1994.

The main counter-claim is that VAT applied in this way is a very blunt instrument and is probably regressive as low-income households which, according to the Gas Consumers Council spend some 13% of their income on fuel, are least able to respond to price signals. The political lobbying that took place during late 1993 and early 1994 resulted in a compensation scheme worth some £1.25 billion a year which compares with the £2.85 billion which might have been raised in a year when the tax was at its full rate. Taken together with lower energy prices encouraged by the gas and electricity industry regulators, the full potential effect of VAT on consumption is never likely to be realised. Perhaps some lessons about the future for environmental taxes can be learned from this experience?

Perhaps some lessons will also be learned in the future from Belgium which introduced a number of environmental taxes on a wide range of packaging and products containing hazardous substances in 1993. The Belgian aim is to set environmental taxes at a level that will bring about change. If a producer does not meet the standards required he will pay the appropriate tax thereby placing his products at a competitive disadvantage.

For throw-away beverage packaging, for example, the object is to stimulate reuse and to recycle the remaining packaging. By 1997, all Belgian drink containers will attract a tax of about 30p per litre bottle which producers will not have to pay if they raise the percentage of reusable soft drink bottles from 40% to 60% by 1997 and from 93% to 95% for beer. Producers are exempt if they set up a deposit/refund system for their packaging. Similar taxes have been introduced for paper, throw-away products such as razors, batteries, industrial packaging and pesticides. All products to which environmental taxes have been applied carry mandatory labels.

Turning now to the wider range of other economic instruments that are being applied to bring about environmental change, a review based on the categories identified in the UK government's 1990 White Paper, This Common Inheritance, is helpful. It covers a very wide range of instruments, which are beyond the scope of this chapter but, by their inclusion, illustrate the UK government's attitude.

Administrative controls—Although included here as an economic instrument these appear to be regulations in the conventional sense of the word. The White Paper states that they 'will for the foreseeable future remain at the heart of Britain's system of environmental control—just as they are in many other countries of the world'. Environmental taxation, then, was not a top priority.

Correcting market distortions—This too seems to stretch the definition of economic instrument to its limit in that this is said to be about 'making existing markets work better' by, for example, privatisation. It is claimed that privatisation of the water industry has brought into the open the scale of the investment needed—£28 billion (in 1989 prices) over 10 years—and borne by the customer. Taken together with the actions of the appropriate regulator to control prices, market transparency is said to play an important role in bringing about the environmental changes desired. The electricity supply industry and waste disposal activities are both included under this heading.

Charges to recover the costs of administration—Examples given in the White Paper include HMIP process licensing fees and the NRA's charges as a part of issuing discharge consents. The Paper does suggest, however, that 'higher charges related to the amount of pollution or of abstraction might be . . . worth considering for the longer term'.

Industry levies, product levies and deposit/refund schemes—These are defined as being charges imposed on the outputs of a homogeneous group of polluters and the proceeds devoted to the cost of clean-up or to expenditure to reduce the level of emissions within the group. They are used in France, Germany and The Netherlands, but only now are being considered for the UK. The proposal for a landfill tax described later comes into this category.

Charges on producers for damage to the environment—Charges such as these are intended to place on polluters the costs which their use of the environment imposes on the community as a whole. Companies affected are able to choose to use the environment at a given level and pay the charge, or to invest in new, less environmentally damaging, methods of production.

Environmental charges on products or materials—This sort of charge would be instead of a charge levied directly on producers and would, as in the Belgian examples already described, add to the price of materials used or products and services sold. Both a carbon/energy tax, as described below, and the differential tax charged on unleaded as opposed to leaded petrol already discussed, come under this heading.

Tradeable quotas—These can be used where a ceiling on total emissions has been set, either locally or nationally, and market mechanisms are then used to allocate the amounts making up the quota between plants or processes. Active consideration is currently being given in the UK for a scheme such as this for sulphur dioxide emissions and is described more fully later. The idea, however, has been well developed in the USA where, in early 1993, the Environmental Protection Agency granted permits to 110 of the country's largest producers of sulphur dioxide for the rights to emit 276 000 tonnes of sulphur dioxide into the air each year after 1995. The auction, carried out in March 1993, was conducted by the Chicago Board of Trade using sealed bids and a secondary market now exists and provides an economic alternative to pollution abatement expenditure. According to the *Financial Times* (31 March 1993), Illinois Power, a mid-west electricity utility that burns large amounts of high sulphur coal, has bought sulphur dioxide permits so as to enable it to build its financial reserves prior to buying more advanced technology when scrubbers are installed in its smokestacks in 1999.

Legal liability and schemes of private compensation—Again it might be argued that financial penalties for breaching the requirements of both criminal and civil law bear little relation to the sort of tax and economic instruments that are the subject of this chapter. The White Paper includes them, however, on the grounds that their existence influences behaviour in a similar way to the real or threatened payment of taxes. They have been dealt with fully in Chapter 4.

Subsidies and schemes of public compensation—This is the final category of economic instrument identified in the White Paper. Subsidies and compensation schemes do, where they exist, have some impact on environmental behaviour in the same way as taxes but they are not widely used. The only real exceptions are to be found in agriculture and with several environmental grant schemes, such as the Environmental Technology Innovation Scheme (ETIS), the DTI's Environmental Management Options Scheme (DEMOS) and EUROENVIRON, part of the EUREKA programme run in the UK by the DTI.

That ends the White Paper's list of so-called economic instruments. It is too wide ranging in some respects but does clearly illustrate the range of alternatives to direct regulation of which taxation is only one. But what of the future?

9.4 In the future

There are a number of specific proposals for environmental taxes being developed and discussed within the European Community generally and the UK specifically. Before looking at them however it is helpful to consider where such taxes fit in the political programmes of the main parties. Although the timing may vary and the emphasis may be different there are strong signs that none of the three main UK political parties will ignore environmental taxes in the years to come.

Perhaps the main reason for the relatively small number of existing environmental tax based measures in the mid 1990s is the apparent reluctance of the UK Conservative government to use them in spite of certain suggestions in 1992 that there would be a new presumption in favour of economic instruments instead of regulation. This is in contrast to many mainland European countries and the EC itself where the idea of shifting the burden of taxation away from labour and capital and onto pollution and resource consumption has widespread support. On the other hand, the Secretary of State for the Environment, John Gummer, said at the NatWest Lecture on 21 April 1994 that the aim of his government's policy had been:

> to shift the burden of taxation from earning to spending. In itself that is a necessary shift if we are to develop sustainability. To cast our taxes on expenditure in such a way that they also bring environmental benefits is clearly another example of the double dividend.

The Liberal Democrats are much more forthright. In a Green Paper entitled 'Taxing pollution, not people', published in September 1993, they set out their agenda. On the assumption that good ideas, wherever they come from, will eventually be picked up by the party in power it is worthwhile looking at the Liberal Democrats' views which are the most fully developed (or maybe just most publicly stated) of those of the three parties. The central message behind the Liberal Democrats' Green Paper is that environmental taxes would not increase the general tax burden but would replace existing taxes or be recycled to achieve environmental goals. Its main concern, however, is with the proposed EC carbon/energy tax which is described more fully below. The Paper supports the proposed tax in contrast to the UK government which has, as we will see, been a long-term opponent.

There are also many other ideas, not only concerning the carbon/energy tax proposal, but also other forms of tax which are worth mentioning. The list begins with the concept of conditionality—which the Liberal Democrats oppose—whereby the carbon/energy tax, for example, would not be introduced until other industrialised countries had taken similar measures. The Paper would also like to see the level of the tax raised and some of the proposed partial exemptions for major industrial energy consumers removed. These also include proposals for spending the money raised. Other ideas listed include a commitment to encourage local authorities to experiment with road pricing schemes in urban areas and a graduated vehicle excise duty to encourage purchases of more energy-efficient cars. No major increase in fuel tax is recommended other than as a result of the carbon tax. Finally, the Paper suggests that fertilizers and pesticides should be taxed at levels sufficient to 'cover the costs of treatment of polluted water and food' and that taxes on certain forms of packaging would also be introduced.

In contrast, the Labour Party is circumspect and whilst its July 1994 environmental programme introduces a number of new ideas it is almost silent on environmental taxes and economic instruments. It does restate its opposition, however, to the use of domestic energy taxes, including the proposed EC carbon/energy tax, because of the low price elasticity of demand for energy and the hardship they impose on many householders. In other respects, however, achieving the ambitious environmental targets set is almost certainly going to require some form of environmental taxation or levy should Labour win power.

It would be wrong, however, to leave this review of environmental taxes and economic instruments giving the impression that no changes are likely in the short term. There are several which warrant a mention beginning with the EC proposals for a carbon/energy tax that have been around in one form or another for several years and ending with a recent call for a timber tax. Only time will tell which of the list will eventually become a reality.

A carbon/energy tax

As long ago as June 1992 the EC put forward a proposed Directive for a combined carbon and energy tax. Its purpose is to reduce carbon dioxide (CO_2) emissions by encouraging both efficient use of energy and switching to less carbon intensive fuels where this is economic.

The proposal involves a tax with equal carbon and energy components. The energy component applies both to fossil fuels and to non-CO_2 emitting energy sources such as nuclear power but most sources of renewable energy are to be exempt. The tax is to be introduced gradually, starting at the equivalent of US$3 per barrel of oil and rising to US$10 per barrel seven years after introduction. At the latter rate the DTI suggests this will imply price rises for the average domestic user of over 15% for both gas and electricity and over 25% for coal and oil. For the average user in the manufacturing industries, price rises would be over 30% on electricity and gas oil, over 45% on gas, about 60% on fuel oil and 70% on coal. Petrol price rises will be under 10%.

With possible cost increases of this order of magnitude, it is perhaps not surprising that the EC proposes that the tax should only be implemented if other OECD countries have introduced similar taxes or measures with an equivalent financial impact. It also proposes a number of other mechanisms aimed at protecting businesses which might be damaged by imports from non-OECD countries without similar taxes or measures.

In the light of all this it is perhaps not surprising that the UK government has resisted the proposals consistently since they were first made and finally announced that it would not accept them in May 1993. In fact the UK is not completely alone because France is still demanding that the tax should fall only on carbon so as to protect its nuclear industry while Spain, Portugal, Eire and Greece maintain that their energy consumption must be allowed to grow so that their economies can catch up with the rest of the European Community.

In spite of many political efforts to resolve the deadlock no substantive progress has been made but lessons, economic and fiscal as well as political, have been learned. It is not impossible that some form of less ambitious tax might find favour in due course. Indeed, without some such tax it may be almost impossible for the EC to achieve its commitment under the 1992 UN Convention on Climate Change to return its CO_2 emissions to 1990 levels by 2000.

Sulphur dioxide permit trading

The promise of some form of UK trading system in surplus emission quotas has, like the proposed EC carbon/energy tax, been around for at least two years. The UK government's intention to introduce a system was first announced in its 1992 progress report on the 1990 White Paper but real action only began in March 1994 when a seminar on the idea took place. The Department of the Environment (DoE) and representatives from industry were present according to *ENDS Report 230*, March 1994.

The UK government had two ideas in mind when it first proposed a permit trading or quota switching system in 1992. The first was to achieve the SO_2 emission targets laid down in the 1988 EC Directive on large combustion plants and the second was to encourage maximum emission reductions at those plants contributing most to acid rain damage. The 1988 Directive, however, is being superseded by a new Europe-wide UN protocol on sulphur emissions requiring the UK to cut its SO_2 emissions by 80% by 2010 from a baseline of 1980 compared with only 60% by 2003 in the Directive. There may also be difficulties in introducing a system of weighting or exchange rates in the quota system to reflect the capacity of an individual plant to cause acid rain damage, in reconciling a permit trading system with the regulation of SO_2 emissions from large bodies under integrated pollution control and in deciding on whether or not switching should be allowed across the whole of the UK or restricted geographically or by industrial sector.

At this stage the difficulties seem to exceed the benefits—in practical terms at any rate. Just as in the case of a carbon/energy tax, however, SO_2 permit trading is now on the agenda. The question is more 'when' rather than 'if' it will be introduced.

Road transport taxes

Perhaps changes in road transport taxes to bring about environmental policy changes will be easier to achieve than either a carbon/energy tax or a system of SO_2 permit trading. After all, real progress has been made already with the introduction of differential tax rates to encourage the use of unleaded petrol.

But there is more progress to be made and three principal reasons why. In the first place there are already significant taxes on motor vehicles so there is no need to take on the political and administrative problems of introducing a wholly new tax. Second, road transport is seen to be a major source of the 'externalities' described at the beginning of this chapter. These are basically costs which are not subject to the price mechanism and include such things as road congestion as well as pollution. Third, there is every sign that there will be a further significant rise in road traffic over the next few years which is bound to increase public awareness of the problems associated with road transport and an acceptance that taxes are a way of dealing with them.

At present there are two major UK road taxes—those on hydrocarbon oils (petrol and diesel fuel with a lower rate for unleaded petrol) and vehicle excise duty. In addition, VAT is charged on the duty as well as the cost of the product. Some two-thirds of the cost of a gallon of petrol is accounted for already by one form of tax or another. So what is the scope for further increasing or altering taxes such as these to promote the greening of road transport?

There are several ways in which this might be done although there are no immediate plans to introduce any of them. The first is to raise the level of duty on petrol so as to either encourage vehicles that use less fuel or to encourage owners to use them less. A second way might be to use the vehicle excise duty to discriminate in favour of smaller engines. Increasing petrol duty bears as heavily on rural residents who have high mileages with little scope for alternative use of public transport. Increasing vehicle excise duty on larger engined cars would help fuel economy without taxing high-mileage car users more heavily than other car users.

A third way might be to introduce some form of road pricing which is now technically possible if in-vehicle microprocessors and sensors are used. Differential pricing policies could have significant effects on the levels of road usage and levels of pollution. And finally the introduction of some form of CO_2-based purchase tax or an annual tax based on CO_2 emission per kilometre is already under active consideration by the EC. Building a consensus about the way forward among EC Member States, however, is likely to prove difficult.

A landfill levy

Another form of economic instrument which, to many people's surprise, will be introduced in 1996, is some form of landfill levy. The exact details of the levy are not known at the time of writing but they will no doubt draw heavily on the independent research commissioned by the DoE and published by HMSO in late 1993.

The underlying aim of a levy on the use of landfill for waste disposal is to discourage it on the grounds that when the externalities of unpriced environmental costs and benefits are quantified, landfills cost between £1 and £4 per tonne of waste in comparison with net environmental benefits of some £4 per tonne from waste incineration. It has been suggested that a levy could be imposed at £5 per tonne of waste. One idea was to use the estimated £500 million a year raised in this way for spending on environmental objectives such as support for recycling or remediation of contaminated land but the UK Government's announcement about the levy, made in November 1994, says that the money will be used to cut taxes on jobs. Nevertheless such hypothecation is often discussed in the context of environmental taxation of one form or another.

At present, the proposal for a landfill levy is the subject of much debate both internally at the DoE and externally through organisations such as the National Association of Waste Disposal Contractors. A key area for discussion is the level of confidence that can be applied to the quantitative results of the research not least because they take no account of local disamenities caused by either landfills or incinerators.

The research also identified methane emissions as the single most important externality associated with landfill. But some producers of landfill waste argue that their wastes contribute little or nothing in this way. They would want to be exempted, at least in part, from any levy which might make it much more complex to administer. There is clearly scope for much debate before the proposal is put in place.

A groundwater clean-up levy

Another form of levy that is also discussed from time to time and for which there appears to be a real need would be a charge on companies using polluting chemicals which find their way into groundwater. There may be real practical problems in devising such a scheme but it has been noted in two 1993 reports from the British Geological Survey as a way of raising a fund for the NRA to pay for groundwater pollution investigations, clean-ups and prosecutions through the Courts.

Under Section 161 of the Water Resources Act 1991, the NRA has the powers to intervene to remedy pollution of groundwater and, most importantly, to seek to recover the costs from the landowner. In practice, however, the NRA has no budget for remediation and is unable to spend what are sometimes the large sums of money needed—even if there is a good chance of recovering the costs involved through the Courts. It has asked the Government for funds to do this but has so far been refused. Perhaps a levy is the way forward.

Recycling credits

Before leaving this brief review of various actual and proposed forms of environmental taxes, levies, etc., a mention should be made of the use of credits (as opposed to charges) as a means of encouraging the implementation of environmental policy. The best example, of which there is now several years of experience, is the use of credits or payments made to collectors of recyclable waste by Waste Disposal Authorities (WDAs).

Recycling credits were introduced on 1 April 1992 under Section 52 of the Environmental Protection Act 1990 and represent the net savings in disposal costs of removing materials from the waste stream so as to recycle them. Payments by WDAs to Waste Collection Authorities (WCAs) are mandatory but at the WDAs discretion in the case of third parties such as commercial recyclers and voluntary groups. They are based, since April 1994, on the most expensive route for disposal of a WDA's waste, having been at half that level until then.

Whether or not the idea is bringing about an increase in recycling activity is far from certain, but it may be that the higher level of payments from April 1994 will make an impact that the DoE's earlier research showed to be uncertain. There has also been controversy over the way in which credits are passed on to third parties. The DoE's research showed that waste merchants and the secondary material industry had cut the prices they would pay in order to get at the value of the credits.

A timber tax

Finally, a word is needed about EC attitudes to environmental taxes and in particular those of the EC Environment Commissioner Paleokrassas, who appears to see them having a central role. In January 1994 he suggested that a tax could be introduced to discriminate between timber from virgin and cultivated forests and might be applied to both imports and wood from European sources.

Whilst superficially attractive, a little further thought reveals a number of potential problems not least in relation to GATT and claims that such a tax would be protectionist as well as actually reducing incentives for sustainable timber management.

This was the line taken by the International Institute for Environment and Development which argues that, in the short term, a tax would cut timber-producing countries' earnings which might then encourage that country to increase timber exports to countries not imposing a tax so as to maintain its foreign exchange earnings. In the longer term a tax would cut producers' profitability and might encourage them to convert forests, both cultivated and virgin, to other uses. To a large extent this is speculation but it illustrates how environmental taxes and other related economic instruments might have unwarranted and unforeseen consequences not only at home but elsewhere in the world.

In spite of all these practical problems, there is every sign that green taxes in one form or another will arrive soon. If they bring about better and more sensitive environmental management of the economy they could be attractive so long as they replace, and not add to, some existing forms of taxation, are administratively straightforward to operate and are fair. The challenge for UK business is to take a positive and constructive part in the debates locally, nationally and internationally.

Perhaps the best summary of the requirements of European business in those matters, and an appropriate way of ending this chapter, is provided by a statement from the International Chamber of Commerce on The Use of Economic and Fiscal Instruments in Environmental Policy (April 1992) in which it emphasises that

> economic and fiscal instruments should not be seen as a universal panacea. They should only be considered on a case-by-case basis, taking into account the complex nature of the particular environmental problems and the various markets where such instruments will play their role.

The ICC then goes on to say that green taxes, or, in its words, economic and fiscal instruments, should only be used in environmental policy if it is reasonable to expect that they will be really effective from an environmental point of view, that they will not degenerate into another method of collecting additional budgetary resources for governments, that they do not impair the internal or external competitiveness of industry, that equivalent provisions should impact on all other sectors in addition to the business sector and that they are cost-effective having regard to both the yield and the cost.

If these requirements are met, UK business will have little cause to complain but, as has been seen, doing so is going to be far from easy.

10

The Way Forward

This book is written for finance directors, accountants and financial auditors. It should also be of interest to a wider business audience who want to look at the financial aspects of the environmental issues affecting UK business in the mid-1990s. It is highly eclectic and has passed over briefly, or left out altogether, some of the environmental concerns that are widely reported in the media. But that is part of the problem—the 'environment' is so broad a concept that it sometimes seems to cover every aspect of human life on Earth.

The environmental way forward for the rest of the 1990s for the financial community, however, is becoming clearer and more focused. Legislation and regulation are the main driving forces. Demands for reliable environmental management systems, hard financial data and guidance on what to say and how to say it to the outside world are also increasing. The financial community is well placed to respond.

Financial management systems, internal controls and their audit are normally relatively easily adapted to deal with environmental requirements, as are annual reports and accounts in reporting to shareholders and the outside world. External financial accounting and auditing standards too can be added to or clarified without undue difficulty to meet the growing demands for environmental information.

There are also important emerging policy areas such as the recognition, measurement and allocation of responsibility for environmental liabilities which need proper input from the financial community. New concepts for green taxes and related economic instruments also need that input to ensure that they are administratively practical and well thought through.

The way forward, therefore, is for the accountancy profession to get its act together so as to provide the leadership necessary. The wider business community and government increasingly need guidance from the profession and the profession has a large commercial opportunity if it is prepared to seize it. Providing high quality, professionally managed and properly regulated environmental auditing and reporting services represent a major long term opportunity for the accounting profession.

Appendices

Appendix A

UNCED 1992: Agenda 21 chapter headings

1. Preamble

Section I, Social and economic dimensions
2. International co-operation to accelerate sustainable development in developing countries and related domestic policies
3. Combating poverty
4. Changing consumption patterns
5. Demographic dynamics and sustainability
6. Protecting and promoting human health conditions
7. Promoting sustainable human settlement development
8. Integrating environment and development in decision-making

Section II, Conservation and management of resources for development
9. Protection of the atmosphere
10. Integrated approach to the planning and management of land resources
11. Combating deforestation
12. Managing fragile ecosystems: combating desertification and drought
13. Managing fragile ecosystems: sustainable mountain development
14. Promoting sustainable agriculture and rural development
15. Conservation of biological diversity
16. Environmentally sound management of biotechnology

17. Protection of the oceans, all kinds of seas, including enclosed and semi-enclosed seas, and coastal areas and the protection, rational use and development of their living resources
18. Protection of the quality and supply of freshwater resources: application of integrated approaches to the development, management and use of water resources
19. Environmentally sound management of toxic chemicals, including prevention of illegal international traffic in toxic and dangerous products
20. Environmentally sound management of hazardous wastes, including prevention of illegal international traffic in hazardous wastes
21. Environmentally sound management of solid wastes and sewage-related issues
22. Safe and environmentally sound management of radioactive wastes

Section III, Strengthening the role of major groups
23. Preamble
24. Global action for women towards sustainable and equitable development
25. Children and youth in sustainable development
26. Recognising and strengthening the role of indigenous people and their communities
27. Strengthening the role of non-governmental organisations: partners for sustainable development
28. Local authorities' initiatives in support of Agenda 21
29. Strengthening the role of workers and their trade unions
30. Strengthening the role of business and industry
31. Scientific and technological community
32. Strengthening the role of farmers

Section IV, Means of implementation
33. Financial resources and mechanisms
34. Environmentally sound technology; transfer, co-operation and capacity-building
35. Science for sustainable development
36. Promoting education, public awareness and training
37. National mechanisms and international co-operation for capacity-building in developing countries
38. International institutional arrangements
39. International legal instruments and mechanisms
40. Information for decision-making

Separate item, Forest principles

Appendix B

UK Ethical and Environmental Funds

	Launch date	Fund size in March 1994
Abbey Ethical Trust	September 1987	£24.2m
Abtrust Ethical Fund	September 1992	£1.3m
Acorn Ethical Unit Trust	December 1989	£4.0m
Allchurches Amity Fund	March 1988	£19.8m
CIS Environ Trust	May 1990	£28.7m
Clerical Medical Evergreen Trust	February 1990	£16.7m
Co-Operative Bank Ethical Unit Trust	November 1993	£12.2m
Credit Suisse Fellowship Trust	July 1986	£5.7m
CU Environmental Exempt Pension Fund	December 1989	£10.0m
Eagle Star Environmental Opportunities Trust	June 1989	£14.4m
Equitable Ethical Trust	January 1994	£15.9m
Ethical Investment Fund (Bromidge & Partners)	January 1986	£1.4m
Fidelity UK Growth Trust	June 1985	£100.9m
Framlington Health Fund	April 1987	£12.8m
Friends Provident Stewardship Income Trust	October 1987	£49.3m
Friends Provident Stewardship Pension Fund	June 1984	£153.8m
Friends Provident Stewardship Unit Trust	June 1984	£168.4m
Friends Provident North American Stewardship	October 1987	£5.3m
Henderson Green PEP	September 1991	£7.0m
HFS Green Chip Fund	November 1989	£13.5m
Jupiter Merlin Ecology Fund	April 1988	£14.1m
Merlin International Green Investment Trust	December 1989	£28.9m
NM Conscience Fund	September 1987	£12.3m
NPI Global Care Unit Trust	August 1991	£7.6m
Scottish Equitable Ethical Pension Fund	April 1988	£13.3m
Scottish Equitable Ethical Unit Trust	April 1989	£14.1m
Skandia Ethical Selection Life Fund	February 1992	£3.2m
Skandia Ethical Selection Pension Fund	February 1992	£0.9m
Sovereign Ethical Fund	May 1989	£9.6m
Sun Life Global Management Ecological Fund	January 1993	DM7.2m
TSB Environmental Investor Fund	June 1989	£24.7m

Source: Ethical Investment Research Service

Appendix C

EC Eco-management and Audit Regulation: environmental management systems requirements

Annex 1 (B) to the EC Eco-Management and Audit Regulation requires that a company's environmental management system be designed, implemented and maintained in such a way as to ensure the fulfilment of the requirements defined below:

(1) Environmental policy, objectives and programmes

The establishment and periodical review and revision as appropriate, of the company's environmental policy, objectives and programmes for the site, at the highest appropriate management level.

(2) Organisation and personnel

Responsibility and authority
  Definition and documentation of responsibility, authority and interrelations of key personnel who manage, perform and monitor work affecting the environment
Management representative
  Appointment of a management representative having authority and responsibility for ensuring that the management system is implemented and maintained.
Personnel, communication and training
  Ensuring among personnel, at all levels, awareness of:

1. the importance of compliance with the environmental policy and objectives, and with the requirements applicable under the management system established;
2. the potential environmental effects of their work activities and the environmental benefits of improved performance;
3. their roles and responsibilities in achieving compliance with the environmental policy and objectives, and with the requirements of the management system;
4. the potential consequences of departure from the agreed operating procedures.

Identifying training needs, and providing appropriate training for all personnel whose work may have a significant effect upon the environment.

The company shall establish and maintain procedures for receiving, documenting and responding to communications (internal and external) from relevant interested parties concerning its environmental effects and management.

(3) Environmental effects

Environmental effects evaluation and registration
Examining and assessing the environmental effects of company's activities at the site, and compiling a register of those identified as significant. This shall include, where appropriate, consideration of:

(a) controlled and uncontrolled emissions to atmosphere;
(b) controlled and uncontrolled discharges to water or sewers;
(c) solid and other wastes, particularly hazardous wastes;
(d) contamination of land;
(e) use of land, water, fuels and energy, and other natural resources;
(f) discharge of thermal energy, noise, odour, dust, vibration and visual impact;
(g) effects on specific parts of the environment and ecosystems.

This shall include effects arising, or likely to arise, as consequences of:

1. normal operating conditions;
2. abnormal operating conditions;
3. incidents, accidents and potential emergency situations;
4. past activities, current activities and planned activities.

Register of legislative, regulatory and other policy requirements
The company shall establish and maintain procedures to record all legislative, regulatory and other policy requirements pertaining to the environmental aspects of its activities, products and services.

(4) Operational control

Establishment of operating procedures
Identification of functions, activities and processes which affect, or have the potential to affect, the environment, and are relevant to the company's policy and objectives.
Planning and control of such functions, activities and processes, and with particular attention to:

(a) documented work instructions defining the manner of conducting the activity, whether by the company's own employees or by others acting on its behalf. Such instructions shall be prepared for situations

in which the absence of such instructions could result in infringement of the environmental policy;
(b) procedures dealing with procurement and contracted activities, to ensure that suppliers and those acting on the company's behalf comply with the company's environmental policy as it relates to them;
(c) monitoring and control of relevant process characteristics (e.g. effluent streams and waste disposal);
(d) approval of planned processes and equipment;
(e) criteria for performance, which shall be stipulated in written standards.

Monitoring

Monitoring by the company of meeting the requirements established by the company's environmental policy, programme and management system for the site; and for establishing and maintaining records of the results.

For each relevant activity or area, this implies:

(a) identifying and documenting the monitoring information to be obtained;
(b) specifying and documenting the monitoring procedures to be used;
(c) establishing and documenting acceptance criteria and the action to be taken when results are unsatisfactory;
(d) assessing and documenting the validity of previous monitoring information when monitoring systems are found to be malfunctioning.

Non-compliance and corrective action

Investigation and corrective action, in case of non-compliance with company's environmental policy, objectives or standards, in order to:

(a) determine the cause;
(b) draw up a plan of action;
(c) initiate preventive actions, to a level corresponding to the risks encountered;
(d) apply controls to ensure that any preventive actions taken are effective;
(e) record any changes in procedures resulting from corrective action.

(5) Environmental management documentation records

Establishing documentation with a view to:

(a) present in a comprehensive way the environmental policy, objectives, and programme;
(b) document the key roles and responsibilities;

(c) describe the interactions of system elements.

Establishing records in order to demonstrate compliance with the requirements of the environmental management system, and to record the extent to which planned environmental objectives have been met.

(6) Environmental audits

Management, implementation and review of a systematic and periodical programme concerning:

(a) whether or not environmental management activities conform to the environmental programme, and are implemented effectively;
(b) the effectiveness of the environmental management system in fulfilling the company's environmental policy.

Appendix D

UK Statements of Financial Auditing Standards

Introductory matters

    010 Scope and authority of APB pronouncements (May 1993)

Responsibility

    100 Objective and general principles (ED June 1993)
    110 Fraud and error (ED October 1993)
    120 Consideration of law and regulations (ED October 1993)
    130 Going concern (ED December 1983)
    140 Engagement letters (ED November 1993)
    150 Post-balance sheet events (ED August 1993)
    160 Other information in documents containing audited financial statements (ED August 1993)
    170 Comparative figures (not yet issued)

Planning, control and recording

    200 Planning (ED April 1993)
    210 Knowledge of the business (ED November 1993)
    220 Audit materiality (ED August 1993)
    230 Documentation (ED April 1993)
    240 Quality control for audit work (ED August 1993)

Accounting systems and internal control

    300 Audit risk assessment (ED August 1993)
    310 Auditing in an EDP environment (not yet issued)

Evidence

    400 Audit evidence (ED April 1993)
    410 Analytical procedures (ED April 1993)
    420 Audit of accounting estimates (ED April 1993)
    430 Audit sampling (ED August 1993)
    440 Management representations (ED August 1993)
    450 First year engagements—opening balances (ED November 1993)
    460 Related parties (not yet issued)
    470 Review of financial statements (ED June 1993)

Using the work of others

500 Considering the work of internal audit (ED June 1993)
510 The relationship between principal auditors and other auditors (ED June 1993)
520 Using the work of an expert

Reporting

600 The auditors' report on financial statements (May 1993)
610 Reports to directors or management (ED November 1993)
620 The auditors' right and duty to report to regulators in the financial sector (March 1994)

Audit engagements other than of financial statements

(Series 700—not yet issued)

Particular industries and sectors

(Series 800—not yet issued)

Glossary of terms

(not yet issued)

Source: Auditing Practices Board: Revision of Auditing Standards and Guidelines

Appendix E

UK Financial Reporting and Accounting Standards

Financial Reporting Standards

1   Cash flow statements
2   Accounting for subsidiary undertakings
3   Reporting financial performance
3A Amendment to FRS 3 in respect of insurance companies
4   Capital instruments
5   Reporting the substance of transactions
6   Acquisitions and mergers
7   Fair values in acquisition accounting

Statements of Standard Accounting Practice

1   Accounting for associated companies
2   Disclosure of accounting policies
3   Earnings per share
4   Accounting for government grants
5   Accounting for value added tax
8   The treatment of taxation under the imputation system in the accounts of companies
9   Stocks and long-term contracts
12 Accounting for depreciation
13 Accounting for research and development
15 Accounting for deferred tax
15A Amendment to SSAP 15: Accounting for deferred tax
17 Accounting for post-balance sheet events
18 Accounting for contingencies
19 Accounting for investment properties
20 Foreign currency translation
21 Accounting for leases and hire purchase contracts
22 Accounting for goodwill
23 Accounting for acquisitions and mergers
24 Accounting for pension costs
25 Segmental reporting
26 Interim statement—consolidated accounts

Urgent issues task force

3   Treatment of goodwill on disposal of a business
4   Presentation of long-term debtors in current assets
5   Transfers from current assets to fixed assets
6   Accounting for post-retirement benefits other than pensions
7   True and fair override disclosures
9   Accounting for operations in hyper inflationary economies

Accounting Standards Board Statements

Early adoption of Financial Reporting Exposure Drafts
Exemption of prior transactions from the provisions of accounting standards
Application of UITF abstracts
Operating and financial review

Accounting Recommendations

The interpretation of 'material' in relation to accounts
   The determination of realised profits and disclosure of distributable profits in the context of the Companies Acts 1948–1981
   Valuations of company property assets and their disclosure in directors' reports or accounts of companies
   Accounting for goods sold subject to reservation of title
   Trust accounts
   Trustee Investments Act 1961
   Disclosure of accounting policies—effect of introduction of paragraph 36A of schedule 4 to the Companies Act 1985
   FRAG 3/93: Provisions for claims in the financial statements of non-life insurance companies

Statements of Recommended Practice

Explanatory foreword
Pension scheme accounts
Accounting by charities

Source: *Members' Handbook 1994* Volume II. Institute of Chartered Accountants in England and Wales (amended as necessary for subsequent pronouncements)

Appendix F

ICC Business Charter for Sustainable Development: principles for environmental management

(1) Corporate priority

To recognise environmental management as among the highest corporate priorities and as a key determinant to sustainable development; to establish policies, programmes and practices for conducting operations in an environmentally sound manner.

(2) Integrated management

To integrate these policies, programmes and practices fully into each business as an essential element of management in all its functions.

(3) Process of improvement

To continue to improve corporate policies, programmes and environmental performance, taking into account technical developments, scientific understanding, consumer needs and community expectations, with legal regulations as a starting point; and to apply the same environmental criteria internationally.

(4) Employee education

To educate, train and motivate employees to conduct their activities in an environmentally responsible manner.

(5) Prior assessment

To assess environmental impacts before starting a new activity or project and before decommissioning a facility or leaving a site.

(6) Products and services

To develop and provide products or services that have no undue environmental impact and are safe in their intended use, that are efficient in their consumption of energy and natural resources, and that can be recycled, reused, or disposed of safely.

(7) Customer advice

To advise, and where relevant educate, customers, distributors and the public in the safe use, transportation, storage and disposal of products provided; and to apply similar considerations to the provision of services.

(8) Facilities and operations

To develop, design and operate facilities and conduct activities taking into consideration the efficient use of energy and materials, the sustainable use of renewable resources, the minimisation of adverse environmental impact and waste generation, and the safe and responsible disposal of residual wastes.

(9) Research

To conduct or support research on the environmental impacts of raw materials, products, processes, emissions and wastes associated with the enterprise and on the means of minimising such adverse impacts.

(10) Precautionary approach

To modify the manufacture, marketing or use of products or services or the conduct of activities, consistent with scientific and technical understanding, to prevent serious or irreversible environmental degradation.

(11) Contractors and suppliers

To promote the adoption of these principles by contractors acting on behalf of the enterprise, encouraging and, where appropriate, requiring improvements in their practices to make them consistent with those of the enterprise; and to encourage the wider adoption of these principles by suppliers.

(12) Emergency preparedness

To develop and maintain, where significant hazards exist, emergency preparedness plans in conjunction with the emergency services, relevant authorities and the local community, recognising potential transboundary impacts.

(13) Transfer of technology

To contribute to the transfer of environmentally sound technology and management methods throughout the industrial and public sectors.

(14) Contributing to the common effort

To contribute to the development of public policy and to business, governmental and intergovernmental programmes and educational initiatives that will enhance environmental awareness and protection.

(15) Openness to concerns

To foster openness and dialogue with employees and the public, anticipating and responding to their concerns about the potential hazards and impacts of operations, products, wastes or services, including those of transboundary or global significance.

(16) Compliance and reporting

To measure environmental performance; to conduct regular environmental audits and assessments of compliance with company requirements, legal requirements and these principles; and periodically to provide appropriate information to the Board of Directors, shareholders, employees, the authorities and the public.

Appendix G

Environmental Action Checklists

(Based on *Your Business and the Environment—an executive guide*. Business in the Environment, 1990)

The basic questions

Does your business . . .

- Adopt and aim to apply the principles of sustainable development—that is, development which meets the needs of the present, without compromising the abilities of future generations to meet their own needs?
- Strive to adopt the highest available environmental standards in all countries in which it operates?
- Adopt a total cradle-to-grave assessment and responsibility for its products and services?
- Aim to minimise the use of all materials, supplies and energy, wherever possible using renewable or recyclable materials and components?
- Minimise waste produced in all parts of its business aiming for waste-free processes wherever possible?
- Expect similar environmental standards to its own from all third parties—suppliers, vendors, contractors?
- Publicise its environmental position annually, preferably in its annual report, including a statement by independent auditors?
- Aim to include environmental considerations in investment decisions?
- Assess on a continuous basis the environmental impact of all its operations?
- Assist in developing solutions to environmental problems as well as supporting the development of public policies?
- Some action checklists to help you answer these questions are attached.

Performance checklist

- Are the relevant external standards and legal requirements being met?
- Are any particular products or processes at risk, whether from potential legislation, consumer pressure, or through sensitivity to energy or material costs?
- Could progress be ensured by setting short, medium and long-term targets to improve environmental performance, and meet company policies and objectives?

- Do environmental issues provide new opportunities, or open new markets?
- How do technology and production processes compare to best available techniques (BAT)?
- Is an audit or review by an external organisation appropriate?
- What monitoring procedures are to be used?
- How are environmental protection procedures and specifications to be enforced? What are the penalties for not meeting standards?
- What contingency plans are in place for accidents? Are these practised?
- Do all managers have environmental responsibilities and objectives?
- Are all operations reviewed and assessed?

  Consider:
  - Site locations and design
  - Buildings
  - Office environment, furniture and supplies, catering products
  - Production processes
  - Emissions—air, water, land
  - Marketing
  - Distribution and transport
  - Finance and investment
  - Community relations
  - Education and training

- Are there plans to repeat the self assessments or audits on a regular basis, for example, yearly?
- Are there plans to up-date regularly your policies and actions?

Standards checklist

- How do you intend to keep abreast of legislative plans, at international, European and UK levels?
- Do you understand, and where possible implement, the best available technology?
- Are you proactive, adopting the precautionary principle, or do you wait for standards to be imposed?
- Do you aim to improve on, and go beyond, existing standards? Could you set company standards in areas of operation where no external standards already exist?
- Have you considered sharing your technology and processes, to raise general standards of operation (both nationally and internationally)?
- Are you tracking current thinking and scientific advances, and anticipating potential changes in standards required?

- Have you identified the highest, most stringent environmental standards available worldwide?
- Are you implementing the highest standards in all countries of operation, irrespective of local requirements?
- Could you act as an agent of change, encouraging others to raise their standards?

Product checklist

- Is the effect of a product on the environment, from production to use through to disposal, considered at the design stage?
- Are products designed with recyclability in mind, for example, to enable recycling of components?
- Does the product damage the environment in which it is used?
- What impact does production have on the environment?
- Have you examined the technology used in production processes?
- Could cleaner production methods be used?
- Are products designed to facilitate disposal? Are safe disposal instructions or an end-of-life disposal service provided?
- What testing procedures are used? Do these impact adversely on the environment?
- Is built-in obsolescence avoided?
- Are environmental impact considerations built into all product feasibility assessments at initial business case review?
- Does the product damage health?

Materials and supplies checklist

- Do you record materials used in all parts of your business?

    Consider:
    - Building materials, for example insulating, lighting, paints.
    - Office environment, for example furniture, cleaning supplies, paper, files, glues, correction-fluid.
    - Catering.
    - Production.
    - Packaging.

- Are the materials used renewable resources?
- Are materials reusable? If not, are re-usable alternatives available?
- Are materials over specified? Could lower grade or waste materials be used instead?
- Are components recyclable?
- Is packaging excessive?
- What packaging materials are used—are they reusable or recyclable?

- Can products be reduced in size, or reshaped, to minimise materials and packaging?
- Are by-products recycled or used elsewhere?
- Are disposal requirements considered before introducing any material?
- Are particularly hazardous materials used? Could they be replaced?
- How are regulations on materials and supplies enforced?

Energy checklist

- How much energy is used in each area of the business? Is it continually assessed and reviewed?
- Can the use of fossil fuels be reduced? Are alternative renewable sources available?
- Are buildings, processes and appliances as energy efficient as possible?
- Could excess heat be re-used as energy? Is there a possibility of using combined heat and power?
- Could energy be saved by:
  - Reviewing the physical construction of buildings to reduce heat loss?
  - Insulating external walls and roofs? Installing double glazing?
  - Fitting thermostats or time controls?
  - Installing more energy efficient lighting?
  - Switching off lights and equipment when not required?
  - Turning off heating in unused rooms?
  - Installing draught lobbies, fitting automatic door closure devices or draught-proof external doors and windows?
  - Improving the insulation of boilers and pipework?
  - Improving the maintenance of boilers and plant?
  - Replacing or upgrading energy consuming equipment and controls to make it more efficient?
  - Installing heat recovery devices in ventilation systems?
  - Using free cooling from outside air when conditions allow?
- Could a total Building Energy Management system be justified?

Water checklist

- How much water is used in each part of the business?
- Have you considered separating your water supply by quality, i.e. drinking, service, industrial?
- Could you install water treatment plants to recycle water?
- Could water be saved by:
  - Placing flow restricters on taps?

- Repairing leaking pipes more quickly?
- Installing thermometers, flowmeters, and flow restricters wherever feasible?
- Installing re-cooling plants instead of using the water supply?
- Adjusting the quantities needed for WCs, showers and rinsing baths?

Waste checklist

- What waste is produced and how is it handled?
- Could waste be totally eliminated? Could production designers be given a 'no drain' objective to encourage elimination of waste? Could production processes be redesigned to minimise waste at source?
- Are useful substances recovered for re-use?
- Have you explored the potential for recycling or reprocessing the waste, or transforming it into harmless substances or energy?
- Have you explored the possibility of participating in waste-exchange schemes (either by selling your waste to other businesses to use as raw materials in their production processes, or by buying waste in for your own use)?
- Have you reviewed spillage procedures for environmental impact (as well as health and safety)?
- Do you re-circulate water where possible?
- Is extra waste being generated by mixing recyclable materials with non-recyclable?
- Do you enable the recycling of office waste, such as the re-use of scrap paper? Have you considered, for example, a colour-coded system for waste bins to differentiate types of waste?
- Have you reviewed alternatives for waste disposal?
- Do you actually ensure the safe disposal of your waste?
- Is your intended disposal facility licensed to deal with your waste?

Suppliers/contractors/vendors checklist

- Have you established environmental standards, and the criteria by which they will be assessed, for the third parties involved with your business?
- How are those standards to be applied?
    - Will you give preference to those who meet standards?
    - Should some standards be mandatory, others merely preferable?
    - Over what timescales will the standards be introduced?

- How can you best collect environmental information from suppliers— covering their products, materials, processes and overall company policies and operations?
- How can you best collect information on alternatives available?
- Can you offer financial or technical assistance to suppliers to help them raise standards?
- Should you impose compliance auditing on suppliers, contractors and vendors?

Communications checklist

- Consider communicating
  - Company policies
  - Plans and targets for improving environmental performance
  - Content and environmental impact of product
  - Investment in environmental improvement
- Consider communicating to and consulting with
  - Employees
  - Customers
  - Suppliers
  - Shareholders
  - Local communities
  - Industry bodies
  - Environmental groups
  - Government
  - General public
- Could you publish information on performance and plans in your annual report?
- Could your packaging or vehicles carry an environmental message?
- How will you restrict PR statements on environmental activity unless they are thoroughly researched and consistent with actual actions?
- Is your environmental labelling relevant, accurate and not misleading?

People/organisation checklist

- Does a member of the board have responsibility for company environmental performance?
- Is environmental awareness training provided?
- Is more detailed education provided where necessary?
- Do employees have environmental objectives and responsibilities?
- Could suggestion schemes be established relating to environmental activities?

- Is environmental education a part of management training?
- Are time, money, and facilities made available to enable employee participation in voluntary environmental activities?
- Is information on the environmental position of the company included in recruitment material?

Community affairs checklist

- What positive environmental contributions could be made to the local community?
- Is it possible to provide information to the local community and consult on plans in advance?
- Are local groups involved in planning and implementation where feasible?
- Do you liaise with the environmental groups, local authorities, etc., on a regular basis?
- Could company sites be used for local environmental activities?
- Is care and consideration given to the external appearance of sites and buildings, and to the preservation of natural habitats?
- Could the local community make use of company facilities, e.g. waste recycling?

Transport checklist

- Is it possible to provide incentives for your employees to minimise the use of cars, by switching to foot, bicycle, public transport? (Could you encourage this with season ticket loans, or by restricting parking spaces?)
- Have you considered converting your car fleet to lead-free petrol, or switching to vehicles with smaller engines or catalytic converters? Are the highest environmental standards available being met by the vehicles distributing your goods?
- Have you reviewed the traffic implications of your site, in terms of location, access and management?
- Could your employees be educated in environmentally aware and economical driving?
- Do you have controls which avoid empty vehicles?
- Do you encourage car pooling?
- Do you ensure cars are well maintained?
- Do you consider distribution implications in the siting of new buildings, for example, factories next to railways?
- What hazards are involved in your transportation of goods?

- Have you reviewed the opportunities for teleconferencing, etc., as an alternative to travelling to meetings, or arranging for staff to work from home (teleworking, telecommuting)?

Finance/investment checklist

- Should investment criteria include requirements on company environmental policies and plans? Consider all forms of investment—acquisition programmes, strategic development, reserves, pension fund etc.
- Have you reviewed how environmental protection may be costed?
- Could the use of non-financial indicators be included in business cases?
- Should you consider investment in research and development of environmentally sound processes and products?
- Would you review all new projects and acquisitions for future environmental liabilities or advantages?
- Has sponsorship of environmental programmes and agencies been considered?
- Are sites checked prior to acquisition for existing pollution problems?

Index

Absolute liability, 75
Accidental damage, 14
Accounting and Environmentalism, 182
Accounting policies, disclosure of, 166
Accounting profession, 2
Accounting Recommendations, 210
Accounting Standards, 165
Accounting Standards Board, 160, 175, 210
Accreditation, 104-7
Acid deposition control programme, 26
Acid rain, 63
Acquisition framework, environmental issues, 158-63
Acquisitions and mergers, 170
Activity audits, 135
Administration costs, 188
Administrative controls, 187-8
Advertising, 112-14
Advertising Standards Authority (ASA), 113
Advisory Committee on Business and the Environment (ACBE), 48, 70, 75-80, 108-9, 129
Agenda 21, 53-4, 200-1
Air Law 1968, 31
Air pollution control, 10-11
Air quality standards, 31
Alkali, etc., Works Regulation Act 1906, 10
Allied Chemical, 132
Alternative forms of energy, 43
American Bankers Association, 69
American Institute of Certified Public Accountants (AICPA), 173
Analytical procedures, 151-2
Annual Reports, 108, 119-21, 123, 124, 126
'Anticipating the Future EC Environmental Policy Agenda', 33

Arthur D Little, 54
Associate Environmental Auditor, 107
Assurpol, 74
Audit sampling techniques, 152
Auditing Practices Board (APB), 136-41
Auditing Standards and Auditing Guidelines, 136, 207-8

Banks, 67-70
BATNEEC, 7, 34, 35, 160, 167
BEO (Best Environmental Option), 35
Black Country Development Corporation, 46
Black list, 9, 111
Blue Angel award, 114-15
Blueprint for a Green Economy, 181
Bodyshop, 86, 117, 160
Bowman's Harbour, 46
BPEO (Best Practicable Environmental Option) Index, 35
British Airways, 160
British Gas, 126, 127
Brown, Alex, 70
Brundtland Conference, 51
BS 5750, 94
BS 7750, 2, 82-95, 104, 106, 107, 129, 134, 136, 142, 144, 153
  Annex A, 93
  commitment, 85-6
  environmental management audits, 91-3
  environmental management manual and documentation, 89-90
  environmental management programme, 89
  environmental management records, 91
  environmental management reviews, 93-4
  environmental objectives and targets, 89

Index

BS 7750 (cont'd)
  environmental policy, 87
  fundamental concept underlying, 84
  initial review, 86–7
  links to BS 5750, 94
  links to EMAR, 94–5
  operational control, 90–1
  organisation and key personnel, 87–8
  overall objective, 84
  register of environmental effects, 88
BSO/Origin, 183
Business Charter for Sustainable Development, 180
Business Council for Sustainable Development, 51, 121
Business Strategy for Sustainable Development, 121, 180
Buyer Beware: A guide to finding out about contaminated land, 45

Cambridge Water Company (CWC) v *Eastern Counties Leather* (ECL), 15, 48, 79
Canadian Institute of Chartered Accountants, 173
Capitalisation of Costs to Treat Environmental Contamination, 173
Carbon taxes, 18
Carbon tetrachloride, 11
Carbon/energy tax, 190, 191–2
CFCs, 11, 62, 114, 115
Chartered Association of Certified Accountants, 128, 182
Charterhouse, 70
Chemical industry, 111, 133
Chemicals corporations, 122
Chemicals Industry Association (CIA), 35
Civil liability
  for damage caused by waste, 18, 73, 78
  for environmental damage, 69
Civil penalties for violations, 25
Clean Air Acts, 11, 25
Clean Systems, 41
Clean Water Act, 26
Clean-up operations, 28, 45, 46, 68–73, 160, 175, 194–5
CO_2 emissions, 43, 52, 58, 112, 183, 191, 194
Coal Board, 64
Coats Viyella, 126
Codex Alimentarius, 60
Commercial opportunities, 62–3
Commercial Union, 63
Committee on Advertising Practice (CAP), 113
Common Law, 14–15, 75, 77
  and statutory framework, 47

Communications, checklist, 218–19
Community affairs, checklist, 219
Companies Act 1989, 142
Compensation funds and schemes, 79–80, 189
Compliance audits, 135
Compliance costs, 33–7
Comprehensive Environmental Response Compensation and Liability Act 1980 (CERCLA), 27, 28, 71
Comprehensive General Liability (CGL) insurance policies, 72
Confederation of British Industry (CBI), 103, 127, 133–4
Conference of the World Committee on Environment and Development, 50
Conservative government, 190
Consumer Protection Act 1987, 76
Contaminated land, 13, 23, 44–9
  funds for remediation, 49
  information provision, 49
  policy objectives, 46–7
  reclamation, 13, 31
  registers of, 69, 72, 162
  remediation services, 45
  responsiblity for remediation, 48–9
  risk of recontamination, 70
  roles of public sector bodies, 49
  statutory framework, 47
  see also Clean-up operations
'Contaminated land and the water environment', 47
Contingencies, 169–70
Contractors, checklist, 218
Control of Pollution Act 1974, 161
Control of Pollution (Amendment) Act, 39
Controlled waste, 38
'Convention on Civil Liability for Damage resulting from activities dangerous to the environment', 46
Copenhagen Agreement, 11
Corporate audits, 135
Court of Appeal, 15
Cowans v *Scargill*, 64

Declaration of Principles on Forests, 53
Deferred tax, 168
Denmark, 45
Department of the Environment (DoE), 33, 104
Depreciation, 167
Desulphurisation equipment, 34
Developing countries, 53, 57
Dewe Rogerson, 62
Documentation, 148, 205
Dow Chemical Company, 40
Due diligence, 135, 157–63
Duty of Care, 11–12, 37–9, 76

Eagle Star Environmental Opportunities
    Trust, 65-6
Earth Summit, 50-4, 63, 67
Eastern Electricity, 112
Eastern Europe, 57
EC, 4, 16
EC Common Agricultural Policy, 58
EC Directive on the Freedom of Access to
    Information on the Environment, 109
EC Directives, 17
EC draft Directive on Civil Liability for
    Damage caused by Waste, 69, 73, 78
EC Eco-Management and Audit Regulation
    (EMAR), 82-4, 92, 94-102, 104-6, 121,
    134, 136, 142, 144, 153, 162
  Annex A, 96
  Annex I, 98, 100
  Annex I (B), 202-6
  Annex II, 98, 100
  Annex V, 100
  Article 4, 101
  Article 5, 99-100
  site registration, 101
  steps to registration, 96-102
EC environmental laws, 16-19, 33-4
EC Framework Directive on waste, 12
EC Green Paper on 'Remedying
    Environmental Damage', 46
EC Large Combustion Plant Directive, 43
EC Pollution Directive, 9
EC Regulations, 17
Eco-labelling, 114-17
Ecofin, 63
Economic development, 57
Economic growth, 56
Ecotec, 45
Effluents. *See* Trade effluents
EIRIS (Ethical Investment Research
    Service), 66
Emerging Issues Task Force, 173
Emissions control programme, 31
Employees, 117-19
Enduring Principles of Auditing, 141
Energy checklist, 217
Energy conservation, 43
Energy efficiency, 34, 42-4, 117
Energy management, 179
Energy monitoring, 179
Energy pricing, 43
Energy utilisation, 179
Engagement letters, 144-5
English Partnerships, 49
E-numbers, 59
Environment Action Programmes, 18
Environment Agency, 15-16, 49, 81
Environment Bill 1994, 13, 49
Environment Label Jury, 114

'Environment Means Business', 133-4
Environment Research Group, 171
Environmental accounting, 164-83
  and financial auditing, 142-67
  existing conventions, 165-76
  future directions, 198-9
  interpretation of 'material', 166
Environmental Accreditation Criteria, 104
Environmental Accreditation Panel, 104
Environmental action checklists, 214-21
Environmental auditing, 1, 98-9, 123,
    131-63, 206
  competition, 140
  definition, 134-5
  future directions, 198-9
  governance and regulation, 140
  history, 132-4
  litigation, 140
  objectives, 137
  reporting, 139
  requirements, 137
  role and scope, 139
  training, 141
  types of audit, 134-6
  USA, 133
Environmental Auditors, 107, 137
  independence, 139
Environmental Auditors Registration
    Association (EARA), 106-7
Environmental Auditors Registration
    Scheme, 106
Environmental awards, 112
Environmental bookkeeping, 181-3
Environmental charges, 188
Environmental consultancies, 133, 134, 140,
    141
Environmental damage
  charges, 188
  responsiblity for remediation, 48-9
Environmental Data Services (ENDS), 35, 134
Environmental effects, 204
Environmental funds, 202
Environmental Impact Assessment
    Directive, 17
Environmental Impact Assessments (EIAs),
    30, 135-6, 162
Environmental Impairment Liability (EIL)
    policies, 72, 73
Environmental information
  confidential, 109
  demand for, 108
  disclosure of, 120-2, 125, 160
  financial statements, 145
  for employees, 118
  for shareholders, 119
  freedom of access to, 109, 162
  public sources, 163

Environmental Information Regulations 1992, 18, 109, 110, 162
Environmental laws, 4–31
European Community, 16–19, 33–4
Germany, 21–4
industrial processes, 7–8
Japan, 29–31
Netherlands, The, 19–21
United Kingdom, 5–16
USA, 24–9
worldwide, 19–31
Environmental liabilities, 61, 68, 69, 75–81
Environmental management, 178
Environmental Management Options Scheme, 189
Environmental management systems, 97–8, 104
Environmental organisation and personnel, 203
Environmental performance, 99, 123, 127
checklist, 214–15
guidelines for measuring, 177–9
hierarchy, 178
measurement approaches, 176–80
people/organisation checklist, 219
Environmental policy, 96, 203
BS 7750, 87
Environmental Policy Consultancy (EPC), 33, 34
Environmental policy statement, 123
Environmental Pollution Control Committee, 30
Environmental programmes, 97–8, 133–4
Environmental Protection Act 1990, 6–14, 16, 18, 34, 37, 44, 49, 72, 78, 127, 160, 161, 167
Environmental Protection Agency (EPA), 25–8, 34, 44, 68, 71, 189
Environmental Protection (Prescribed Processes and Substances) Regulations 1990, 7–8
Environmental reporting, 108–30
future, 127
international, 119–24
obligations, 162
recommendations, 130
United Kingdom, 124–7
Environmental Reporting Award, 128
Environmental review, 97, 125
Environmental standards, 59
checklist, 215
Environmental statement, 99–100
preparation, 137
Environmental strategies, 179
Environmental surveys, 74
Environmental systems, 82–107

Environmental Technology Innovation Scheme (ETIS), 189
Ethical funds, 202
Ethical screening, 63–4
EUREKA programme, 189
EUROENVIRON, 189
Europe
environmental liabilities, 69
insurance, 74–5
see also EC
European Action Programmes, 16
European Better Environment Awards for Industry, 112
European Community. *See* EC
European Community Scheme, 114
European Environment Agency, 17–18
European Lighting Council, 117
Evidence, audit, 150–1
Expert services, 155
Exxon, 62–3

Fault-based liability, 76
Federal Environment Agency (UBA), 114–15
Financial accounting, future directions, 198–9
Financial Accounting Standards Board (FASB), 173
Financial auditing, 136–41
and environmental accounting, 142–67
audit report, 139
auditors' right and duty to report to regulators, 157
competition, 140
future direction, 138–41
governance and regulation, 140
independence, 139
litigation, 140
materiality, 147
objectives and general principles, 142–3
reporting to directors or management, 156–7
role and scope, 139
training, 140
Financial community, 61
Financial performance, 171–2
Financial reporting, 119, 128
Financial Reporting Standards (FRS), 165–6, 209
Financial review, 157–8
Financial Sector Working Group, 70, 75, 108, 129
Financial Services Act 1986 (FSA), 162
Financial statements, 145
USA, 174–5

'Firm Foundations: CBI proposals for environmental liability and contaminated land', 45
First Analysis Corporation, 70
Fleet Factors, 68
Food additives, 59
Food and Environment Protection Act 1985, 162
Food standards, 60
Foreningen of Statsautoriserede Revisorer (FSR), 104
Forest management, 53
Fraud and error, 143
Free trade, 57
Friends of the Earth, 45, 110, 112
Friends Provident, 64
Friends' Stewardship Unit Trust, 64
FRS 2, 170
FRS 3, 171–2
Fuels, sulphur in, 34
Fund managers, 66
Fundamental uncertainty, 155–6
Funds, sources of, 202
Future Development of Auditing, 138

Gaia theory, 181
General Agreement on Tariffs and Trade (GATT), 32, 57–60, 196
General Public Liability policies, 73–4
German Institute for Quality Control and Labelling (RAL), 114, 115
Germany, 36
  environmental laws, 21–4
Global Environmental Facility, 54
Global environmental market, 36
Global warming, 112
GMB 'Green Works' initiative, 118
GMB Model Environment Agreement, 118
Gray, Rob, 182
Green Book, 63
Green funds, 64
Green Party, 5
Greenhouse effect, 43
Greenhouse gases, 63, 112
Greening of Accountancy, The, 182
Greenpeace, 110, 111
Grey list, 9, 111
Gross Domestic Product, 33
Gross National Product (GNP), 54
Groundwater
  clean-up levy, 194–5
  contaminations, 23
Gummer, John, 190

Halons, 11
Hazardous and Solid Waste Amendment 1984, 27

Hazardous waste control, 27, 71
  disposal, 31, 111
  remediation, 174
  rules concerning, 133
Henley Centre for Forecasting, 117
Her Majesty's Inspectorate of Pollution (HMIP), 7–10, 14, 16, 18, 34, 35, 157, 167, 188
House of Lords Select Committee on the European Communities, 80
Hundred Group's Good Practice recommendations, 128
Hydro Aluminium Metals Ltd, 179

ICI, 126, 127, 160
Incorporated Society of British Advertisers (ISBA), 113
Independent Broadcasting Authority (IBA), 113
Industrial processes, environmental laws, 7–8
Information access, 18
Inquimamento, 74
Institute of Chartered Accountants in England and Wales (ICAEW), 128, 129, 166, 171
Institute of Fiscal Studies (IFS), 185
Institution of Chemical Engineers Register of Environmental Professionals, 106
Insurance, 71–5
  company share prices, 63
  Europe, 74–5
  UK, 72–4
  USA, 71
Integrated Pollution Control (IPC), 7–10, 33, 34, 61, 160, 167
Internal auditors, 153–4
International Chamber of Commerce (ICC), 51, 134, 180, 196
  Business Charter for Sustainable Development, 211
International developments, 50–60
International environmental reporting, 119–24
International Institute for Environment and Development, 196
International trade, 57–60
Investment, 61–81
  checklist, 219
  future, 65–6
  opportunities, 63
  properties, 170
  returns, 65
Irrecoverable economic loss, 77
Issues audits, 135

Japan, 36
  environmental laws, 29–31
Joint and several liability, 76–7

Knowledge of the business, 146–7
KPH Marketing, 117
KPMG International Environmental Network, 122–3

Labelling. *See* Eco-labelling
Labour Party, 191
Laender, 23
Land contamination. *See* Contaminated land
Land Quality Statement, 49
Land reclamation. *See* Contaminated land
Landfill levy, 194
Landfill sites, 12, 42
Landfill tax, 188
Lebin, Eberhard, 111
Legal liability, 189
Levies, 188
Liberal Democrats, 190
Life Cycle Analysis (LCA), 83, 102–3, 116, 134, 135
  cost aspects, 103
  stages of, 102–3
  use in marketing, 103
Litter, 13–14
Local authorities, guidance to, 109
Local Authority Air Pollution Control (APC), 10
Local authority waste disposal companies (LAWDCs), 12, 73
Long stop date for personal injury claims, 78
Long-term contracts, 167
Lovelock, James, 181

Making a Corporate Commitment Campaign, 44
Management
  representations, 152–3
  responsibilities, 39
Managing Waste: Guidelines for Business, 39
Market distortions, 188
MAS, 74
Materials checklist, 216
Measurement approaches, environmental performance, 176–80
Mergers. *See* Acquisitions and mergers
Merlin Research Unit, 66
Methane emissions, 194
Mobile sources program, 26
Montreal Protocol, 11
Moral judgements, 66

Motor industry, 122
Multilateral Trade Organisation (MTO), 59

National Accreditation Council for Certification Bodies (NACCB), 104–7, 142
  organisations giving qualifications, 106
National Ambient Air Quality Standards programme, 25
National Emission Standards for Hazardous Air Pollutants, 25
National Environmental Agency, 30
National Pollutant Discharge Elimination System permit programme, 26
National Priorities List (NPL), 27
National Rivers Authority (NRA), 8–10, 14, 16, 18, 45, 47, 69, 111, 157, 161, 195
National Trust, 110
National Union of Mineworkers, 64
Negligence, 14
Netherlands, The, 19–21, 36, 45
Nissan UK, 36
Non-renewable energy sources, 43
Norwich Union, 62
NO_x emissions, 43, 183
NPI, 62
Nuclear Installations Act 1965, 78

Occidental Petroleum, 132
OECD, 57
Oele Committee, 20
Official development assistance, 54
'Operating and Financial Review' (OFR), 160–1, 172–6
Operational control, 204–5
Outboard Marine Corporation, 72
Ozone-depleting substances, 11
Ozone layer, 114

Packaging materials
  comparison of, 103
  recycling, 18, 20, 22, 41–2, 187
Paper and board, recycling, 40–1
'Paying for our Past', 44, 46
Pearce, David, 181
Personal injury claims, long stop date for, 78
Petrochemical industry, 41, 122
Pilot projects, 178
Planning applications, 49
Planning (Hazardous Substances) Act 1990, 162
Planning permission, 15
Planning process, 146, 162
Plastics recycling, 41
Police Acts, 23

Index

Polluter pays principle, 48
Pollution Adjusting Committee, 30
Polychlorinated biphenyls (PCBs), 72
Pools, 74, 79
Post-balance sheet events, 168–9
Powergen, 127
Pressure groups, 110–12, 157
Principal Environmental Auditor, 107, 154–5
Private agreements, 30
Private-citizen led enforcement suits, 25
Private compensation, 189
Private nuisance, 14
Procter & Gamble, 103
Producer Responsibility Industry Group (PRG), 41–2
Product checklist, 216
PRP (Potentially Responsible Parties), 28
Public compensation, 189
Public nuisance, 14
Public participation, 25
Public registers, 161

Quality control, 148–9

Radioactive substances, 13–14
Radioactive Substances Act 1960, 162
Rand Institute, 28
Reclaimed materials, 40
Reclamation of contaminated land. *See* Contaminated land
Recognised Supervisory Body (RSB), 142, 149
Recoverable economic loss, 77
Recycling
  credits, 12, 195
  materials, 40
  packaging materials, 18, 20, 22, 41–2, 187
  paper and board, 40–1
  plastics, 41
Red list, 9
Register of Eco-Audit Specialists (Royal Society of Chemistry), 106
Registration Board for Assessors, 106
Relief for environmental impairment, 77
Renewable energy sources, 43
Resource Conservation and Recovery Act 1976 (RCRA), 27, 71
Retrospective liability, 78–9
Return, 67–8
Rio Declaration on Environment and Development, 51–2
Risk assessment, 149–50
Risk management, 67–8, 74
River systems, 9
Road transport
  checklist, 220
  taxes, 193–4
Roddick, Anita, 86
Royal Commission on Environmental Pollution, 111
Royal Institute of Chartered Surveyors, 49
Royal Insurance, 63
Royal Society for Nature Conservation, 110
Royal Society for the Protection of Birds, 110
Rylands v *Fletcher*, 14–15

SAS 100, 142–3
SAS 110, 143
SAS 120, 144
SAS 140, 144–5
SAS 160, 145
SAS 200, 146
SAS 210, 146–7
SAS 220, 147–8
SAS 230, 148
SAS 240, 148–9
SAS 300, 149–50
SAS 400, 150–1
SAS 410, 151–2
SAS 430, 152
SAS 440, 152–3
SAS 500, 153–4
SAS 510, 154–5
SAS 520, 155
SAS 600, 155
SAS 610, 156–7
SAS 620, 157
Scale of charges, 8
Securities and Exchange Commission (SEC), 132, 174
Security, 67–8
Segmental reporting, 171
Sewage treatment, 10
Share prices, 63
Shareholders, 119–27
Single European Act 1987, 16
Site audits, 135
S-K 101, 174
S-K 103, 174
SmithKline Beecham, 126
SO_2 emissions, 43, 192
Society for the Promotion of Lifecycle Development, 103
Soviet Union, 57
SSAP 2, 166
SSAP 9, 167
SSAP 12, 167
SSAP 15, 168
SSAP 15A, 168
SSAP 17, 168–9
SSAP 18, 169–70
SSAP 19, 170

SSAP 23, 170
SSAP 25, 171
Standards. *See* BS; Environmental standards
Statements of Auditing Standards, 137
see also SAS
Statements of Financial Accounting Concepts, 173
Statements of Financial Auditing Standards, 137–8, 142, 207–8
Statements of Recommended Practice, 210
Statements of Standard Accounting Practice (SSAP), 165, 209
see also SSAP
Statutory nuisances, 11
Stock Exchange Yellow Book, 161
Stock Market, 61–6
Stockholm Conference on the Human Environment, 50–1
Strict liability, 48, 75
Subsidiary undertakings, 170
Subsidies, 189
Sulphur dioxide permit trading, 192–3
Sulphur in fuels, 34
Superfund, 27, 28, 44, 49, 68, 71
Superfund Amendments and Reauthorization Act of 1986 (SARA), 28
Suppliers
  checklist, 218
  performance, 179
Supplies checklist, 216
Survey of Ethical and Environmental Funds in Continental Europe, 66
Sustainable development, 121, 165, 180–1, 211–13
Sweden, 36
SWOT analysis, 86

Taxation, 184–97
  future, 189–97
  practical issues, 186–9
  theory, 185–6
'Taxing pollution, not people', 190
Technical Waste Instruction, 22
Third-World lending, 66
'This Common Inheritance' (White Paper), 6, 187
Timber tax, 195–7
Town and Country Planning (Assessment of Environmental Effects) Regulations 1988, 17, 162
Toxic waste, 71
Trade, 57–60
Trade effluents
  consents, 161
  management, 179

Tradeable quotas, 188–9
Trades Unions, 118
Treatment, storage and disposal (TSD) facilities, 27
1,1,1–Trichloroethane, 11
TUC, 118
Turner & Newall, 63

UN Commission on Sustainable Development, 54
UN Conference on Environment and Development (UNCED). *See* Earth Summit
UN Conference on Trade and Development (UNCTAD), 58
UN Convention on Protection of Biodiversity, 53
UN Economic Commission for Europe (UNECE) Protocol, 11
UN Framework Convention on Climatic Change, 52
UN Intergovernmental Working Group of Experts on International Standards of Accounting and Reporting, 119
UNCED 1992: Agenda 21, 53–4, 200–1
Unit trusts, 65
United Kingdom
  environmental laws, 5–16
  environmental reporting, 124–7
  insurance, 72–4
Urban Development Corporations, 46
Uruguay Round, 57
US Steel, 132
USA, 36
  clean-up operations, 68–9
  company reporting, 161
  environmental auditing, 133
  environmental laws, 24–9
  financial statements, 174–5
  insurance, 71
'Use of Economic and Fiscal Instruments in Environmental Policy', 196

VALPAK, 41
Value-added statement, 183
VAT, 187, 193
Vendors, checklist, 218
Venture capital, 70
Verification examination, 100–1
Verpackungsverordnung, 22
VNO, commission on the environment, 20
Volatile organic compounds (VOCs), 11

Waste Collection Authorities (WCAs), 12–13, 38, 195

Waste disposal, 11–13, 22
  checklist, 218
  licences, 161
  policy, 39
  practices, 39
Waste Disposal Authorities (WDAs), 12–13, 195
Waste generation, 37
Waste Law 1970, 31
Waste management, 11–13, 39–40, 63
  licences, 161
Waste Management Licensing Regulations 1994, 12
Waste minimisation programme, 40
Waste Regulation Authorities, 12, 16, 38, 39

Water
  checklist, 217–18
  pollution control, 9–10, 26
Water Acts, 9, 16, 18, 69, 161
Water Law 1970, 31
Water Resources Act 1991, 9, 10, 161, 195
Welsh Development Agency, 49
World Bank, 54–7
World Development Report, 56
World Energy Council, 43
Worldwide environmental laws, 19–31
Worldwide Fund for Nature (WWF), 110
WRAP (Waste Reduction Always Pays), 40

Yellow Book, 163